Third Edition

EDUCATIONAL
FOUNDATIONS

*For James and Naomi and the countless families
everywhere simply fighting for a quality education.*

Third Edition

EDUCATIONAL
FOUNDATIONS

An Anthology of Critical Readings

EDITORS

Alan S. Canestrari & Bruce A. Marlowe

Roger Williams University

Los Angeles | London | New Delhi
Singapore | Washington DC

Los Angeles | London | New Delhi
Singapore | Washington DC

FOR INFORMATION:

SAGE Publications, Inc.

2455 Teller Road

Thousand Oaks, California 91320

E-mail: order@sagepub.com

SAGE Publications Ltd.

1 Oliver's Yard

55 City Road

London EC1Y 1SP

United Kingdom

SAGE Publications India Pvt. Ltd.

B 1/I 1 Mohan Cooperative Industrial Area

Mathura Road, New Delhi 110 044

India

SAGE Publications Asia-Pacific Pte. Ltd.

3 Church Street

#10-04 Samsung Hub

Singapore 049483

Acquisitions Editor: Diane McDaniel

Editorial Assistant: Megan Koraly

Production Editor: Libby Larson

Copy Editor: Megan Markanich

Typesetter: C&M Digitals (P) Ltd.

Proofreader: Dennis W. Webb

Indexer: Diggs Publications

Cover Designer: Gail Buschman

Marketing Manager: Terra Schultz

Permissions Editor: Adele Hutchinson

Copyright © 2013 by SAGE Publications, Inc.

Printed in the United States of America

A catalog record of this book is available from the Library of Congress.

9781452216768

This book is printed on acid-free paper.

Certified Chain of Custody
Promoting Sustainable Forestry
www.sfiprogram.org
SFI-01268

SUSTAINABLE
FORESTRY
INITIATIVE

SFI label applies to text stock

14 15 16 17 18 10 9 8 7 6 5 4 3

Contents

Preface

Ten, nine, eight, seven, six, five, four, three, two, one . . . Happy New Year. (Applause.) January rings in a brand new year: a time to make resolutions, an opportunity to imagine a new self, a chance to eat better, get some regular exercise, and lose a little weight . . . feel a little better about yourself. (Confident applause.) But, as everyone knows, resolutions are promises that, more often than not, get broken. (Silence.)

All promises? Even ones made by President Obama in his 2012 State of the Union address? Like the rest of us, tradition dictates that even presidents make January resolutions that speak to the potential of the nation. A time to redouble our efforts as we imagine a brighter future . . . spend more efficiently, celebrate bipartisanship, feel a little better about the nation's economy. Linking jobs and education together, President Obama had this to say:

> A great teacher can offer an escape from poverty to the child who dreams beyond his circumstance. Every person in this chamber can point to a teacher who changed the trajectory of their lives. Most teachers work tirelessly, with modest pay, sometimes digging into their own pocket for school supplies, just to make a difference.

Then, later, he added this:

> Teachers matter. So instead of bashing them or defending the status quo, let's offer schools a deal. Give them the resources to keep good teachers on the job and reward the best ones. (Applause.) And in return, grant schools flexibility: to teach with creativity and passion, to stop teaching to the test, and to replace teachers who just aren't helping kids learn.

Even if true to his word, does such a resolution deserve applause? Let's examine the resolution closely. For example, doesn't offering to "reward the best" teachers beg the question (as it assumes we know, and can agree upon) what constitutes good teaching? How do *you* define good teaching? Do you know it when you see it? Can it be measured, and if so, how? Think carefully about the terms used by the President in his proposed deal. Is such an offer an acknowledgment that teachers are currently denied the resources they need? And if teachers were to reject such a deal, are we to assume the President's fallback position is to continue denying them resources and "teaching to the test" as the only other alternative? Moreover, does the President's exhortation that teachers teach with "creativity and passion" assume this is not currently the case? When he says we should replace teachers who aren't helping kids learn, what does he mean? Learn what? Measured how? By whom?

As you will soon discover, these important questions—as well as questions about what schools should look like, about curriculum, and assessment—are being answered, increasingly, by people furthest removed from schools, teachers, and young people. And the ways in which these questions are answered is based, more than ever, on political calculations. Remarkably, there is a broad consensus among those in the political class and agreement too among the membership of the nation's corporate elite about how to best answers these questions. Indeed, when it comes to education policy, there is no longer an ideological clash between Democrats and Republicans, who are further apart on the issues of the day now than perhaps at any time in our nation's history.

Instead, there is bipartisan support over what students should learn and how they should learn it, about what good schools look like, about how we should assess student learning. . . . Since our second edition, the neoconservative reform agenda has come to completely dominate American public education. Their "at-risk" mind-set, characterized by an almost singular focus on how our schools are failing, has resulted in narrow directives now firmly embedded within public education. What once appeared as isolated news stories and cause for local embarrassment—teaching to the test, scripted curricula, mindless repetition of facts—is now openly advocated without chagrin by local and state school officials. Yearly test results have emerged as the most important measure of the worth of our schools despite the fact that the numbers such assessments provide obfuscate the complexity of schooling and serve to short-circuit deeper understanding of student learning and high quality teaching.

Can such an at-risk educational vision serve to renew and sustain our nation, our democracy, and our schools? Does the current model of accountability serve the public interest? Is there another way to frame reform?

Fortunately, there are still many thoughtful, progressive administrators, teachers, and parents. You will read their words in the pages that follow. In different ways, and at different times, they have refused to blindly accept an at-risk perspective, questioned uncritical compliance, and challenged the notion that there is, of necessity, a singular path to learning that requires rigid adherence to state directives. We have chosen these authors because, like Thoreau, they worry that public education is in jeopardy of making "a straight-cut ditch of a free, meandering brook."

But how does one begin to walk down an alternative path? Why aren't teachers at the forefront of the debate? How can we prepare beginning teachers to move purposefully in another direction, to ask questions, to challenge assumptions . . . to be involved? What questions should teachers ask? What answers should teachers accept?

We hope that new teachers will consider asking whether their instruction promotes the status quo. How deliberate are their efforts to promote equality and to include the experiences of traditionally marginalized groups in the curriculum? Is their instruction implemented at a transformational, social action level? New teachers need models of critical reflection (and even dissent) in order to help them develop their own critical questions and voices.

Like the first two editions, the major purpose of this third edition is to help teachers develop habits of critical reflection about schools and schooling before entering the classroom. It is for this reason that we have deliberately chosen authors with strong views that reflect these particular biases. We hope that these readings will offer a platform for discussion and debate that may be used by instructors to increase student knowledge of pedagogy and to provide authentic opportunities for potential teachers to think critically about teaching and learning. For example, we are very concerned about the current trend toward standardization of curriculum and instruction—a trend that we believe devalues teaching and increases the distrust of teachers. We believe, like Deborah Meier, that this trend had manifested itself in schools organized around testing and that it is imperative for teachers to actively critique such events and recapture some of the control and power over their work.

We assembled this book because we believe that the current textbooks written on the foundations of education are too broad and too politically cautious to engage students or help them develop their own critical voices. Such texts do a good job of providing a survey of practices but with very limited reference to the social contexts of teachers and their students, without taking a strong stance in favor of one practice or another. In these texts' attempt to cover everything in a curriculum, students have little opportunity to delve deeply into any substantive issues. Instead, they are exposed, in only the most superficial ways, to the important issues facing the field. While the scope of the typical course has become broader in the past several years, the tone has become more dispassionate. As textbook content demands expand, students become responsible for knowing less and less about more and more. The texts on the market, like the textbooks in many fields, are so cursory that they leave professors few options other than assuming highly didactic, teacher-directed approaches to instruction. The texts also tend to promote practices that are antithetical to meaningful instruction: lecture, memorization, and multiple-choice assessment. Finally, the texts, because of their size and scope and their neutral stance, foster acceptance of the status quo without opportunity for in-depth examination, reflection, and discussion.

What you have in your hands is a book that we hope you will find as exciting as we do: an anthology of critical readings for students about to enter the teaching profession and for students interested in carefully examining schools and schooling. We feature provocative, engaging authors whose views are politicized but whose writing and opinions matter not simply because they are gadflies but because their ideas work and because their achievements as teachers, principals, and policy shapers are so notable.

The anthology continues to be organized around essential questions. They are: Why teach? Who are today's students? What makes a good teacher? What do good schools look like? How should we assess student learning? How does one develop a critical voice? How do we move forward? Our authors' answers continue to be bold and refreshing. They eschew the unquestioning compliance so characteristic of new teachers and, by taking a hard look at traditional educational practice, they serve as models for the kind of reflective practitioners we hope our students will become when they enter the field. We frame each chapter with a very brief introductory vignette that provides context for the issues that the authors' essays address and that also serves to raise probing questions about teaching and learning.

After several years on the market, we have had plenty of feedback to our first two editions. While the responses to our book have been overwhelmingly positive, we also received a number of very specific, constructive recommendations from valued colleagues, critics, and the students with whom we have had the pleasure of working. Principal among these were recommendations for essays that more directly "answer" the questions posed at the outset of each chapter. To address this suggestion, we removed essays that were only tangentially related to each chapter's opening question and substituted them with pieces that more directly address the content of each chapter's focus. In addition to most of the fine essays contained in our original edition, you will now also find works new to this edition by Diane Ravitch; Alfie Kohn; Corrine Munoz-Plaza, Sandra C. Quinn, and Kathleen A. Rounds; William Johnson; and Lois Weiner. We also commissioned two pieces for the third edition by imaginative teacher educators Darlene Witte-Townsend and Kelly Donnell, both of whom have long experience working in schools and with children and young people. Finally, and as previously noted, we have added a new chapter that imagines a different future and an essay about the experiences of lesbian, gay, bisexual, and transgender students.

HOW *NOT* TO USE THIS BOOK

If you are a professor who adopted our previous editions, you can rest assured that we have not changed our perspective concerning the use of this book. You won't find any direct instruction here. Instead, we hope that you, like those who have found the anthology useful, will think critically about the most effective ways to engage your students with these readings and the issues they raise, without simply telling. Let's once again be clear: Simply walking through the table of contents, chapter by chapter, and expounding on the views of the authors contained in these pages is not what we had in mind.

If you are a student, you hold our third edition in your hands for the first time; we challenge you to ensure that your professors practice what they preach about instruction. Are you sitting through long and boring lectures about why teachers should not lecture? Are you engaged in discussion? If not, perhaps it is time to ask your professor, "Why not?"

Acknowledgments

Our thinking regarding teaching and learning continues to be shaped, reshaped, and supported by our colleagues and our work with children. Like the first and second editions, this anthology is composed of the writing of those who have had a profound influence on our understanding of what is most important for learners, parents, teachers, and schools. We also want to thank Kelly Donnell and Ann Winfield, two of our colleagues here at Roger Williams University. Kelly Donnell offers an optimistic urban education essay, and Ann Gibson Winfield closes the anthology with an inspirational message to teachers.

Great teachers and writers, however, are not our only sources of inspiration or support: Special thanks go to Pam and Nancy for their criticisms of the manuscript at its various stages. We are also grateful to Gary Canestrari for his artistic sense and input regarding the design of the book's cover and to Janet Foulger for the final product.

We are extremely fortunate to have wonderful administrative support here at Roger Williams University. Mary Gillette, as always, was extremely helpful using her manuscript wizardry and her artistic sense to make our new chapters visually appealing.

We would also like to thank James Brown and his daughter Naomi for sharing their story with us.

At SAGE, Diane McDaniel has been a continuous source of encouragement and support. Several others at SAGE were instrumental in shepherding the project through all its phases. They include Brian Normoyle, Megan Koraly, and Libby Larson. The reviewers of the manuscript are gratefully acknowledged:

Jennifer L. Allen
University of Akron

Kate Kauper
Cornell College

Elaine Bacharach Coughlin
Pacific University

John Petrovic
The University of Alabama

Martha L. Wall-Whitfield
Virginia Commonwealth University

Dr. Edna Theresa West
Ursuline College

About the Editors

Alan S. Canestrari is a veteran social studies practitioner and professor of education at Roger Williams University. He earned his EdD from Boston University. He has had a long career in public schools and universities as a history teacher and department chair, as adjunct professor at Rhode Island College, and as mentor in the Brown University Masters of Teaching Program. In 1992, he was recognized as the Rhode Island Social Studies Teacher of the Year. He is the editor (with Bruce Marlowe) of *Educational Psychology in Context: Readings for Future Teachers* (SAGE).

Bruce A. Marlowe is the author (with Marilyn Page) of *Creating and Sustaining the Constructivist Classroom* (Corwin Press) and of a six-part video series titled *Creating the Constructivist Classroom* (The Video Journal of Education). He earned his PhD in educational psychology from The Catholic University of America in Washington, D.C., where he also completed 2 years of postdoctoral training in neuropsychological assessment. He has taught at the elementary, secondary, and university levels and is currently professor of educational psychology and special education at Roger Williams University.

Alan and Bruce have both taught courses in the foundations of education; neither is satisfied with any of the foundations texts currently available on the market. Both authors can be reached by mail at Roger Williams University, School of Education, One Old Ferry Road, Bristol, Rhode Island 02809, and also by telephone and e-mail: Alan Canestrari at (401) 254–3749 and acanestrari@rwu.edu and Bruce Marlowe at (401) 254–3078 and bmarlowe@rwu.edu.

About the Contributors

Lisa Delpit is an eminent scholar and executive director of the Center for Urban Education and Florida International University. She has a new book titled, *Multiplication Is for White Kids: Raising Expectations for Other People's Children* (2012).

Robert DiGiulio (deceased), former professor of education at Johnson State College in Vermont, was the author of numerous books, including *Great Teaching: What Matters Most in Helping Students Succeed* (2004), *Educate, Medicate, or Litigate? What Teachers, Parents, and Administrators Must Do About Student Behavior* (2001), and *Positive Classroom Management: A Step-by-Step Guide to Successfully Running the Show Without Destroying Student Dignity* (2006).

Kelly Donnell, a former elementary schoolteacher, teaches at Roger Williams University. Her research interests include urban education, practitioner inquiry, and induction for beginning teachers. She is coauthor, with Andrea J. Stairs and Alyssa Hadley Dunn, of *Urban Teaching in America: Theory, Research, and Practice in K-12 Classrooms* (2012).

Paulo Freire (deceased) was arguably one of the founding fathers of critical pedagogy. He was an author and social activist in Brazil.

John Taylor Gatto is a former New York City and New York State Teacher of the Year. He is currently at work on a documentary film about the nature of modern schooling titled *The Fourth Purpose*, with his friend and former student, Roland Legiardi-Laura.

Henry Giroux is a professor at McMaster University in Hamilton, Ontario, where he currently holds the Global Television Network Chair in English and Cultural Studies. He is a prolific writer. He is author of *Youth in a Suspect Society* (2009).

William Johnson is a special education teacher at a public high school in Brooklyn who writes on education for the website Gotham Schools.

Herbert Kohl's *On Teaching* remains a classic response to the perennial question: Why teach? He is the author of more than 40 books on education. He and his wife, Judy, were the recipients of the National Book Award in 1978 for *The View From the Oak*.

Alfie Kohn, a self-described "gadfly," was described in *Time* magazine as "perhaps the country's most outspoken critic of education's fixation on grades [and] test scores." He writes and speaks widely on human behavior, education, and parenting.

Jonathan Kozol's experience as a fourth-grade substitute teacher in Boston inspired his first major exposé on the effects of segregation on children, *Death at an Early Age*. He continues to be an outspoken critic of American public education.

Deborah Meier is currently on the faculty of New York University's Steinhardt School of Education, as senior scholar and adjunct professor as well as board member and director of New Ventures at Mission Hill, director and advisor to Forum for Democracy and Education, and on the board of the Coalition of Essential Schools.

Corrine Munoz-Plaza is a principal research associate with the National Development and Research Institutes in New York City. Her current work involves data collection and analysis on the STOP Hepatitis C Project.

A. S. Neill (deceased), founder of Summerhill School, a classic and radical experiment in child rearing, cared deeply about children's freedom and happiness.

Thomas Newkirk's most recent books include *The Art of Slow Reading* (2011), *Holding Onto Good Ideas in a Time of Bad Ones* (2009), and *Teaching the Neglected "R"* (2007, coedited with Richard Kent). He is a professor of English at the University of New Hampshire.

Sonia Nieto, professor emerita of language, literacy, and culture at the University of Massachusetts School of Education, Amherst, speaks and writes on multicultural education.

Susan Ohanian, freelance writer and former teacher, is an outspoken critic of "stir and serve recipes" for teaching. In 2003, she won the National Council of Teachers of English George Orwell Award for Distinguished Contribution to Honesty and Clarity in Public Language.

Marilyn Page, a former professor of education at Penn State, consults on novice teacher mentoring, school reform, classroom management, and technology issues in education. She is the author of *You Can't Teach Until Everyone is Listening*.

Sandra C. Quinn is the associate dean for Public Health Initiatives, professor in the Department of Family Science, and senior associate director of the Center for Health Equity at the School of Public Health, University of Maryland, College Park.

Diane Ravitch is research professor of education at New York University and a historian of education. She is also a nonresident senior fellow at the Brookings Institution. She is an outspoken critic of the charter school movement.

Kathleen A. Rounds is a professor at the School of School of Social Work, University of North Carolina at Chapel Hill, director of the Public Health Social Work Leadership Training Program, and cochair of the Dual Degree Program between the School of Social Work and the MCH Department, School of Public Health.

Lois Weiner is a professor in the Department of Elementary and Secondary at New Jersey City University. She teaches courses in social foundations of education and curriculum and instruction and is the coordinator of the Masters Degree Program in Urban Education/ Teaching and Learning in Urban Schools. Her research currently explores the "global assault" on teaching, teachers, and their unions.

Ann Gibson Winfield, associate professor of historical and philosophical foundations of education at Roger Williams University, recently returned from a Fulbright-Hayes Group Project visit to Egypt. Her book *Eugenics and Education in America* (2007) is considered a seminal work by eugenic historians.

Darlene Witte-Townsend is a former professor of education at Johnson State College in Vermont. Her research has included examinations of children's play, literacy, language, spirituality, and development, as well as educational philosophy, communication, practices, and the effects of No Child Left Behind (NCLB).

PART I

Why Teach?

S tudents file into a crowded lecture hall at a small liberal arts college in the Northeast. The class, Foundations of Education, is a prerequisite for acceptance into the School of Education program, and it is enrolled at maximum capacity. It is the first day of class. Students are expecting that the syllabus for the course will be distributed and read aloud, and if no one asks any questions about the requirements of the class, then the students can cut out early and enjoy the warm September sunshine. After all, nobody bought the book yet. The professor arrives and greets the students.

"Good morning. So, you are all interested in becoming teachers? Wonderful. We need bright, energetic, young teachers in the profession today. Teaching can be a very rewarding career, but I must warn you that it is a challenging time for teachers, especially beginning teachers. Teachers are under tremendous scrutiny. There are also increasing concerns about the deplorable condition of our schools, the lack of parental support, the disturbing behavior of the children, and the general disrespect for teachers by the public at large. So, why teach?"

A long silence fills the hall.

"This is not a rhetorical question. Tell us, why do you want to teach?"

More silence . . . long silence.

Finally, Jennifer offers, "My mom is a teacher. So is my aunt. I guess I have grown up around teaching, and ever since I can remember, I've wanted to teach, too."

Then Erin says, "I just love kids. Like, I just want to make a difference in their lives. I want to teach elementary school. The kids are so cute at that age."

Robert adds, "I work as a camp counselor in the summers. My cabin always wins the camp contest. I really connect with kids. I mean, I just know what they like. It is not so hard, plus teachers have summers off."

Sound good? Do Jennifer, Erin, and Robert have it right? Are these the reasons to teach?

1

Letters to a Young Teacher

Why New Recruits Leave Inner-City Classrooms—and What It Will Take to Keep Them There

Jonathan Kozol

The truth about the flight of teachers from our public schools has been obscured by lack of clear distinctions between schools of very different kinds. The loss of first-year teachers from suburban schools is not particularly high. In inner-city neighborhoods, by contrast, on the basis of my conversations with at least 200 of these young recruits, I would estimate that upwards of one-half decide to leave the school in which they're placed by the end of their third year.

This is why, in my newest book, which represents a year of correspondence with a highly motivated 1st grade teacher whom I call Francesca, I try to share with her the strategies I've learned from other urban teachers who have managed to resist the inclination to throw up their hands and leave their jobs, no matter what frustrations they experience.

Talkback

Why do bright young teachers leave urban schools, and what will it take to keep them there?

NOTE: From the book *Letters to a Young Teacher,* Crown Publishing Company, 2007.

In these letters, I take issue with the common explanation, one I hear repeatedly from those who do not seem to know too many of these bright young people, that the major cause of their frustrations is an inability to relate successfully to children of minorities. At least in the case of the better-educated and more idealistic teachers—and there are more of them than ever nowadays—who come into the classroom steeped in civil rights traditions and the values of their frequently pro-gressive parents, they enter public education with a purposeful and even preferential option for the children of the black and brown and poor.

The most frequently reiterated reason for discouragement that they express has nothing to do with "relating to their students," with whom they tend to strike an almost instantaneous rapport. Instead, it has to do with the systematic crushing of their creativity and intellect, the threatened desiccation of their personalities, and the degradation of their sense of self-respect under the weight of heavy-handed, business-modeled systems of Skinnerian instruction, the cultural denuding of curriculum required by the test-prep mania they face, and the sense of being trapped within "a state of siege," as one teacher puts it, all of which is now exacerbated by that mighty angst machine known as No Child Left Behind.

The challenge for such teachers, as they convey it to me in our conversations, is: (1) to hold fast to the pedagogic principles they value and the tenderness of their attachment to young people that has brought them to the classroom in the first place, (2) to do so in a way that will not isolate them in their schools and leave them feeling all the more discouraged as a consequence. I urge these teachers, for example, not to turn their backs on veteran instructors in their schools, a com-mon error made by inexperienced idealists. Although, in any given school, there are bound to be some older teachers who may not be help-ful allies or ideal role models for beginning teachers, the best among them bring a sense of personal stability and of assimilated selflessness into a school and, when younger teachers treat them with respect and turn to them as friends, typically respond with the protective kindness that can be a salvatory comfort for a novice teacher under stress.

I also urge these teachers: Reach out as quickly as you can to the parents of your students, especially those parents who initially are least responsive. Give them your cellphone number. Visit them in after-noons or evenings. And, in the case of young white teachers serving children of minorities, learn to cross the lines of race and class in sensi-tive but determined ways that lower the barriers between your class-room and your children's homes. Winning the solidarity of parents is one of the best ways, in my own experience, of building a structure of defense against potential critics in the upper levels of bureaucracy who may not appreciate a youthful teacher's healthy instinct for dissent.

Most of all, I encourage in these teachers a sense of what I like to call "enjoyable and mischievous irreverence" in the course of navigating those mandated miseries introduced by federal pressure into many inner-city schools but, at the same time, a mature sophistication and respectfulness in dealing with their principals, who often view the policies they must enforce with the very same distaste their younger teachers do. Many good principals, while they'd seldom say this openly at school, tell me in private that the burden of anxiety about the threat of sanctions that hang constantly like sharpened swords above their heads is leading them to foist upon their teachers practices they pedagogically abhor. Some tell me that they secretly applaud those teachers who are not afraid to undermine the stern intentionality of these mandated practices with thinly veiled lightheartedness, so long as they can teach the skills their students need and have a sensible regard for classroom management. They know these are the teachers who will not quit in despair.

In Francesca's case, none of this proved difficult, in part because she'd been superbly grounded both in educational techniques and in the critical consciousness derived from her immersion in political science and the other areas of liberal arts and sciences during her college years. She was also blessed with the kind of incandescent personality that won the adoration of her children almost from the minute that they walked into her room.

Firm when she needed to be, she quickly learned that look of earned authority that, with a single glance, could bring a slightly wild and rambunctious little boy out of his periodic episodes of orbiting the room and get him back into his chair to work, reluctantly, at putting vowels in between his consonants, as 6-year-olds quite stubbornly refuse to do at first. But she never sacrificed the sheer aesthetic merriment of being with small children, and she built her literacy lessons not out of a scripted text of grunts and chants but, as much as possible, out of the words her children actually selected and enjoyed ("wiggly" and "wobbly," when teeth were coming loose) or sometimes very big words, like "bamboozle" or "persnickety," the sounds of which had stirred their curiosity when they had heard them spoken by their grandma, for example.

Even when she spoke to me about the most draconian requirements "aligned"—to use a mechanistic piece of jargon she deplored—with state exams, her voice still had that energetic sound of somebody who never lets herself be beaten down but keeps on coming back with a nice sense of lively combat and delicious bits of irony about the contradictions that she had to deal with. I tell young teachers, "You are going to need a good big helping of Francesca's sly, subversive sense of humor in the face of state-ordained absurdities like being told to write across your chalkboard the 'official number' for each mini-chunk of amputated knowledge you're obliged to teach, in case a clipboard bureaucrat walks into your room and wants to know which 'state proficiency' you are 'delivering' at the specific minute of the morning."

Francesca, I am glad to say, refused to put those numbers on her wall because, she said, their only purpose was "to cover my rear end— they have zero value to my children." And although her students mastered all the skills they needed to do well on their exams, she refused to turn her class into a test-prep factory or allow the fear of failure to be substituted, as a motivating principle, for the natural rewards of learning for its own inherent sake alone.

She also refused to genuflect before the business-driven values that have penetrated many inner-city schools, where I routinely see embarrassing and mawkish posters telling kids the "mission" of their school is to "produce" the "workers" that our nation needs in order to "compete in global markets." Upper-middle-class suburban schools, she scathingly observed, would "never stoop to put that kind of gibberish on the wall."

Inspired teachers of young children, like Francesca, ardently refuse to see themselves as servants of the global corporations or drill sergeants for the state. They disdain to be regarded chiefly as technicians of utilitarian proficiency. And they stalwartly refuse to see their pupils as so many future economic units for a corporate society, into whom they are expected to pump "added value," as the number-crunchers who determine much of education policy demand.

Few of these technocrats appear to recognize much pre-existing value in the young mentalities of children or, indeed, to be acquainted closely with the personalities and character of children. Rarely, if ever, do they ask if children ought to have some opportunity for happiness during the hours that they spend with us in school. (I cannot find that word in any sentence of the No Child Left Behind Act.)

Faced with these pathogenic pressures, teachers of young children in particular need to learn not only to prevail in the quite literal respect of keeping their jobs and staying in their schools, but also to retain their sense of playful energy and fascination in the unexpected offerings of all those pint-sized packages of whim and curiosity who are entrusted to their care. This is why I fervently encourage them, even in the most decrepit and depressive-looking of our urban schools, to fight with every bit of courage they command to defend the right to celebrate each perishable day and hour in a child's life, which, in the current climate of opinion, may be one of the greatest challenges they have.

Schools can probably survive quite well without their rubrics charts, their AYPs, and their obsessive lists of numbered categories and containers, reminiscent of the lists severe psychotics make in efforts to control the uncontainable and, for healthy people, wonderful disorder of reality. They can't survive without excited teachers who take satisfaction in the beautiful vocation they have chosen. Keeping young teachers in our schools is of immense importance, but keeping them there with spirits strong and souls intact is more important still. If we lose this, we lose everything.

FOR FURTHER EXPLORATION

Kozol, J. (1991). *Savage inequalities: Children in America's schools.* New York: Harper Perennial.

Kozol, J. (2000). *Ordinary resurrections: Children in the years of hope.* New York: Harper Perennial.

Kozol, J. (2005). *The shame of the nation: The restoration of apartheid schooling in America.* New York: Broadway.

Kozol, J. (2007). *Letters to a young teacher.* New York: Broadway.

Jonathan Kozol is a National Book Award-winning author of 12 books on education. His newest work, *Letters to a Young Teacher,* was released in 2007 by Crown. The supportive network he recently created for teachers in the public schools may be reached at EducationActionInfo@gmail.com.

2

The Green Monongahela

John Taylor Gatto

I n the beginning I became a teacher without realizing it. At the time, I was growing up on the banks of the green Monongahela River forty miles southwest of Pittsburgh, and on the banks of that deep green and always mysterious river I became a student too, master of the flight patterns of blue dragonflies and cunning adversary of the iridescent ticks that infested the riverbank willows.

"Mind you watch the ticks, Jackie!" Grandmother Mossie would call as I headed for the riverbank, summer and winter, only a two-minute walk from Second Street, where I lived across the trolley tracks of Main Street and the Pennsylvania Railroad tracks that paralleled them. I watched the red and yellow ticks chewing holes in the pale green leaves as I ran to the riverbank. On the river I drank my first Iron City at eight, smoked every cigarette obtainable, and watched dangerous men and women make love there at night on blankets—all before I was twelve. It was my laboratory: I learned to watch closely and draw conclusions there.

How did the river make me a teacher? Listen. It was alive with paddle-wheel steamers in center channel, the turning paddles churning up clouds of white spray, making the green river boil bright orange where its chemical undercurrent was troubled; from shore you could clearly hear the loud *thump thump thump* on the water. From all over town young boys ran gazing in awe. A dozen times a day. No one ever became indifferent to them because nothing important can ever really be boring. You can see the difference, can't you? Between those serious boats and the truly boring spacecraft of the past few decades, just flying junk without a purpose a boy can believe in; it's hard to feign an interest even now that I teach for a living and would like to pretend for the sake of the New York kids who won't have paddle-wheelers in their lives. The rockets are dull toys children in Manhattan put aside the day after Christmas, never to touch again; the riverboats were serious magic, clearly demarcating the world of boys from the world of men. Levi-Strauss would know how to explain.

In Monongahela by that river everyone was my teacher. Daily, it seemed to a boy, one of the mile-long trains would stop in town to take on water and coal or for some mysterious reason; the brakeman and engineer would step among snot-nosed kids and spin railroad yarns, let us run in and out of boxcars, over and under flatcars, tank cars, coal cars, and numbers of other specialty cars whose function we memorized as easily as we memorized enemy plane silhouettes. Once a year, maybe, we got taken into the caboose that reeked of stale beer to be offered a bologna on white bread sandwich. The anonymous men lectured, advised, and inspired the boys of Monongahela—it was as much their job as driving the trains.

Sometimes a riverboat would stop in mid-channel and discharge a crew, who would row to shore, lying their skiff to one of the willows. That was the excuse for every rickety skiff in the twelve-block-long town to fill up with kids, pulling like Vikings, sometimes with sticks instead of oars, to raid the "Belle of Pittsburgh" or "The Original River Queen." Some kind of natural etiquette was at work in Monongahela. The rules didn't need to be written down: if men had time they showed boys how to grow up. We didn't whine when our time was up—men had work to do—we understood that and scampered away, grateful for the flash of our own futures they had had time to reveal, however small it was.

I was arrested three times growing up in Monongahela, or rather, picked up by the police and taken to jail to await a visit from Pappy to spring me. I wouldn't trade those times for anything. The first time I was nine, caught on my belly under a parked car at night, half an hour after curfew; in 1943 blinds were always drawn in the Monongahela Valley for fear Hitler's planes would somehow find a way to reach across the Atlantic to our steel mills lining both banks of the river. The Nazis were apparently waiting for a worried mother to go searching for her child with a flashlight after curfew, then *whammo!* down would descend the Teutonic air fleet!

Charlie was the cop's name. Down to the lockup we went—no call to mother until Charlie diagrammed the deadly menace of Goering's Luftwaffe. What a geopolitics lesson that was! Another time I speared a goldfish in the town fishpond and was brought from jail to the library, where I was sentenced to read for a month about the lives of animals. Finally, on VJ Day—when the Japanese cried "Uncle!"—I accepted a dare and broke the window of the police cruiser with a slingshot. Confessing, I suffered my first encounter with employment to pay for the glass, becoming sweep-up boy in my grandfather's printing office at fifty cents a week.

After I went away to Cornell, I saw Monongahela and its green river only one more time, when I went there after my freshman year to give blood to my dying grandfather, who lay in the town hospital, as strong in his dying as he had ever been in his living. In another room my grandmother lay dying. Both passed within twenty-four hours, my grandad, Harry Taylor Zimmer, Sr., taking my blood to his grave in the cemetery there. My family moved again and again and again, but in my own heart I never left Monongahela, where I learned to teach from being taught by everyone in town, where I learned to work from being asked to shoulder my share of responsibility, even as a boy, and where I learned to find adventures I made myself from the everyday stuff around me—the river and the people who lived alongside it.

In 1964, I was making a lot of money. That's what I walked away from to become a teacher. I was a copywriter on the fast track in advertising, a young fellow with a knack for writing thirty-second television commercials. My work required about one full day a month to complete, the rest of the time being spent in power breakfasts, after-work martinis at Michael's Pub, keeping up with the shifting fortunes of about twenty agencies in order to gauge the right time to jump ship for more money, and endless parties that always seemed to culminate in colossal headaches.

It bothered me that all the urgencies of the job were generated externally, but it bothered me more that the work I was doing seemed to have very little importance—even to the people who were paying for it. Worst of all, the problems this work posed were cut from such a narrow spectrum that it was clear that past, present, and future were to be of a piece: a twenty-nine-year-old man's work was no different from a thirty-nine-year-old man's work, or a forty-nine-year-old man's work (though there didn't seem to be any forty-nine-year-old copywriters—I had no idea why not).

"I'm leaving," I said one day to the copy chief.

"Are you nuts, Jack? You'll get profit sharing this year. We can match any offer you've got. Leaving for who?"

"For nobody, Dan. I mean I'm going to teach junior high school."

"When you see your mother next, tell her for me she raised a moron. Christ! Are you going to be sorry! In New York City we don't have schools; we have pens for lost souls. Teaching is a scam, a welfare project for losers who can't do anything else!"

Round and round I went with my advertising colleagues for a few days. Their scorn only firmed my resolve; the riverboats and trains of Monongahela were working inside me. I needed something to do that wasn't absurd more than I needed another party or a new abstract number in my bankbook.

And so I became a junior high school substitute teacher, working the beat from what's now Lincoln Center to Columbia, my alma mater, and from Harlem to the South Bronx. After three months the dismal working conditions, the ugly rooms, the torn books, the repeated instances of petty complaints from authorities, the bells, the buzzers, the drab teacher food in the cafeterias, the unpressed clothing, the inexplicable absence of conversation about children among the teachers (to this day, after twenty-six years in the business, I can honestly say I have never once heard an extended conversation about children or about teaching theory in any teachers' rooms I've been in) had just about done me in.

In fact, on the very first day I taught I was attacked by a boy waving a chair above his head. It happened in the infamous junior school Wadleigh, on 113th Street. I was given the eighth grade typing class—seventy-five students and typewriters—with this one injunction: "Under no circumstances are you to allow them to type. You lack the proper license. Is that understood?" A man named Mr. Bash said that to me.

It couldn't have taken more than sixty seconds from the time I closed the door and issued the order not to type for one hundred and fifty hands to snake under the typewriter covers and begin to type. But not all at once—that would have been too easy. First, three machines began to *clack clack* from the right rear. Quick, who were the culprits? I would race to the corner screaming *stop!*—when suddenly, from behind my back, three other machines would begin! Whirling as only a young man can do, I caught one small boy in the act. Then, to a veritable symphony of machines clicking, bells ringing, platens being thrown, I hoisted the boy from his chair and announced at the top of my foolish lungs I would make an example of this miscreant.

"Look out!" a girl shouted, and I turned toward her voice just in time to see a large brother of the little fellow I held heading toward me with a chair raised above his head. Releasing his brother, I seized a chair myself and raised it aloft. A standoff! We regarded each other at a distance of about ten feet for what seemed forever, the class jeering and howling, when the room door opened and Assistant Principal Bash, the very man who'd given the no-typing order, appeared.

"Mr. Gatto, have these children been typing?"

"No, sir," I said, lowering my chair, "but I think they want to. What do you suggest they do instead?"

He looked at me for signs of impudence or insubordination for a second, then, as if thinking better of rebuking this upstart, he said merely, "Fall back on your resources," and left the room.

Most of the kids laughed—they'd seen this drama enacted before.

The situation was defused, but silently I dubbed Wadleigh the "Death School." Stopping by the office on my way home, I told the secretary not to call me again if they needed a sub.

The very next morning my phone rang at 6:30. "Are you available for work today, Mr. Gatto?" said the voice briskly.

"Who is this?" I asked suspiciously. (Ten schools were using me for sub work in those days, and each identified itself at once.)

"The law clearly states, Mr. Gatto, that we do not have to tell you who we are until you tell us whether you are available for work."

"Never mind," I bellowed, "there's only one school who'd pull such crap! The answer is no! I am never available to work in your pig-pen school!" And I slammed the receiver back onto its cradle.

But the truth was none of the sub assignments were boat rides; schools had an uncanny habit of exploiting substitutes and providing no support for their survival. It's likely I'd have returned to advertising if a little girl, desperate to free herself from an intolerable situation, hadn't drawn me into her personal school nightmare and shown me how I could find my own significance in teaching, just as those strong men in the riverboats and trains had found their own significance, a currency all of us need for our self-esteem.

It happened this way. Occasionally, I'd get a call from an elementary school. This particular day it was a third grade assignment at a school on 107th Street, which in those days was nearly one hundred percent non-Hispanic in its teaching staff and 99% Hispanic in its student body.

Like many desperate teachers, I killed most of the day listening to the kids read, one after another, and expending most of my energy trying to shut the audience up. This class had a very low ranking, and no one was able to put more than three or four words together without stumbling. All of a sudden, though, a little girl named Milagros sailed through a selection without a mistake. After class I called her over to my desk and asked why she was in this class of bad readers. She replied that "they" (the administration) wouldn't let her out because, as they explained to her mother, she was really a bad reader who had fantasies of being a better reader than she was. "But look, Mr. Gatto, my brother is in the sixth grade, and I can read every word in his English book better than he can!"

I was a little intrigued, but truthfully not much. Surely the authorities knew what they were doing. Still, the little girl seemed so frustrated I invited her to calm down and read to me from the sixth grade book. I explained that if she did well, I would take her case to the principal. I expected nothing.

Milagros, on the other hand, expected justice. Diving into "The Devil and Daniel Webster," she polished off the first two pages without a gulp. My God, I thought, this is a real reader. What is she doing here? Well, maybe it was a simple accident, easily corrected. I sent her home, promising to argue her case. Little did I suspect what a hornet's nest my request to have Milagros moved to a better class would stir up.

"You have some nerve, Mr. Gatto. I can't remember when a substitute ever told me how to run my school before. Have you taken specialized courses in reading?"

"No."

"Well then, suppose you leave these matters to the experts!"

"But the kid can read!"

"What do you suggest?"

"I suggest you test her, and if she isn't a dummy, get her out of the class she's in!"

"I don't like your tone. None of our children are dummies, Mr. Gatto. And you will find that girls like Milagros have many ways to fool amateurs like yourself. This is a matter of a child having memorized one story. You can see if I had to waste my time arguing with people like you I'd have no time left to run a school."

But, strangely, I felt self-appointed as the girl's champion, even though I'd probably never see her again.

I insisted, and the principal finally agreed to test Milagros herself the following Wednesday after school. I made it a point to tell the little girl the next day. By that time I'd come to think that the principal was probably right—she'd memorized one story—but I still warned her she'd need to know the vocabulary from the whole advanced reader and be able to read any story the principal picked, without hesitation. My responsibility was over, I told myself.

The following Wednesday after school I waited in the room for Milagros' ordeal to be over. At 3:30 she shyly opened the door of the room.

"How'd it go?" I asked.

"I don't know," she answered, "but I didn't make any mistakes. Mrs. Hefferman was very angry, I could tell."

I saw Mrs. Hefferman, the principal, early the next morning before school opened. "It seems we've made a mistake with Milagros," she said curtly. "She will be moved, Mr. Gatto. Her mother has been informed."

Several weeks later, when I got back to the school to sub, Milagros dropped by, telling me she was in the fast class now and doing very well. She also gave me a sealed card. When I got home that night, I found it, unopened, in my suitcoat pocket. I opened it and saw a gaudy birthday card with blue flowers on it. Opening the card, I read, "A teacher like you cannot be found. Signed, Your student, Milagros."

That simple sentence made me a teacher for life. It was the first praise I ever heard in my working existence that had any meaning. I never forgot it, though I never saw Milagros again and only heard of her again in 1988, twenty-four years later. Then one day I picked up a newspaper and read:

Occupational Teacher Award

Milagros Maldonado, United Federation of Teachers, has won the Distinguished Occupational Teacher Award of the State Education Department for "demonstrated achievement and exemplary professionalism." A secretarial studies teacher at Norman Thomas High School, New York City, from which she graduated, Miss Maldonado was selected as a Manhattan Teacher of the Year in 1985 and was nominated the following year for the Woman of Conscience Award given by the National Council of Women.

Ah, Milagros, is it just possible that I was your Monongahela River? No matter, a teacher like you cannot be found.

FOR FURTHER EXPLORATION

Gatto, J.T. (1992). *Dumbing us down: The hidden curriculum of compulsory schooling.* Philadelphia, PA: New Society Publishers.

Gatto, J.T. (1993). *The exhausted school: Bending the bars of traditional education.* Albany, CA: Berkeley Hills Books.

Gatto, J.T. (2000). *A different kind of teacher: Solving the crisis of American schooling.* Albany, CA: Berkeley Hills Books.

Gatto, J.T. (2010). *Weapons of mass instruction: A schoolteacher's journey through the dark world of compulsory schooling.* Gabriola Island, BC: New Society Publishers.

John Taylor Gatto is an author and former New York City and New York State Teacher of the Year.

3

Why Teach?

Herbert Kohl

THERE ARE MANY reasons that lead people to choose elementary and secondary school teaching. Some people choose teaching because they enjoy being with young people and watching them grow. Others need to be around young people and let their students grow for them. Teaching for some is a family tradition, a craft that one naturally masters and a world that surrounds one from childhood. For others teaching is magical because they have had magical teachers whose roles they want to assume. Teaching can be a way of sharing power, of convincing people to value what you value, or to explore the world with you or through you.

There are some cynical reasons for going into teaching, which were much more prevalent when getting a job was not difficult. For example, for some people teaching becomes a matter of temporary convenience, of taking a job which seems respectable and not too demanding while going to law school, supporting a spouse through professional or graduate school, scouting around for a good business connection, or merely marking time while figuring out what one really wants to do as an adult. For others teaching is a jumping-off point into administration, research, or supervision.

Many student teachers I have known over the last five years are becoming teachers to negate the wounds they received when they were in school. They want to counter the racism, the sexual put-downs, all the other humiliations they experienced with new, freer ways of teaching and learning. They want to be teachers to protect and nurture people younger than they who have every likelihood of being damaged by the schools. Some of these people come from poor or oppressed communities, and their commitment to the children is a commitment to the community of their parents, brothers and sisters, and their own children as well. Others, mostly from white middle or upper-class backgrounds, have given up dialogue with their parents and rejected the community they grew up in. Teaching for them becomes a means of searching for ways of connecting with a community they can care for and serve.

There were a number of reasons that led me to choose elementary school teaching. For one, I never wanted to put my toys away and get on with the serious business of being an adult. I enjoy playing games, building things that have no particular purpose or value beyond themselves, trying painting, sculpting, macrame without becoming obsessed by them. I enjoy moving from subject to subject, from a math problem to a design problem, from bead collecting to the classification of mollusks. Specialization does not interest me, and teaching elementary school makes it possible for me to explore many facets of the world and share what I learn. My self-justification is that the games I play and the things I explore all contribute to making a curriculum that will interest and engage my students.

I guess also I became a teacher of young children initially because I thought they were purer, more open, and less damaged than I was. They were the saviors—they could dare to be creative where I was inhibited; they could write well because they didn't know what good writing was supposed to be; they could learn with ease, whereas I was overridden with anxiety over grades and tests. I never forgot the time in high school when I was informed that I missed making Arista, the national high school honor society, by 0.1 of a point. I went into the boys' bathroom and cried, the first time I had cried since being a baby. Neither Hitler's horrors nor the deaths of relatives and friends could cause me to cry because I was a male and was too proud to show sadness and weakness. Yet 0.1 of a grade point could bring tears and self-hatred and feelings of inferiority. And what if I'd made it—would I laugh at my friends' tears because they missed by 0.1 of a point just as they did at me? There is no reward on either side of that cruel system.

When I became a teacher, some of my dreams of free development for my own students came true—they could be open and creative. But they also could be closed, destructive, nasty, manipulating—all the things I wanted to avoid in the adult world. It was important to sort out the romance of teaching from the realities of teaching and discover whether, knowing the problems, the hard work and frustration, it still made sense to teach. For me the answer has been "yes," but there are still times I wish I'd chosen some easier vocation.

Everyone who goes into teaching, even temporarily, has many reasons for choosing to spend five hours a day with young people. These reasons are often unarticulated and more complex than one imagines. Yet they have significant effects upon everyday work with students and on the satisfaction and strength the teacher gets from that work. Consequently, it makes sense, if you are thinking of becoming a teacher, to begin questioning yourself and understanding what you expect from teaching and what you are willing to give to it.

It also is of value to understand what type of children, what age, what setting is most sensible for your temperament and skills. Simple mistakes like teaching children that are too young or too old can destroy promising teachers. I had a friend who was teaching first grade and having a miserable time of it. The class was out of order, the students paid no attention to what she said, and she couldn't understand what the children were talking about. One day in anger, she blurted out to me that her major frustration was that she couldn't hold a good conversation with her class. She wanted to talk about civil rights, racism, about ways of reconstructing our society, about poverty and oppression.

She wanted to read poetry with the children, expose them to music. She prepared each class for hours, put herself into the work, cared about the children—and yet things kept on getting worse. What she wanted and needed from her six-year-olds was simply beyond them. I suggested that she try junior high if she wanted dialogue and challenge from her students. First grade was a mistake. The next year she transferred to one of the most difficult junior high schools in New York City, where she immediately felt at home. She was in the right place—what she offered could be used by the students, and therefore they could reward her with the exchange she needed.

There are a number of questions people thinking of becoming teachers might ask themselves in order to clarify their motives and focus on the type of teaching situations that could make sense for them. These questions do not have simple answers. Sometimes they cannot be answered until one has taught for a while. But I think it makes sense to keep them in mind while considering whether you actually want to teach and then, if you do, during training and the first few years of work.

1. What reasons do you give yourself for wanting to teach? Are they all negative (e.g., because the schools are oppressive, or because I was damaged, or because I need a job and working as a teacher is more

respectable than working as a cab driver or salesperson)? What are the positive reasons for wanting to teach? Is there any pleasure to be gained from teaching? Knowledge? Power? As an elaboration on this, there is another similar question:

2. Why do you want to spend so much time with young people? Are you afraid of adults? Intimidated by adult company? Fed up with the competition and coldness of business and the university? Do you feel more comfortable with children? Have you spent much time with children recently, or are you mostly fantasizing how they would behave? Before deciding to become a teacher, it makes sense to spend time with young people of different ages at camp, as a tutor, or as a playground supervisor. I have found it valuable to spend time at playgrounds and observe children playing with each other or relating to their parents or teachers. One day watch five-, ten-, fifteen-year-olds on the playground or the street, and try to see how they are alike and how they are different. The more you train your eye to observe young people's behavior, the easier it will be to pick up attitudes and feelings and relationships in your own classroom.

Elaborating on the question of why spend so much time with young people, it is important to ask . . .

3. What do you want from the children? Do you want them to do well on tests? Learn particular subject matter? Like each other? Like you? How much do you need to have students like you? Are you afraid to criticize them or set limits on their behavior because they might be angry with you? Do you consider yourself one of the kids? Is there any difference in your mind between your role and that of your prospective students?

Many young teachers are not sure of themselves as adults, feel very much like children and cover over a sense of their own powerlessness with the rhetoric of equality. They tell their students that they are all equal and then are surprised when their students walk all over them or show them no respect. If students have to go to school, if the teacher is paid and the students are not, if the young expect to learn something from the older in order to become more powerful themselves, then the teacher who pretends to be an equal of the student is both a hypocrite and a disappointment in the students' eyes. This does not mean that the teacher doesn't learn with or from the students, nor does it mean that the teacher must try to coerce the students into learning or be the source of all authority. It does mean, however, that the teacher ought to have some knowledge or skills to share, mastery of a subject that the students haven't already encountered and might be interested in. This leads to the next question:

4. What do you know that you can teach to or share with your students? Too many young people coming out of college believe that they do not know anything worth sharing or at least feel they haven't learned anything in school worth it. Teacher training usually doesn't help since it concentrates on "teaching skills" rather than the content of what might be learned. Yet there is so much young people will respond to if the material emerges out of problems that challenge them and if the solutions can be developed without constant judging and testing. I have found that young people enjoy working hard, pushing and challenging themselves. What they hate is having their self-esteem tied up in learning and regurgitating material that bores them. Constant testing interferes with learning.

The more you know, the easier teaching becomes. A skilled teacher uses all his or her knowledge and experience in the service of building a curriculum each year for the particular individuals that are in the class. If you cannot think of any particular skills you have, but just like being with children, don't go right into teaching. Find other ways of spending time with young people while you master some skills that you believe are worth sharing.

Here is a partial list of things one could learn: printing; working with wood, plastic, fabrics, metal; how to run a store; making or repairing cars, shoes, boats, airplanes; playing and teaching cards, board, dice, ball games; playing and composing music; understanding ways of calculating and the use and construction of computers; using closed circuit TV; making films; taking pictures; understanding history, especially history that explains part of the present; knowing about animals and plants; understanding something of the chemistry of life; knowing the law; understanding how to use or care for one's body.

These subjects are intrinsically interesting to many students and can be used as well in teaching the so-called basic skills of reading, writing, and math, which are themselves no more than tools that extend people's power and make some aspects of the world more accessible. Too often these basic skills are taught in isolation from interesting content, leaving students wondering what use phonics or set theory could possibly have in their lives. It is not good enough to tell the class that what they are learning now will be of use when they are grown-ups. Six-year-olds and ten-year-olds have immediate interests, and reading and math ought to be tied to these interests, which range all the way from learning to make and build things to learning to play games and master comic books and fix bicycles and make money and cook and find out about other people's feelings and lives—the list can go on and on. The more time you spend informally with young children, the more you will learn about their interests. Listening carefully and following up on what you hear are skills a teacher has to cultivate. If students are interested in paper airplanes, it is more sensible to build a unit around flying than to ban them and assume police functions.

5. Getting more specific, a prospective teacher ought to consider what age youngster he or she feels greatest affinity toward or most comfortable with. There are some adults who are afraid of high school- or junior high school-aged people (thirteen to seventeen-year-olds), while others are terrified at the idea of being left alone in a room with twenty-four six-year-olds. Fear of young people is neither unnatural nor uncommon in our culture. This is especially true in the schools, where undeclared warfare between the adults and the children defines much of the social climate. As long as young people feel constantly tested and judged by their teacher and have to experience the humiliation of their own or their friends' failures, they try to get even in any ways they can. Teachers who try to be kind often find themselves taken advantage of, while those who assume a strict stand are constantly tricked and mocked. It takes time and experience to win the respect of young people and not be considered their enemy in the context of a traditional American school.

It is very difficult to feel at ease in a classroom, to spend five hours with young people, and not emerge wiped out or exhausted at the end of the day. This is especially true if one is mismatched with the students.

Great patience and humor, an ease with physical contact, and an ability to work with one's hands as well as one's mouth are needed for teachers of five- and six-year-olds. A lack of sexual prudery is almost a prerequisite for junior high school teachers, while physical and personal confidence and the love of some subject make work with high school students much easier.

This does not mean that an adult shouldn't take chances working with students whose age poses a problem. I know this year has been one of the most fulfilling of my teaching years, and yet I was full of anxiety about my ability to be effective with five- and six-year-olds after working with twelve- to eighteen-year-olds for twelve years. I taught myself to be patient, learned to work with my hands, to play a lot, to expect change to develop slowly. The students' ability to express affection or dislike openly and physically moved and surprised me, and initially their energy exhausted me. I must have lost fifteen pounds the first month, just trying to keep up with them.

One way of discovering what age youngster to begin working with is to visit a lot of schools. Try to find teachers you like and respect, and spend a few days working alongside them. Don't visit for an hour or two. It is important to stay all day (or if you have time, all week) to get a sense of the flow of time and energy working with that age person involves. Of course, your rhythm as a teacher might be different, but it is important to have a sense of what it is like to be with young people all day before becoming a teacher.

6. Before becoming a teacher it is important to examine one's attitudes toward racial and class differences. Racism is part of the heritage of white Americans, and though it can be mostly unlearned, it manifests itself in many subtle ways. Some white teachers are overtly condescending toward black and brown and red children, giving them crayons instead of books. Others are more subtly condescending—they congratulate themselves on caring enough to work in a ghetto, choose one or two favorite students and put the rest down as products of a bad environment. They consider themselves liberal, nonracist, and yet are repelled by most of their students while believing that they are "saving" a few. There are ways of picking up racist attitudes in one's own way of talking. When a teacher talks about his or her pupils as "them" or "these kind of children," or when a favorite pupil is described as "not like the rest of them," one is in the presence of a racist attitude. Accompanying this attitude is usually an unarticulated fear of the children. I have seen white kindergarten teachers treat poor black five-year-old boys as if they were nineteen, carried guns and knives, and had criminal intentions at all times. Needless to say, this sort of adult attitude confuses and profoundly upsets the child. It also causes the adult to ignore acts that should otherwise be prevented. Many white teachers in ghetto schools claim they are being permissive and believe in allowing their students freedom when it would be closer to the truth to say that they are afraid that their students will beat them up and that they are afraid to face the moral rage their students have from being treated in brutal and racist ways. When a student destroys a typewriter or brutalizes a smaller student, that is not an acceptable or humane use of freedom.

Young teachers have a hard time knowing how and when to be firm and when to be giving. This becomes even more complex when the teacher is white, of liberal persuasion, afraid of physical violence, and teaching a class of poor children who are not white.

However, fear is not limited to white-nonwhite situations. Many middle-class people have attitudes toward poor people in general that are manifested in the classroom in ways very close to the racist attitudes described above. Poverty is looked upon as a disease that one does not want to have contact with. Many teachers have a hard time touching poor children, as if somehow the poverty can be spread by physical contact. Then there are the condescending liberal attitudes toward "saving" a few good students from the general condition of poverty, as if the rest got what they deserve.

Prospective teachers, especially those who might choose or be assigned to work with poor or nonwhite students have to examine their own attitudes toward class and race. If these people come from isolated white middle-class communities, I would suggest they move into a mixed urban community and live and work there before becoming teachers. Then they might be able to see their students as individuals rather than as representatives of a class or race. And they might also develop insight into the different ways people learn and teach each other and themselves. Good teaching requires an understanding and respect of the strengths of one's pupils, and this cannot develop if they and their parents are alien to one's nonschool experience.

7. Another, perhaps uncomfortable, question a prospective teacher ought to ask him or herself is what sex-based motives he or she has for wanting to work with young people. Do you want to enable young boys or girls to become the boys or girls you could never be? To, for example, free the girls of the image of prettiness and quietness and encourage them to run and fight, and on an academic level, mess about with science and get lost in the abstractions of math? Or to encourage boys to write poetry, play with dolls, let their fantasies come out, and not feel abnormal if they enjoy reading or acting or listening to music?

Dealing with sex is one of the most difficult things teachers who care to have all their students develop fully have to learn how to manage. Often children arrive at school as early as kindergarten with clear ideas of what is proper behavior for boys and girls. The teacher has to be sensitive to parentally and culturally enforced sex roles that schools traditionally enforce, and be able to lead children to choose what they want to learn, free of those encumbrances.

There are other problems teachers have to sort out that are sexual rather than sex-based. Many male teachers enjoy flirting with female students and using flirtation as a means of controlling the girls. Similarly, some female teachers try to seduce male students into learning. All these exchanges are covert—a gesture, a look, a petulant or joking remark.

Children take adult affection very seriously, and often what is play or dalliance on the part of the adult becomes the basis of endless fantasy and expectation on the part of the child. The issue exists in the early grades, but is much more overt on the high school level, where young teachers often naively express affection and concern, which students interpret as sexual overtures (which in some cases they might actually be, however unclear to the teacher).

Entering into an open relationship with a student is another issue altogether. Obviously, love is not bound to age or status. One should be wary, however, of confusing love with conquest and manipulation, but these problems are not limited to one's life as a teacher.

A final question that should be asked with respect to sex in the classroom: do you need to get even with one sex, as a group, for real or fancied injuries you experienced? Do you dislike boys or girls as a group? Do you feel that the girls were always loved too much? That the boys brutalized you and need to learn a lesson? That somehow you have to get even in your classroom for an injury you suffered as a child? There are many good reasons for not becoming a teacher, and the need to punish others for a hurt you suffered is certainly one.

It might seem that I'm being harsh or cynical by raising questions about motives for teaching and suggesting that there are circumstances in which a person either should not become a teacher or should wait a while. If anything, these questions are too easy and can unfortunately be put aside with facile, self-deceiving answers. But teaching young people— i.e., helping them become sane, powerful, self-respecting, and loving adults—is a very serious and difficult job in a culture as oppressive and confused as ours, and needs strong and self-critical people.

There are other questions that ought to be considered. These might seem less charged, but are not less important.

8. What kind of young people do you want to work with? There are a number of children with special needs that can be assisted by adults with particular qualities. For example, there are some severely disturbed children—children whose behavior is bizarre, who are not verbal, who might not yet be toilet-trained at nine or ten, who might be engaged in dialogue for hours at a time with creatures you cannot perceive. My first experience was at a school for severely disturbed children very much like those described above. I liked the children, but lasted only six months since I didn't have the patience. I needed them to recognize and engage me, even through defiance. I couldn't bear their silence or removal, their unrelieved pain. As soon as I changed schools and began to work with normal, though angry and defiant, young people, I felt at home.

My wife, Judy, is different. She has the patience to live with small increments of change, is calm and gentle and nonthreatening to remote and scared children. She feels much more at home in silent or remote worlds than I do, and is an excellent teacher of disturbed children. It is a matter of knowing who you are and what the children need.

These same questions should be raised by people thinking of working with deaf, blind, or physically damaged people. Who are they? What is the world they live in? How can I serve them?

Let me illustrate a perverse way of going about deciding how to serve people in order to point toward a more healthy way of functioning. For a long time most schools for deaf children were controlled by nondeaf teachers, parents, and administrators who advocated the oral, rather than the manual, tradition. The oral tradition maintained that it was necessary for deaf individuals to learn to speak instead of depending on sign language. Many oralist schools prohibited their students from using sign language, and some professionals within that tradition maintained that sign language was not a "real" language at all, but some degenerate or primitive form of communication. All these prohibitions were to no avail—deaf children learned signing from each other and used it when the teachers' backs were turned. Many deaf adults trained in oralist schools ended up despising the language they were forced to learn and retreated into an all-deaf world where communication was in signs. Recently things have begun to change—sign language has been shown to be an expressive, sophisticated language with perhaps even greater potential for communication than oral language. A deaf-power movement has developed which insists that teachers of the deaf respond to the needs of deaf adults and children. It is no longer possible to tell deaf people what they must learn from outside the community. To teach within a deaf community (and, in fact, in all communities) requires understanding the world people live in and responding to their needs as they articulate them. This does not mean that the teacher should be morally or politically neutral. Rather, it means that being a teacher does not put an individual in a position of forcing his or her values on students or community. A teacher must engage in dialogue with the students and parents if he or she hopes to change them—and be open to change as well. Many teachers have been educated in communities they initially thought they would educate.

9. Some people get along well in crowds, and others function best with small groups or single individuals. Before becoming a classroom teacher, it is important to ask oneself what the effect is on one's

personality of spending a lot of time with over twenty people in the same room. Some of the best teachers I know do not feel at ease or work effectively with more than a dozen students at a time. With those dozen, however, they are unusually effective. There are other people who have a gift for working on a one-to-one basis with students no one else seems to reach. There are ways to prepare oneself for individual or small-group work—as skills specialist, remedial teacher, learning disabilities specialist, and so forth. There are also schools where it is possible to work with small groups as a teacher. Once you decide how you want to begin to work in a school, then you can look around and try to discover a situation in which you can be effective.

10. A final, though complex, question is what kind of school one should teach in. This is especially difficult for people like myself, who believe that almost every school in the United States, within and without the public school system, contributes to maintaining an oppressive society based upon an unequal distribution of wealth and a debasement of people's sense of dignity and personal worth. In the next section I will elaborate on this and suggest some ways of infiltrating the system and struggling to change it. It is my conviction that teachers who comply with the values and goals of this culture can only do so at the cost of stripping their students of self-respect and substituting violence in the form of competition in place of knowledge, curiosity, and a sense of community.

Getting a Job. There are not many teaching jobs these days. If you still care to teach, broaden your notion of where you might teach. The schools are only one possible place. Try businesses, social agencies, hospitals, parks, community service organizations. It is, for example, possible to teach literacy to hospitalized children; to use an art and recreation program as a means of teaching most anything; to become associated with a job training program or a prison program. It is possible to set up a child care operation in your home, or turn babysitting into a teaching situation, or set up an after-school tutoring program. Often there are federal or state monies available for reading or child care or delinquency prevention programs. It is important to know how to get access to that money. If necessary, go to the county board of education, to Head Start offices, to regional offices of the Department of Health, Education and Welfare and ask about the programs they sponsor. Often a few weeks of research may open up a number of unexpected possibilities. The Grantsmanship Newsletter is an excellent source of information and is worth having (for subscriptions write to Grantsmanship Center, 1015 W. Olympic Blvd., Los Angeles, CA 90015).

Also think about teaching children with problems—the severely disturbed, retarded, physically handicapped, deaf, or blind. Remember, children are children despite the way in which society labels them. Basically the same techniques and belief in the children's abilities work with all kinds of children. If there are special things one need learn, they are easy to master. The more one thinks of teaching outside the schools, the more imaginative one can be in searching for a job that will allow one to teach, or in defining a job and convincing others that it is worth supporting.

FOR FURTHER EXPLORATION

Kohl, H. R. (1968). *36 children: Innovations in education.* Columbus, OH: Open University Press.

Kohl, H. R. (1969). *The open classroom: A practical guide to a new way of teaching.* New York: New York Review.

Kohl, H. R. (2004). *Stupidity and tears: Teaching and learning in troubled times.* New York: The New Press.

Kohl, H. R., & Holt, J. (1967). *Teaching the "unteachable": The story of an experiment in children's writing.* New York: New York Review.

Herbert Kohl is the author of more than forty books on education. He and his wife, Judy, were the recipients of the National Book Award in 1978 for *The View From the Oak.*

PART II

Who Are Today's Students?

I t was the end of August and Ashley Murphy was headed back to Horace Mann Elementary School for the first time since finishing the fifth grade more than 10 years ago. She was thrilled to be returning as a teacher to the very school where she had so many fond memories as a student. To think that she would be shoulder-to-shoulder with some of her former teachers and that now they would be her colleagues!

Driving up to the old brick building brought back a flood of memories: the smell of chalk dust; the neat rows of desks; Steven Parker teasing her in the third grade about her braces; and the stern and aloof principal, Mr. Dabrowski, walking into the cafeteria and immediately causing a hush to fall over the crowd of excited children's voices. Ashley couldn't wait to reunite with her old teachers, the women whose guidance and inspiration was instrumental in her decision to teach. They will be so proud of me, she thought, to see how I have changed, how I have matured.

Ashley was excited too about sharing what she had learned in her teacher education program. And, even though the principal had called this end of summer orientation meeting simply to introduce the new staff and to acquaint everyone with some new districtwide policies, Ashley came prepared with reams of beautifully prepared lessons and activities she would use to kick off the first few weeks of the year with her class of second graders. She couldn't wait to show her new colleagues what she had brought with her.

Imagine Ashley's despair then when Nancy Rush, *her* former second grade teacher, asked Ashley how she knew her carefully prepared lessons would be appropriate for the students who would soon stream into her classroom.

"But, I don't understand," Ashley said, "I've worked very hard on these lessons and each of them reflects what my professors told us about the importance of inquiry learning and engaging students in hands-on activities."

"Well," Nancy began, "how can you plan a series of lessons when you have not considered the most important question: Who are *your* students? Do you think they will look and act like your friends and you did when *you* were in second grade? Will they come from backgrounds similar to your own? Will they all speak English as a first language? Might they have disabilities or other challenges that affect their learning? Who are your students?"

Why is this such an important question? How do race, ethnicity, and income level, for example, affect the teaching and learning cycle?

4

What Should Teachers Do?

Ebonics and Culturally Responsive Instruction

Lisa Delpit

I will submit that one of the reasons [Ebonics] is a problem, if you will—a controversy—is that you cannot divorce language from its speakers. And if you have people who have been disenfranchised, are neglected, are rejected, it is very difficult for the society at large to elevate their language. And, thus, when you start to try to make a case with legitimizing Ebonics—a way of communicating by some, although not all African-Americans speak it—you, in effect, are talking about legitimizing a group of people. You are talking about bringing them to a status comparable to society at large. And that's always a difficult proposition. So, in a certain sense, we cannot talk about Ebonics separate and distinct from the state of African-American people in the United States as a neglected and as an underclass, marginalized, if you will, people.

—Orlando Taylor
Professor of Communications at Howard University
Emerge *magazine, April 1997*

The "Ebonics Debate" has created much more heat than light for most of the country. For teachers trying to determine what implications there might be for classroom practice, enlightenment has been a completely nonexistent commodity. I have been asked often enough recently, "What do you think about Ebonics? Are you for it or against it?" My answer must be neither. I can be neither for Ebonics or against Ebonics any more than I can be for or against air. It exists. It is the language spoken by many of our African-American children. It is the language they heard as their mothers nursed them and changed their diapers and played peek-a-boo with them. It is the language through which they first encountered love, nurturance, and joy.

On the other hand, most teachers of those African-American children who have been least well-served by educational systems believe that their students' life chances will be further hampered if they do not learn Standard English. In the stratified society in which we live, they are absolutely correct. While having access to the politically mandated language form will not, by any means, guarantee economic success (witness the growing numbers of unemployed African Americans holding doctorates), not having access will almost certainly guarantee failure.

So what must teachers do? Should they spend their time relentlessly "correcting" their Ebonics-speaking children's language so that it might conform to what we have learned to refer to as Standard English? Despite good intentions, constant correction seldom has the desired effect. Such correction increases cognitive monitoring of speech, thereby making talking difficult. To illustrate, I have frequently taught a relatively simple new "dialect" to classes of preservice teachers. In this dialect, the phonetic element "iz" is added after the first consonant or consonant cluster in each syllable of a word. (Maybe becomes miz-ay-biz-ee and apple, iz-ap-piz-le.) After a bit of drill and practice, the students are asked to tell a partner in "iz" language why they decided to become teachers. Most only haltingly attempt a few words before lapsing into either silence or into Standard English. During a follow-up discussion, all students invariably speak of the impossibility of attempting to apply rules while trying to formulate and express a thought. Forcing speakers to monitor their language typically produces silence.

Correction may also affect students' attitudes toward their teachers. In a recent research project, middle school, inner-city students were interviewed about their attitudes toward their teachers and school. One young woman complained bitterly, "Mrs. _____ always be interrupting to make you 'talk correct' and stuff. She be butting into your conversations when you not even talking to her! She need to mind her own business!" Clearly this student will be unlikely to either follow the teacher's directives or to want to imitate her speech style.

GROUP IDENTITY

Issues of group identity may also affect students' oral production of a different dialect. Researcher Sharon Nelson-Barber (1982), in a study of phonologic aspects of Pima Indian language, found that, in grades 1–3, the children's English most approximated the standard dialect of their teachers. But surprisingly, by fourth grade, when one might assume growing competence in standard forms, their language moved significantly toward the local dialect. These fourth graders had the competence to express themselves in a more standard form but chose, consciously or unconsciously, to use the language of those in their local environments. The researcher believes that, by ages eight to nine, these children became aware of their group membership and its importance to their well-being, and this realization was reflected in their language. They may also have become increasingly aware of the school's negative attitude toward their community and found it necessary—through choice of linguistic form—to decide with which camp to identify.

What should teachers do about helping students acquire an additional oral form? First, they should recognize that the linguistic form a student brings to school is intimately connected with loved one's community, and personal identity. To suggest that this form is "wrong" or, even worse, ignorant, is to suggest that something is wrong with the student and his or her family. To denigrate your language is, then, in African-American terms, to "talk about your mama." Anyone who knows anything about African-American culture knows the consequences of that speech act!

On the other hand, it is equally important to understand that students who do not have access to the politically popular dialect form in this country are less likely to succeed economically than their peers who do. How can both realities be embraced in classroom instruction?

It is possible and desirable to make the actual study of language diversity a part of the curriculum for all students. For younger children, discussions about the differences in the ways TV characters from different cultural groups speak can provide a starting point. A collection of the many children's books written in the dialects of various cultural groups can also provide a wonderful basis for learning about linguistic diversity, as can audiotaped stories narrated by individuals from different cultures, including taped books read by members of the children's home communities. Mrs. Pat, a teacher chronicled by Stanford University researcher Shirley Brice Heath (1983), had her students become language "detectives," interviewing a variety of individuals and listening to the radio and TV to discover the differences and similarities in the ways people talked. Children can learn that there are many ways of saying the same thing, and that certain contexts suggest particular kinds of linguistic performances.

Some teachers have groups of students create bilingual dictionaries of their own language form and Standard English. Both the students and the teacher become engaged in identifying terms and deciding upon the best translations. This can be done as generational dictionaries, too, given the proliferation of "youth culture" terms growing out of the Ebonics-influenced tendency for the continual regeneration of vocabulary. Contrastive grammatical structures can be studied similarly but, of course, as the Oakland policy suggests, teachers must be aware of the grammatical structure of Ebonics before they can launch into this complex study.

Other teachers have had students become involved with standard forms through various kinds of role-play. For example, memorizing parts for drama productions allow students to practice and "get the feel" of speaking Standard English while not under the threat of correction. A master teacher of African-American children in Oakland, Carrie Secret, uses this technique and extends it so that students videotape their practice performances and self-critique them as to the appropriate use of Standard English. (But I must add that Carrie's use of drama and oration goes much beyond acquiring Standard English. She inspires pride and community connections that are truly wondrous to behold.) The use of self-critique of recorded forms may prove even more useful than I initially realized. California State University–Hayward professor Etta Hollins has reported that just by leaving a tape recorder on during an informal class period and playing it back with no comment, students began to code-switch—moving between Standard English and Ebonics—more effectively. It appears that they may have not realized which language form they were using until they heard themselves speak on tape.

Young students can create puppet shows or role-play cartoon characters—many "superheroes" speak almost hypercorrect Standard English. Playing a role eliminates the possibility of implying that the child's language is inadequate and suggests, instead, that different language forms are appropriate in different contexts. Some other teachers in New York City have had their students produce a news show every day for the rest of the school. The students take on the personae of famous newscasters, keeping in character as they develop and read their news reports. Discussions ensue about whether Tom Brokaw would have said it that way, again taking the focus off the child's speech.

Although most educators think of Black Language as primarily differing in grammar and syntax, there are other differences in oral language of which teachers should be aware in a multicultural context, particularly in discourse style and language use. Harvard University researcher Sarah Michaels and other researchers identified differences in children's narratives at "sharing time" (Michaels & Cazden, 1986). They found that there was a tendency among young white children to tell "topic-centered" narratives—stories focused on one event—and a tendency among Black youngsters, especially girls, to tell "episodic" narratives—stories that include shifting scenes and are typically longer. While these differences are interesting in themselves, what is of greater significance is adults' responses to the differences. C. B. Cazden (1988) reports on a subsequent project in which a white adult was taped reading the oral narratives of Black and white first graders, with all syntax dialectal markers removed. Adults were asked to listen to the stories and comment about the children's likelihood of success in school. The researchers were surprised by the differential responses given by Black and white adults.

VARYING REACTIONS

In responding to the retelling of a Black child's story, the white adults were uniformly negative, making such comments as "terrible story, incoherent" and "[n]ot a story at all in the sense of describing something that happened." Asked to judge this child's academic competence, all of the white adults rated her below the children who told "topic-centered" stories. Most of these adults also predicted difficulties for this child's future school career, such as "This child might have trouble reading," that she exhibited "language problems that affect school achievement," and that "family problems" or "emotional problems might hamper her academic progress."

The Black adults had very different reactions. They found this child's story "well formed, easy to understand, and interesting, with lots of detail and description." Even though all five of these adults mentioned the "shifts" and "associations" or "nonlinear" quality of the story, they did not find these features distracting. Three of the Black adults selected the story as the best of the five they had heard, and all but one judged the child as exceptionally bright, highly verbal, and successful in school (Cazden, 1988).

This is not a story about racism, but one about cultural familiarity. However, when differences in narrative style produce differences in interpretation of competence, the pedagogical implications are evident. If children who produce stories based on differing discourse styles are expected to have trouble reading and viewed as having language, family, or emotional problems, as was the case with the informants quoted by Cazden, they are unlikely to be viewed as ready for the same challenging instruction awarded students whose language patterns more closely parallel the teacher's.

Most teachers are particularly concerned about how speaking Ebonics might affect learning to read. There is little evidence that speaking another mutually intelligible language form, per se, negatively affects one's ability to learn to read (Sim, 1982). For commonsensical proof, one need only reflect on nonstandard English-speaking Africans who, though enslaved, not only taught themselves to read English, but did so under threat of severe punishment or death. But children who speak Ebonics do have a more difficult time becoming proficient readers. Why? In part, appropriate instructional methodologies are frequently not adopted. There is ample evidence that children who do not come to school with knowledge about letters, sounds, and symbols need to experience some explicit instruction in these areas in order to become independent readers. Another explanation is that, where teachers' assessments of competence are influenced by the language children speak, teachers may develop low expectations for certain students and subsequently teach them less (Sims, 1982). A third explanation rests in teachers confusing the teaching of reading with the teaching of a new language form.

Reading researcher Patricia Cunningham (1976–1997) found that teachers across the United States were more likely to correct reading miscues that were "dialect"-related ("Here go a table" for "Here is a table") than those that were "nondialect"-related ("Here is a dog" for "There is a dog"). Seventy-eight percent of the former types of miscues were corrected, compared with only 27 percent of the latter. She concludes that the teachers were acting out of ignorance, not realizing that "here go" and "here is" represent the same meaning in some Black children's language.

In my observations of many classrooms, however, I have come to conclude that even when teachers recognize the similarity of meaning, they are likely to correct Ebonics-related miscues. Consider a typical example:

TEXT: Yesterday I washed my brother's clothes.

STUDENT'S
RENDITION: Yesterday I wash my bruvver close.

The subsequent exchange between student and teacher sounds something like this:

T: Wait, let's go back. What's that word again? [Points at *washed*.]

S: Wash.

T: No. Look at it again. What letters do you see at the end? You see "e-d." Do you remember what we say when we see those letters on the end of the word?

S: "ed."

T: OK, but in this case we say washed. Can you say that?

S: Wash*ed*.

T: Good. Now read it again.

S: Yesterday I wash*ed* my bruvver.

T: Wait a minute, what's that word again? [Points to *brother*.]

S: Bruvver.

T: No. Look at these letters in the middle. [Points to *brother*.] Remember to read what you see. Do you remember how we say that sound? Put your tongue between your teeth and say /th/. . . .

The lesson continues in such a fashion, the teacher proceeding to correct the student's Ebonics-influenced pronunciations and grammar while ignoring that fact that the student had to have comprehended the sentence in order to translate it into her own language. Such instruction occurs daily and blocks reading development in a number of ways. First, because children become better readers by having the opportunity to read, the overcorrection exhibited in this lesson means that this child will be less likely to become a fluent reader than other children that are not interrupted so consistently. Second, a complete focus on code and pronunciation blocks children's understanding that reading is essentially a meaning-making process. This child, who understands the text, is led to believe that she is doing something wrong. She is encouraged to think of reading not as something you do to get a message, but something you pronounce. Third, constant corrections by the teacher are likely to cause this student and others like her to resist reading and to resent the teacher.

Language researcher Robert Berdan (1980) reports that, after observing the kind of teaching routine described above in a number of settings, he incorporated the teacher behaviors into a reading instruction exercise that he used with students in a college class. He put together sundry rules from a number of American social and regional dialects to create what he called the "language of Atlantis." Students were then called upon to read aloud in this dialect they did not know. When they made errors he interrupted them, using some of the same statements and comments he had heard elementary school teachers routinely make to their students. He concludes:

> The results were rather shocking. By the time these PhD Candidates in English or linguistics had read 10–20 words, I could make them sound totally illiterate. . . . The first thing that goes is sentence intonation: they sound like they are reading a list from the telephone book. Comment on their pronunciation a bit more, and they begin to subvocalize, rehearsing pronunciations for themselves before they dare to say them out loud. They begin to guess at pronunciations.
>
> They switch letters around for no reason. They stumble; they repeat. In short, when I attack them for their failure to conform to my demands for Atlantis English pronunciations, they sound very much like the worst of the second graders in any of the classrooms I have observed.
>
> They also begin to fidget. They wad up their papers, bite their fingernails, whisper, and some finally refuse to continue. They do all the things that children do while they are busily failing to learn to read.

The moral of this story is not to confuse learning a new language form with reading comprehension. To do so will only confuse the child, leading her away from those intuitive understandings about language that will promote reading development and toward a school career of resistance and a lifetime of avoiding reading.

Unlike unplanned oral language or public reading, writing lends itself to editing. While conversational talk is spontaneous and must be responsive to an immediate context, writing is a mediated process that may be written and rewritten any number of times before being introduced to public scrutiny. Consequently, writing is more amenable to rule application—one may first write freely to get one's thoughts down, and then edit to hone the message and apply specific spelling, syntactical, or punctuation rules. My college students who had such difficulty talking in the "iz" dialect found writing it, with the rules displayed before them, a relatively easy task.

To conclude, the teacher's job is to provide access to the national "standard" as well as to understand the language the children speak sufficiently to celebrate its beauty. The verbal adroitness, the cogent and quick wit, the brilliant use of metaphor, the facility in rhythm and rhyme, evident in the language of Jesse Jackson, Whoopi Goldberg, Toni Morrison, Henry Louis Gates, Jr., Tupac Shakur, and Maya Angelou, as well as in that of many inner-city Black students, may all be drawn upon to facilitate school learning. The teacher must know how to effectively teach reading and writing to students whose culture and language differ from that of the school, and must understand how and why students decide to add another language form to their repertoire. All we can do is provide students with access to additional language forms. Inevitably, each speaker will make his or her own decision about what to say in any context.

But I must end with a caveat that we keep in mind a simple truth: Despite our necessary efforts to provide access to Standard English, such access will not make any of our students more intelligent. It will not teach them math or science or geography—or, for that matter, compassion, courage, or responsibility. Let us not become so overly concerned with the language form that we ignore academic and moral content. Access to the standard language may be necessary, but it is definitely not sufficient to produce intelligent, competent caretakers of the future.

FOR FURTHER EXPLORATION

Delpit, L. (1995). *Other people's children: Cultural conflict in the classroom.* New York, NY: The New Press

Delpit, L. (2003). *The skin that we speak: Thoughts on language and culture in the classroom.* New York, NY: W.W. Norton and Company.

Delpit, L. (2012). *Multiplication is for white people: Raising expectations for other people's children.* New York, NY: The New Press.

Perry, T. & Delpit, L. (1998). *The real ebonics debate: Power, language, and the education of African-American children* (Eds.). Boston, MA: Beacon Press.

Lisa Delpit is Eminent Scholar and Executive Director of the Center for Urban Education and Innovation at Florida International University.

5

Racism, Discrimination, and Expectations of Students' Achievement

Sonia Nieto

> *[Racists have power] only if you let them! We'll stick with (the example of striped shirts): If I go where everyone is wearing solids, and I'm wearing a stripe, and someone comes up to me and tells me, "You don't belong here; you're wearing stripes," I'll say, "I belong anywhere I want to belong." And I'll stand right there! But there are some people who just say, "Oh, okay," and will turn around and leave. Then the racist has the power.*
>
> —Linda Howard
> *Interviewee*

Linda Howard is a young woman who has been directly harmed by racism in and out of school, and she has a highly evolved understanding of it on both an individual and an institutional level. As you will see in her case study, Linda has thought very deeply about racism. Many teachers and other educators, however, have not. In this chapter, we will explore the impact that racism, other biases, and expectations of student abilities may have on achievement. We will focus on racism as an example of bias, but I will also point out other kinds of

NOTE: Niteo, Sonia, *Affirming Diversity: The Sociopolitical Context of Multicultural Education*, 4th Edition, © 2004. Reprinted by permission of Pearson Education, Inc., Upper Saddle River, NJ.

personal and situational discrimination when appropriate. These include discrimination on the basis of gender (sexism), ethnic group (ethnocentrism), social class (classism), language (linguicism), or other perceived differences. I will also mention anti-Semitism, discrimination against Jews; anti-Arab discrimination, directed against Arabs; ageism, discrimination based on age; heterosexism, discrimination against gay men and lesbians; and ableism, discrimination against people with disabilities.

DEFINITIONS OF RACISM AND DISCRIMINATION

Discussions of prejudice and discrimination tend to focus on the biases and negative perceptions of individuals toward members of other groups. For example, Gordon Allport, in his groundbreaking work on the nature of prejudice, quotes a United Nations document defining discrimination as "any conduct based on a distinction made on grounds of natural or social categories, which have no relation either to individual capacities or merits, or to the concrete behavior of the individual person." This definition is helpful but incomplete because it fails to describe the harmful effects of such conduct. More broadly speaking, discrimination denotes negative or destructive behaviors that can result in denying some groups' life necessities as well as the privileges, rights, and opportunities enjoyed by other groups. Discrimination is usually based on prejudice, that is, the attitudes and beliefs of individuals about entire groups of people. These attitudes and beliefs are generally, but not always, negative.

Our society, among many others, categorizes people according to both visible and invisible traits, uses such classifications to deduce fixed behavioral and mental traits, and then applies policies and practices that jeopardize some and benefit others. Classifications based on race, ethnicity, gender, social class, and other physical or social differences are all around us. Frequently, they result in gross exaggerations and stereotypes: Girls are not as smart as boys; African Americans have rhythm; Asians are studious; Poles are simple-minded; Jews are smart; and poor people need instant gratification. Although some of these may appear to be "positive" stereotypes, both "negative" and "positive" stereotypes have negative results because they limit our perspective of an entire group of people. There are two major problems with categorizing people in this way: First, people of all groups begin to believe the stereotypes; and second, both material and psychological resources are doled out accordingly.

We see a clear example of the implications of such categorizations in the case study of Rich Miller. Rich was quite severe in his criticism of other African Americans, whom he characterized as "settling for the easiest way out," "lazy," and "tacky." He had internalized the myth of success based completely on individual endeavor rather than as also influenced by structural issues such as institutional racism and lack of opportunity. It is easy to understand how this happens: In our society, the metaphor of "pulling yourself up by your bootstraps" is powerful indeed; it allows little room for alternative explanations based on structural inequality.

Racism and other forms of discrimination are based on the perception that one ethnic group, class, gender, or language is superior to all others. In the United States, the conventional norm used to measure all other groups is European-American, upper-middle class, English-speaking, and male. Discrimination based on perceptions of superiority is part of the structure of schools, the curriculum, the education most teachers receive, and the interactions among teachers, students, and the community. But discrimination is not simply an individual bias; it is above all an institutional practice.

Most definitions of racism and discrimination obscure the institutional nature of oppression. Although the beliefs and behaviors of individuals may be hurtful, far greater damage is done through institutional discrimination, that is, the systematic use of economic and political power in institutions (such as schools) that leads to detrimental policies and practices. These policies and practices have a harmful effect on groups that share a particular identity (be it racial, ethnic, gender, or other). The major difference between individual and institutional discrimination is the wielding of power, because it is primarily through the power of the people who control institutions such as schools that oppressive policies and practices are reinforced and legitimated. Linda Howard, one of our young interviewees, already understood this distinction. In her case study, she distinguished between prejudice and racism in this way: "We all have some type of person that we don't like, whether it's from a different race, or from a different background, or they have different habits." But she went on to explain, as we saw in the quote at the beginning of this chapter, that a racist is someone who has power to carry out his or her prejudices.

Let me give another example: Let's say that I am prejudiced against tall people. Although my bias may hurt individual tall people because I refuse to befriend them or because I make fun of them, I can do very little to limit their options in life. If, however, I belonged to a group of powerful "non-talls" and we limited the access of tall persons to certain neighborhoods, prohibited them from receiving quality health care, discouraged intermarriage with people of short or average height, developed policies against their employment in high-status professions, and placed all children who were the offspring of "talls" (or who showed early signs of becoming above average in height) in the lowest ability tracks in schools, then my bias would have teeth and its institutional power would be clear. In the discussion that follows, we will be concerned primarily with institutional discrimination.

Institutional discrimination generally refers to how people are excluded or deprived of rights or opportunities as a result of the normal operations of the institution. Although the individuals involved in the institution may not be prejudiced or have any racist intentions or even awareness of how others may be harmed, the result may nevertheless be racist. In this sense, intentional and unintentional racism are different. But because they both result in negative outcomes, in the end it does not really matter whether racism and other forms of discrimination are intentional. Rather than trying to figure out whether the intent was to do harm or not, educators would do better to spend their time addressing the effects of racism.

When we understand racism and other forms of discrimination as a systemic problem, not simply as an individual dislike for a particular group of people, we can better understand the negative and destructive effects it can have. Vanessa Mattison provides a good example of a young person struggling to reconcile our country's lofty ideals of equality and fair play with the reality of the injustice she saw around her. Vanessa was committed to social justice, but she saw it primarily as working to change the attitudes and behaviors of individuals. She had not yet made the connection between racism and institutional oppression, and she did not grasp that institutional racism was far more harmful than individual biases or acts of meanness. But she was beginning to see that certain norms existed that were unfair to Blacks, women, and gays and lesbians. In her words: "There's all these underlying rules that if you're not this, you can't do that."

This is meant neither to minimize the powerful effects of individual prejudice and discrimination, which can be personally painful, nor to suggest that discrimination occurs only in one direction, for example, from Whites toward Blacks. There is no monopoly on prejudice and individual discrimination; they happen in all directions, and even within groups. However, interethnic and intraethnic biases and personal prejudices, while negative and hurtful, simply do not have the long-range and life-limiting effects of institutional racism and other kinds of institutional discrimination.

As an illustration of institutional racism, let us look at how testing practices are sometimes used in schools: Students from dominated groups may be stigmatized and labeled because of their performance on standardized tests. What places these students at a disadvantage is not that particular teachers have prejudiced attitudes about them; teachers may, in fact, like the students very much. What places the students at jeopardy is the fact that they may be labeled, grouped, and tracked, sometimes for the length of their schooling, because of their score on an ethnocentric and biased test. In this case, it is institutions—schools and the testing industry—that have the major negative impact on students from culturally dominated groups.

Prejudice and discrimination, then, are not just personality traits or psychological phenomena; they are also a manifestation of economic, political, and social power. The institutional definition of racism is not always easy to accept because it goes against deeply held notions of equality and justice in our nation. According to Beverly Tatum, "An understanding of racism as a system of advantage presents a serious challenge to the notion of the United States as a just society where rewards are based solely on one's merits." Racism as an institutional system implies that some people and groups benefit and others lose. Whites, whether they want to or not, benefit in a racist society; males benefit in a sexist society. Discrimination always helps somebody—those with the most power—which explains why racism, sexism, and other forms of discrimination continue.

According to Meyer Weinberg, racism is a system of privilege and penalty. That is, one is rewarded or punished in housing, education, employment, health, and so on, by the simple fact of belonging to a particular group, regardless of one's individual merits or faults. He goes on to explain, "Racism consists centrally of two facets: First, a belief in the inherent superiority of some people and the inherent inferiority of others; and second, the acceptance of distributing goods and services—let alone respect—in accordance with such judgments of unequal worth." In addressing the institutional nature of racism, he adds, " . . . racism is always collective. Prejudiced individuals may join the large movement, but they do not cause it." According to this conception, the "silence of institutional racism" and the "ruckus of individual racism" are mutually supportive. It is sometimes difficult to separate one level of racism from the others, as they feed on and inform one another. What is crucial, according to Weinberg, is understanding that the doctrine of White supremacy is at the root of racism.

THE HISTORY AND PERSISTENCE
OF RACISM IN U.S. SCHOOLS

As institutions, schools respond to and reflect the larger society. It therefore is not surprising that racism finds its way into schools in much the same way that it finds its way into other institutions such as housing, employment, and the criminal justice system. Overt expressions of racism may be less frequent in schools today than in the past, but racism does not just exist when schools are legally segregated or racial epithets are used against Black students. Racism is also manifested in rigid ability tracking, low expectations of students based on their identity, and inequitably funded schools.

Racism and other forms of discrimination—particularly sexism, classism, ethnocentrism, and linguicism—have a long history in our schools and their effects are widespread and long lasting. The most blatant form of discrimination is the actual withholding of education, as was the case with African Americans and sometimes with American Indians during the nineteenth century. To teach enslaved Africans to read was a crime punishable under the law and it became a subversive activity that was practiced by Blacks in ingenious ways. Other overt forms of discrimination include segregating students, by law, according to their race, ethnicity, or gender, as was done at one time or another with African American, Mexican American, Japanese, and Chinese students, as well as with females; or forcing them into boarding schools, as was done with American Indian students. In such groups, children have been encouraged to adopt the ways of the dominant culture in sundry ways, from subtle persuasion to physical punishment for speaking their native language. This, too, is a bitter reminder of the inequities of U.S. educational history.

Unfortunately, the discrimination that children face in schools is not a thing of the past. School practices and policies continue to discriminate against some children in very concrete ways. Recent studies have found that most students of color are still in schools that are segregated by race and social class, and the situation is worsening rather than improving. At the impetus of the civil rights movement, many school systems throughout the United States were indeed desegregated. But less than rigorous implementation of desegregation plans, "White flight," and housing patterns have succeeded in resegregating many schools. Segregation invariably results in school systems that are "separate and unequal" because segregated schools are differently funded, with fewer resources provided to schools in poor communities and vastly superior resources provided to schools in wealthier communities.

Segregation often results in students receiving differential schooling on the basis of their social class, race, and ethnicity. In addition, schools that serve students of color tend to provide curricula that are watered down and at a lower level than schools that serve primarily White students. Also, teachers in poor urban schools tend to have less experience and less education than colleagues who teach in schools that serve primarily European American and middle-class students. Even when they are desegregated, many schools resegregate students through practices such as rigid ability tracking. Consequently, desegregating schools in and of itself does not guarantee educational equity.

MANIFESTATIONS OF RACISM AND DISCRIMINATION IN SCHOOLS

Racism and discrimination are manifested in numerous school practices and policies. Policies most likely to jeopardize students at risk of educational failure are most common precisely in the institutions in which those students are found. For example, many studies have found that rigid tracking is most evident in poor communities with large numbers of African American, Latino, and American Indian students.

It is sometimes difficult to separate what is racist or discriminatory from what appear to be neutral school policies and practices or behaviors of individual teachers. An early study cited by Ray McDermott can help illustrate this point. Through filmed classroom observations, he found that a White teacher tended to have much more frequent eye contact with her White students than with her Black students. Was this behavior the result of racism? Was it because of cultural and communication differences? Or was poor teacher preparation responsible for her behavior?

David and Myra Sadker cite many anecdotes in their powerful report on sexism in schools that bring up similar questions. They found that well-intentioned and otherwise excellent teachers often treat their female students far differently from their male students, interacting with them less frequently, asking them fewer questions, and giving them less feedback than they give male students. Because boys are expected to be more verbal and active and are both praised and reproached more often by their teachers, girls become invisible in the classroom. Girls are singled out neither for praise nor for disciplinary action. They are simply expected, as a group, to be quiet, attentive, and passive. Is this because of inherent sexism? Are teachers simply unaware of how such practices may jeopardize girls and, in a different way, boys as well?

In another example of how difficult it is to separate racism from individual teachers' behaviors or seemingly neutral policies, Patricia Gandara found, in a study of 50 low-income and high-achieving Mexican Americans, that most were either light-skinned or European-looking. Few of the sample, according to Gandara, looked "classically Mexican in both skin color and features." Does this mean that teachers intentionally favored them because of their light skin? Did teachers assume that their light-skinned students were smarter?

These questions are impossible to answer in any conclusive way; it is probable that institutional racism and teachers' biases both play a role in negative outcomes such as those described in the studies. The results, however, are very clear: In the study by McDermott, the Black children had to strain three times as hard to catch the teacher's eye, looking for approval, affection, and encouragement. In the Sadker and Sadker report, the researchers concluded that girls are frequently denied an equal education simply because of their gender, rather than because of any personal talents or deficits. In Gandara's study, the light-skinned students were able to derive more benefits from their schooling than their darker-skinned peers.

Thus students' educational success or failure cannot be explained solely by family circumstance, social class, race, gender, or language ability. Racism and other forms of institutional discrimination also play a part. African American, Latino, American Indian, and poor children in general continue to achieve below grade level, drop out in much greater numbers, and go to college in much lower proportion than their middle-class and European American peers. Two concrete examples illustrate this point: Black students are chronically underrepresented in programs for the gifted and talented, being only half as likely to be placed in a class for the gifted as are White students, even though they may be equally gifted. Latino students drop out of school at a rate higher than any other major ethnic group; and in some places, the rate has been as high as 80 percent. If educational failure were caused only by students' background and other social characteristics, it would be difficult to explain why similar students are successful in some classrooms and schools and not in others. For instance, students at Central Park East High School in East Harlem, one of the most economically impoverished communities in New York City, have reached unparalleled levels of success compared to their peers in other neighborhood schools who are similar to them in every way.

School structures have also proved to be sexist in organization, orientation, and goals. Most schools are organized to meet best the needs of White males; that is, the policy and instruction in schools generally reflect what is most effective for the needs of their male students, not the needs of either females or students of color. This organization includes everything from the curriculum, which follows the developmental level of males more closely than that of females, to instructional techniques, which favor competition as a preferred learning style, although it is not necessarily the best learning environment for either females or most students of color. The effect of such discrimination on female students is to reinforce the persistent message that they are inferior. In fact, high-achieving female students tend to receive the least attention of all from their teachers.

Discrimination based on social class is also prevalent in our public schools. In a study of affluent and low-income youth in a secondary school, Ellen Brantlinger found that students' social class was highly correlated with their academic placement, with most low-income students in special education or low tracks and all the high-income students in college preparatory classes. This was the case in spite of the fact that two of the high-income students were classified as "learning disabled." Using data from 1993, the National Center for Education Statistics also found a significant correlation between social class and dropping out of school. While only 6 percent of high-income students dropped out, over 40 percent of low-income students did so.

The hidden curriculum, that is, subtle and not-so-subtle messages that are not part of the intended curriculum, may also have an impact on students. These messages may be positive (e.g., the expectation that all students are capable of high quality work) or negative (e.g., that children of working-class backgrounds are not capable of aspiring to professional jobs), although the term is generally used to refer to negative messages. These frequently unintentional messages may contradict schools' stated policies and objectives. For instance, Carolyn Persell found that, in spite of schools' and teachers' stated commitment to equal education, social class is repeatedly related to how well students do in school. In fact, she found that students are more different from one another when they leave school than when they enter it, thus putting to rest the myth of school as the "great equalizer." Persell found that differences in academic achievement experienced by students of different economic and cultural backgrounds are due primarily to a number of specific factors: the kinds of schools the students attend, the length of time they stay in school, the curriculum and pedagogy to which they are exposed, and societal beliefs concerning intelligence and ability.

Rather than eradicate social class differences, then, it appears that schooling reflects and even duplicates them. This finding was confirmed by Samuel Bowl and Herbert Gintis in their ground-breaking class analysis of schooling. They compared the number of years of schooling of students with the socioeconomic status of their parents and found that students whose parents were in the highest socioeconomic group tended to complete the most years of schooling. They concluded that schooling in and of itself does not necessarily move poor children out of their parents' low economic class. More often, schooling maintains and solidifies class divisions.

Intentional or not, racism, classism, and other forms of discrimination are apparent in the quality of education that students receive. A graphic example of discrimination based on both race and class is found in the differential resources given to schools. As is evident in Jonathan Kozol's searing indictment of the funding of public education, the actual money spent on schools is very often directly correlated with the social class and race of the student body. Furthermore, a review of relevant literature by Carol Ascher and Gary Burnett reported that disparities in funding between rich and poor states, and between rich and poor districts in the same state, have actually grown in the recent past.

In the case of African American youth, Angela Taylor found that to the extent that teachers harbor negative stereotypes about them, African American children's race alone is probably sufficient to place them at risk for negative school outcomes. Of course, many teachers and other educators prefer to think that students' lack of academic achievement is due solely to conditions inside their homes or inherent in their cultures. But the occurrence of racism in schools has been widely documented. In a report about immigrant students in California, more than half of the students interviewed indicated that they had been the victims of teachers' biases, citing instances where they were punished, publicly embarrassed, or ridiculed because of improper use of English. They also reported that teachers had made derogatory comments about immigrant groups in front of the class. Most of the middle and high school students interviewed in a study by Mary Poplin and Joseph Weeres also had witnessed incidents of racism in school. And in a study in an urban high school in the Northeast, Karen Donaldson found that an astounding 80 percent of students surveyed said they had experienced or witnessed racism or other forms of discrimination in school.

Studies focusing specifically on Latino youth have reported similar results. Marietta Saravia-Shore and Herminio Martinez interviewed Puerto Rican youths who had dropped out of school and were currently participating in an alternative high school program. These youths keenly felt the discrimination of their former teachers, who they said were "against Puerto Ricans and Blacks." One young woman said that a former teacher had commented, "Do you want to be like the other Puerto Rican women who never got an education? Do you want to be like the rest of your family and never go to school?" In Virginia Zanger's study of high-achieving Latino and Latina high school students in Boston, one young man described his shock when his teacher called him "spic" right in class. Although the teacher was later suspended, the incident had clearly affected how this young man perceived school and his teachers. If we keep in mind that these are successful students, who are apt to hear far fewer of such damaging comments than other students, we can begin to grasp the enormity of the problem confronted by young people who are not as successful in school.

The effect of discrimination on students is most painfully apparent when students themselves have the opportunity to speak. Their thoughts concerning their education are revealing. In her study, Karen Donaldson found that students were affected by racism in three major ways: White students experienced guilt and embarrassment when they became aware of the racism to which their peers were subjected; students of color sometimes felt they needed to compensate and overachieve to prove they were equal to their White classmates; and at other times, students of color said that their self-esteem was badly damaged. However, self-esteem is a complicated issue that includes many variables. It does not come fully formed out of the blue, but is created in particular contexts and responds to conditions that vary from situation to situation. Teachers' and schools' complicity in creating negative self-esteem cannot be discounted. This point was illustrated by Lillian, a young woman in a study of an urban high school by Nitza Hidalgo. Lillian commented, "That's another problem I have, teachers, they are always talking about how we have no type of self-esteem or anything like that . . . But they're the people that's putting us down. That's why our self-esteem is so low."

RACISM, DISCRIMINATION, AND SILENCE

Many times, unintentional discrimination is practiced by well-meaning teachers who fear that talking about race will only exacerbate the problem. As a consequence, most schools are characterized by a curious absence of talk about differences, particularly about race. The process begins with the preparation of teachers. In one study, Alice Mcintyre interviewed a group of White female student teachers working in urban schools in order to understand how they made meaning of their Whiteness in relation to teaching. She found that these preservice teachers were reluctant to discuss racism or to consider their individual or collective role in perpetuating it. Because they saw their students primarily as victims of poverty and parental neglect, these student teachers preferred to place themselves in relationship to their students as protective "White Knights." This patronizing stance facilitated their denial of racism.

Silence and denial about racism are still quite prevalent when student teachers become teachers. In a follow-up study to her initial research concerning students' experiences with racism, Karen Donaldson had a hard time recruiting White teachers to take part in an antiracist education teacher study because most White teachers were not aware (or claimed not to be aware) of racial biases in schools and of how these biases could influence students' achievement. In another study, Julie Wollman-Bonilla found that a sizable proportion of the teachers in her children's literature courses explicitly rejected children's books about race and racism or use with their students. Whether it was to shield their students from unpleasant realities, or to uphold particular societal myths, Wollman-Bonilla concluded that many teachers lack the courage to present views that differ from the mainstream perspective. As a result, their role becomes one of maintaining the status quo rather than helping children question social inequality and injustice. That this attitude can be taken to an extreme is evident in research by Ellen Bigler: When she asked a middle school librarian in a town with a sizable Puerto Rican community if there were any books on the Hispanic experience, the librarian answered that carrying such books was inadvisable because it would interfere with the children's identification of themselves as "American"!

Silence pervades even schools committed to equity and diversity. This was a major finding in a study by Kathe Jervis of the first year of a New York City middle school consciously designed to be based on these principles. Although she had not originally intended to focus her study on race, Jervis found that there was an odd silence on the part of most teachers to address it. Their reluctance to discuss race resulted in their overlooking or denying issues of power that are imbedded in race. Jervis concluded that "even in the 'best' schools, where faculty try hard to pay attention to individuals, Whites' blindness to race clouds their ability to notice what children are really saying about themselves and their identities."

Failure to discuss racism, unfortunately, will not make it go away. Linda Howard's close relationship with Mr. Benson, her English teacher, was no doubt partly due to the fact that they were able to talk openly about racism and other biases. Racism, classism, and other forms of discrimination play a key role in setting up and maintaining inappropriate learning environments for many students. A related phenomenon concerns the possible impact of teachers' expectations on student achievement.

EXPECTATIONS OF STUDENTS' ACHIEVEMENT

Much research has focused on teachers' interactions with their students, specifically teacher expectations. The term *self-fulfilling prophecy*, coined by Robert Merton in 1948, means that students perform in ways that teachers expect. Student performance is based on both overt and covert messages from teachers about students' worth, intelligence, and capability. The term did not come into wide use until 1968, when a classic study by Robert Rosenthal and Lenore Jacobson provided the impetus for subsequent extensive research on the subject. In this study, several classes of children in grades one through six were given a nonverbal intelligence test (the researchers called it the "Harvard Test of Influenced Acquisition"), which researchers claimed would measure the students' potential for intellectual growth. Twenty percent of the students were randomly selected by the researchers as "intellectual bloomers," and their names were given to the teachers. Although the students' test scores actually had nothing at all to do with their potential, the teachers were told to be on the alert for signs of intellectual growth among these particular children. Overall these children, particularly in the lower grades, showed considerably greater gains in IQ during the school year than did the other students. They were also rated by their teachers as being more interesting, curious, and happy, and thought to be more likely to succeed later in life.

Rosenthal and Jacobson's research on teacher expectations caused a sensation in the education community, and controversy surrounding it continues to be present. From the beginning, the reception to this line of research has been mixed, with both supporters and detractors. But one outcome was that the effect of teachers' expectations on the academic achievement of their students was taken seriously for the first time. Before this research, students' failure in school was usually ascribed wholly to individual or family circumstances. Now, the possible influence of teachers' attitudes and behaviors and the school's complicity in the process had to be considered as well. The most compelling implications were for the education of those students most seriously disadvantaged by schooling, that is, for students of color and the poor.

Early research by Ray Rist on teachers' expectations is also worth mentioning here. In a groundbreaking study, he found that a kindergarten teacher had grouped her class by the eighth day of class. In reviewing how she had done so, Rist noted that the teacher had already roughly constructed an "ideal type" of student, most of whose characteristics were related to social class. By the end of the school year, the teacher's differential treatment of children based on who were "fast" and "slow" learners became evident. The "fast" learners received more teaching time, more reward-directed behavior, and more attention. The interactional patterns between the teacher and her students then took on a "castelike" appearance. The result after three years of similar behavior by other teachers was that teachers' behavior toward the different groups influenced the children's achievement. In other words, the teachers themselves contributed to the creation of the "slow" learners in their classrooms.

In the research by Rist, all the children and teachers were African American but represented different social classes. But similar results have been found with poor and working-class children of any race. Persell, in a review of relevant research, found that expectations for poor children were lower than for middle-class children even when their IQ and achievement scores were similar. Teachers' beliefs that their students are "dumb" can become a rationale for providing low-level work in the form of elementary facts, simple drills, and rote memorization. Students are not immune to these messages. On the other hand, a study by Diane Pollard found that the academic performance of African American students is enhanced when they perceive their teachers and other school staff to be supportive and helpful.

Some of the research on teacher expectations is quite old. Although it is reasonable to expect that, with the increasing diversity in our schools, it no longer holds true, there are still numerous examples of teachers' low expectations of students. A recent study by Francisco Rios underscores the problem. Rios studied teachers in an urban city in the Midwest to determine what principles of practice they used for teaching in culturally diverse classrooms. Among the 16 teachers he studied, he found that most of the comments they made about their students were negative; further, none of the teaching principles that they identified focused on academic achievement and only one teacher said that her students wanted to learn.

These findings are particularly problematic when we consider the impact that such beliefs can have on students. Given the increasing diversity in our public schools, the problem is even more acute because many teachers know little or nothing about the background of their students. Consequently, teachers may consider their students' identity to be at fault. This was the result found by Bram Hamovitch in an ethnographic study of an urban after-school program for adolescents at risk of dropping out of school. In his study, Hamovitch concluded that the program failed to meet its objective of motivating students to continue their education because "it allegorically asks them to dislike themselves and their own culture."

Teachers' attitudes about the diversity of their students develop long before they become teachers, however. In a review of recent literature, Kenneth Zeichner found that teacher education students, who are mostly White and monolingual, by and large view diversity of student backgrounds as a problem. He also found that the most common characteristics of effective teachers in urban schools are a belief that their students are capable learners, and an ability to communicate this belief to the students. Martin Haberman reached a similar conclusion, identifying a number of functions of successful teachers of the urban poor. Most significant, he found that successful teachers did not blame students for failure and they had consistently high expectations of their students. Rich Miller offers compelling evidence of this reality. According to Rich, standards would be higher in his high school if there were more White students. But the reason was not because White students are smarter, but because White teachers don't push the Black students as much as they push White students. On the other hand, Black teachers, Rich said, have "expectations that are higher than White teachers . . . because they know how it was for them."

What happens when teachers develop high expectations of their students? In a wonderful example of how changing the expectations of students can influence achievement in a positive direction, Rosa Hernandez Sheets recounted her own experience with five Spanish-speaking students who had failed her Spanish class. Just one semester after placing them in what she labeled her "advanced" class, the very same students who had previously failed, passed the AP Spanish language exam, earning college credits while just sophomores and juniors. A year later, they passed the AP Spanish Literature exam. As a result of the change in her pedagogy, over a three-year period, Latino and Latina students who had been labeled "at risk" were performing at a level commonly expected of honors students.

The issue of labeling is key in this situation. In a similar case, Ruben Rumbaut found that the self-esteem of immigrant students is linked to how they are labeled by their schools. Specifically, he found that students' self-esteem is diminished when they are labeled "Limited English Proficient." If this is the case with a seemingly neutral term, more loaded labels no doubt have a much greater impact. But explicit labeling may not even be needed. According to Claude Steele, the basic problem that causes low student achievement is what he terms "stigma vulnerability" based on the constant devaluation faced by Blacks and other people of color in society and schools. In schools, this devaluation occurs primarily through the harmful attitudes and beliefs that teachers communicate, knowingly or not, to their students. Steele maintains, "Deep in the psyche of American educators is a presumption that black students need academic remediation, or extra time with elemental curricula to overcome background deficits."

Although disadvantage may contribute to the problem, Steele contends that Blacks underachieve even when they have sufficient material resources, adequate academic preparation, and a strong value orientation toward education. To prove his point, he reviewed a number of programs that have had substantial success in improving the academic achievement of Black students without specifically addressing either their culturally specific learning orientations or socioeconomic disadvantage. What made the difference? In these programs, student achievement was improved simply by treating students as if they were talented and capable. Steele concludes, "That erasing stigma improves black achievement is perhaps the strongest evidence that stigma is what depresses it in the first place."

Research on teachers' expectations is not without controversy. First, it has been criticized as unnecessarily reductionist because, in the long run, what teachers expect matters less than what teachers do. Second, the term itself and the research on which it is based imply that teachers have the sole responsibility for students' achievement or lack of it. This is both an unrealistic and an incomplete explanation for student success or failure. The study by Rosenthal and Jacobson, for example, is a glaring indication of the disrespect with which teachers have frequently been treated and raises serious ethical issues in research. Blaming teachers, or "teacher bashing," provides a convenient outlet for complex problems, but it fails to take into account the fact that teachers function within contexts in which they usually have little power.

There are, of course, teachers who have low expectations of students from particular backgrounds and who are, in the worst cases, insensitive and racist. But placing teachers at the center of expectations of student achievement shifts the blame to some of those who care most deeply about students and who struggle every day to help them learn. The use of the term *teachers' expectations* distances the school and society from their responsibility and complicity in student failure. That is, teachers, schools, communities, and society interact to produce failure.

Low expectations mirror the expectations of society. It is not simply teachers who expect little from poor, working-class, and culturally dominated groups. Garfield High School in East Los Angeles, a school made famous by the extraordinary efforts of Jaime Escalante and other teachers in propelling an unprecedented number of students to college in spite of poverty and discrimination, was visited by George Bush when he was running for U.S. president. Rather than build on the message that college was both possible and desirable for its students, Bush focused instead on the idea that a college education is not needed for success. He told the largely Mexican American student body that "we need people to build our buildings . . . people who do the hard physical work of our society." It is doubtful that he would even have considered uttering these same words at Beverly Hills High School, a short distance away. The message of low expectations to students who should have heard precisely the opposite is thus replicated even by those at the highest levels of a government claiming to be equitable to all students.

THE COMPLEX CONNECTIONS
BETWEEN DIVERSITY AND DISCRIMINATION

Because societal inequities are frequently reflected in schools, institutional racism and other biases are apparent in inequitable school policies and practices in complex ways. Let us take the example of language. The fact that some children do not enter school speaking English cannot be separated from how their native language is viewed by the larger society or from the kinds of programs available for them in schools. Each of these programs—whether ESL, immersion, or two-way bilingual education—has an underlying philosophy with broad implications for students' achievement or failure. As a consequence, each approach may have a profound influence on the quality of education that language minority children receive. But linguistic and other differences do not exist independently of how they are perceived in the general society or by teachers; there is a complex relationship between students' race, culture, native language, and other differences with institutional discrimination, school practices, and teachers' expectations.

Social class provides another example of the complex links between difference and discrimination. In spite of the firm belief in our society that social class mobility is available to all, classism is a grim reality because economic inequality is now greater in the United States than in any other industrial or postindustrial country in the world; in fact, social class inequality has actually increased in the past 20 years. Related to this reality is the widely accepted classist view among many educators that poverty causes academic failure. Yet although poverty may have an adverse effect on student achievement, the belief that poverty and failure go hand-in-hand is questionable. Research by Denny Taylor and Catherine Dorsey-Gaines provides evidence that by itself poverty is not an adequate explanation for the failure to learn. In their work with Black families living in urban poverty, they found inspiring cases of academically successful students. They discovered children who consistently did their homework, made the honor roll, and had positive attitudes about school. The parents of these children motivated them to learn and study, had high hopes for their education, were optimistic about the future, and considered literacy an integral part of their lives—this in spite of such devastating conditions as family deaths; no food, heat, or hot water; and a host of other hostile situations.

Similarly, an in-depth study by David Hartle-Schutte of four Navajo students, who might be identified as "at risk" by their teachers because of poverty and culture, found that these students came from homes where literacy was valued. But their school failed to recognize and build on the many literacy experiences they had in their homes to help them become successful readers. These cases point out that home background can no longer be accepted as the sole or primary excuse for the school failure of large numbers of students.

Examples such as these demonstrate that although poverty is certainly a disadvantage, it is not an insurmountable obstacle to learning. The economic condition of African American and other poor students has often been used as an explanation for academic failure, but as Kofi Lomotey, in a review of the education of African American youths, states: "... there are clear examples of environments that have, over long periods of time, been successful in educating large numbers of African-American students. These models can be replicated; the situation is not hopeless." In fact, one major explanation for students' lack of academic achievement lies in the lack of equitable resources given to students of different social classes and cultural backgrounds. For instance, one of the most disturbing patterns found in the 1997 National Condition of Education report was that, compared with middle-class White children, children of color and low-income students were much more likely to be taught by teachers who had little academic preparation for their teaching field. Furthermore, the skills differentials that result from this inequity will lead to earnings differentials as adults to a much greater extent than was the case even 20 years ago.

In the ideal sense, education in the United States is based on the lofty values of democracy, freedom, and equal access. Historically, our educational system proposed to tear down the rigid systems of class and caste on which education in most of the world was (and still is) based and to provide all students with an equal education. Education was to be, as Horace Mann claimed, "the great equalizer." On the other hand, some educational historians have demonstrated that the common school's primal purposes were to replicate inequality and to control the unruly masses. Thus, the original goals of public school education were often at cross purposes.

Mass public education began in earnest in the nineteenth century through the legislation of compulsory education and its most eloquent democratic expression is found in the early-twentieth-century philosophy of John Dewey. The commitment that Dewey articulated for educational equity continues today through policies such as desegregation and nonsexist education and through legislation and policies aimed at eradicating many existing inequalities. But the legacy of inequality also continues through policies and practices that favor some students over others, including unequal funding, rigid tracking, and unfair tests. As a result, schools have often been sites of bitter conflict.

Race is another pivotal way in which privilege has been granted on an unequal basis. Based on his research, the historian David Tyack asserts that the struggle to achieve equality in education is nothing new, and that race has often been at the center of this struggle. He adds: "Attempts to preserve white supremacy and to achieve racial justice have fueled the politics of education for more than a century." But resistance on the part of parents, students, and teachers has been crucial in challenging the schools to live up to their promise of equality. That is, schools were not racially desegregated simply because the courts ordered it, and gender-fair education was not legislated only because Congress thought it was a good idea. In both cases, as in many others, educational opportunity was expanded because many people and communities engaged in struggle, legal or otherwise, to bring about change.

Although in theory education is no longer meant to replicate societal inequities but rather to reflect the ideals of democracy, we know that such is not always the reality. Our schools have consistently failed to provide an equitable education for all students. The complex interplay of student differences, institutional racism and discrimination, teachers' biases that lead to low expectations, and unfair school policies and practices all play a role in keeping it this way.

CONCLUSION

Focusing on the persistence of racism and discrimination and low expectations is meant in no way to deny the difficult family and economic situation of many poor children and children of color, or its impact on their school experiences and achievement. Drug abuse, violence, and other social ills, as well as poor medical care, deficient nutrition, and a struggle for the bare necessities for survival harm children's lives, including their school experiences. The fact that poor children and their parents do not have at their disposal the resources and experiences that economic privilege would give them is also detrimental.

But blaming poor people and people from dominated racial or cultural groups for their educational problems is not the answer to solving societal inequities. Teachers can do nothing to change the conditions in which their students may live, but they can work to change their own biases as well as the institutional structures that act as obstacles to student learning. As we have seen, racism and other forms of discrimination play a central role in educational failure, as does the related phenomenon of low expectations.

FOR FURTHER EXPLORATION

Nieto, S. (1992). *Affirming diversity: The sociopolitical context of multicultural education*. Boston, MA: Pearson Custom Publishing.

Nieto, S. (1999). *The light in their eyes: Creating multicultural learning communities*. New York, NY: Teachers College Press.

Nieto, S. (2005). *Why we teach*. New York, NY: Teachers College Press.

Nieto, S. (2010). *Language, culture, and teaching: Critical perspectives* (2nd ed.). Oxford, UK: Routledge.

Sonia Nieto is a professor of Teacher Education at the University of Massachusetts.

6

Inclusion

Rejecting Instruction That Disables

Bruce Marlowe and Marilyn Page

I n 1997, when her world was still fresh and ripe with possibility, Bruce's six-year-old daughter Rachel ran off the school bus one windy October afternoon waving a single sheet of paper high over her head. "I have homework! I have homework!" she shouted excitedly. Now, seven years later, her delight in school learning has been replaced with ennui, languor, and a precocious world-weariness about formal education. Rachel's school narrative lumbers forward, plodding predictably to its tedious, anticlimactic finish. But, she will survive. Unfortunately for students with disabilities, their school stories are considerably less sanguine, even for the fewer than half that finish high school. And, what of students who are gifted and talented?

If you've read this far into the book, you're probably feeling as if you need no further justification to build your instruction around constructivism. In this chapter, we're going to try to convince you otherwise because students who don't fit the mold, for whatever reasons, need good teachers who understand that the *questions students ask* are the most central issue to knowledge construction and active engagement. You already know that teachers who simply deliver information, or provide all of the questions without ever turning to student-developed inquiries (even if the teacher-created questions are interesting), will invariably face students who are unmotivated, disengaged, and perhaps even hostile. For students with disabilities and other learning differences, the stakes are even higher and the need more urgent.

NOTE: From Marlowe, B. & Page, M. (2005). *Creating and sustaining the constructivist classroom*. Thousand Oaks, CA: Corwin.

SHAM INQUIRY

As noted in previous chapters, in spite of the avalanche of both anec-
dotal and empirical reports (Capraro, 2001; Cole & McGuire, 2004;
Fraser & Spinner, 2002; Thomason, 2003; Marlowe & Page, 1998) concerning the positive results of progressive, inquiry-based learning, passive traditional practices appear firmly entrenched (Goodlad, 1984;
Cuban, 1990, 2001; Apple, 2001). In fact, the repertoire of most teachers
continues to be limited strictly to the familiar cycle of information
transmission and evaluation.

More chillingly, there is a relatively new trend taking place in our
schools, one that arose, ostensibly, to counter the perception of teacher
over-reliance on *talk and chalk*. And it is this trend that, perhaps more
than any other reason, accounts for the scarcity of constructivist pedagogy in our classrooms. For lack of a better term, we refer to it simply
as *sham inquiry*—that is, teaching practices that look like inquiry, sound
like inquiry, but on closer inspection are revealed to be just as unhealthy
to student learning as a steady, uniform diet of teacher telling. In its
various guises, sham inquiry gives no one solace but the teacher, who,
thinking she has refined her practice, continues to ignore, discount, or
put aside the questions *students ask* in favor of those she believes are
more valuable.

At the root of sham inquiry is the fundamental misunderstand-
ing that constructivism is largely about what teachers do, as opposed
to what their students do. From at least the time of Dewey, progressive educational movements have always been co-opted by a large
set of players who, historically, have viewed teachers simply as technicians. In an effort to codify good practice, school administrators,
teacher education programs, state licensing agencies, professional
developers, and textbook publishers have become overly preoccupied with the *how to*, often producing scripted materials, teacher
prompts, protocols, and other programmed forms of instruction
what Ohanian (see chapter 9) refers to as "Stir-and-Serve Recipes for
Teaching." Such approaches are based on the erroneous assumption
that all students can learn from the same materials, classroom
instructional techniques, and modes of evaluation. Nowhere is this
sort of sham inquiry more prevalent than in its use with students
with disabilities and other learning differences. This appears to be
true for two separate but related reasons: First, the predominance of
low expectations by teachers of low-achieving students (particularly
those who are African-American and Latino); and second, a fix

which is worse than the problem: "teaching styles that stress drill, practice, and other mind-numbing strategies" based on the mistaken belief that "such children lack ability" (Berliner & Biddle in Kohn, 1999, p. 99).

TOUGH QUESTION:

Why are students with disabilities less likely to have constructivist learning experiences than nondisabled students? Is this justifiable?

SHAM INQUIRY IN PRACTICE

> . . . inquiry is the way people learn when they're left alone.
> (Suchman, 1966, p. 2)

Consider Jonah, a highly gifted fifth-grade student in a mixed-ability classroom. His school story captures the need for constructivist classrooms, as well as the seduction and danger of sham inquiry. Jonah's teacher, Mr. Stevens—young, energetic, charismatic—began his review of fractions and their relationships one Friday by passing out a variety of materials to each of the cooperative groups he had previously established: poster board, empty egg cartons, calculators, construction paper, markers, scissors. He asked simply, "Using the strategies we have talked about all week, please demonstrate that three-fourths is greater than two-thirds." As Mr. Stevens circled the room, checking for understanding and periodically asking probing questions to individual groups about their work, the students attacked the problem with vigor, applying what they had been taught during the last four days. They divided the fractions (in order to compare the decimal amounts), filled the egg cartons, drew pie charts, and found common denominators. Mr. Stevens was thrilled that the students seemed to remember everything he had *covered* and as he made the rounds, he expressed his pride in them with great enthusiasm.

Jonah sat pensively, immobile.

While his group was busy pasting their work onto the poster board, he seemed to just stare at the numbers. And then, 15 minutes after the activity had begun, he said to Mr. Stevens, "I just noticed something. . . . That's *so* cool. Look, Mr. Stevens, if you multiply from the bottom-up and across like this:

You get 9 on the left side and 8 on the right side. That's *really* cool. Is that a way to show that three-fourths is greater than two-thirds? I mean will this always work? I think it will, but I'm not sure I really get it yet. Why does this work? I think I can figure it out. Can I work on this instead? Can I?" Uncertain of where Jonah was going, and nervous about his taking of such a divergent path, Mr. Stevens reminded Jonah that he was to use the strategies he had taught the class during the week. Mr. Stevens pointed out that there was no evidence that Jonah had done any work at all. Besides, Mr. Stevens had no idea if Jonah was on to something or not.

In the span of 15 minutes, Mr. Stevens communicated several potent lessons to Jonah; lessons that distinguish sham inquiry from a true constructivist classroom and underscore the need for real inquiry for students with learning differences. Mr. Stevens believes, mistakenly, that his classroom provides opportunities for all students to engage in constructivist activities.

But, here is what Jonah learned:

1. It is more important that I answer my teacher's questions than my own.

2. Independent thinking and problem solving is not to be pursued, unless my teacher understands it and/or it conforms to teacher-approved methods and strategies.

3. It is very important that I move at the same pace and produce the same products as my peers.

4. And, my understanding can only be demonstrated by repeating back what has been transmitted and nothing more.

There is another, subtler message often embedded in practices that masquerade as constructivism as well, a message to which Mr. Stevens probably does not ascribe. The message, delivered inadvertently, but powerfully through his words and actions, is that memorization is more important than deep understanding; that activity, simply for the sake of activity, leads to greater comprehension than deep reflection and inquiry. To wit, teacher-directed activities often sabotage real inquiry. As Sewall (2000) has noted:

> Activity based learning is vain . . . At rock bottom, projects and activities provide mere entertainment. Teachers . . . seek to fill dead time in the classroom. Projects and activities keep kids occupied and unmutinous.

TOUGH QUESTION:

When is activity learning in vain and when is it not?

Clearly, Jonah is a remarkably bright and unusually perceptive student. Yet, there is something all too familiar about his developing school story, a story that most of us remember from our own school experiences, or see in our children, or, worse, watch unfold on the faces of our students.

Many students are essentially teacher-proof; they will survive years of bad schooling relatively unscathed. Students like Jonah, however, and those with a myriad of other learning differences, often get trampled in school. As noted above, although constructivist educational practices clearly benefit all students, its implementation is considerably more urgent for our students who learn differently than their peers. That is, while the implications of poor instruction for most students' learning is relatively benign, the relationship between such traditional notions of teaching and learning and the outcomes for students with exceptionalities is much more dire. And, because special education law now requires that students with disabilities be educated with their nondisabled peers to the maximum extent appropriate (i.e., in the least restrictive environment), all teachers, regardless of their politics about inclusion, must assume responsibility for the learning of all students.

FULL INCLUSION IS CHANGING CLASSROOMS

For the last 20 years, most special education students received a large part of their education in public schools—but on a *pull-out* basis. Most still do. That is, students leave their regular classrooms for part or all of the day to work with a special education teacher or aide in a resource room on individual academic skills or behavioral goals; however, including students with disabilities in regular classrooms for most or all of their day (regardless of the severity of their disability) has become increasingly popular around the nation and about 80% of students with disabilities spend at least some of their day in a regular classroom. (That means they are in *your* classroom.) This change in thinking has been variously described as the *full inclusion* or *mainstreaming* movement. Several persuasive arguments have driven this change. For example, special education is prohibitively expensive, stigmatizes students, fragments instruction, and contributes to a high drop-out rate.

Although research shows (Henley, Ramsey, & Algozzine, 1993; Giangreco et al., 2004) that special-needs students appear to do better in regular classrooms than in special education settings, recent surveys indicate that most teachers are still uncomfortable with special education students in their classrooms because they feel that they do not have the proper training to work with students with disabilities. Are these fears justified? Perhaps, but in some sense, this appears irrelevant because virtually every public school classroom (K-12) has at least one student with a disability; teachers must learn to adjust to mainstreaming, regardless of their politics. Still, legitimate questions remain.

TOUGH QUESTIONS:

Do students with disabilities require something regular education teachers cannot provide?

What is it that special education teachers provide that is so critical to the needs of students with disabilities?

What additional training do regular education teachers need to ensure that students with disabilities receive an appropriate education in their classrooms?

WHAT'S SO SPECIAL ABOUT SPECIAL EDUCATION?

As it turns out, very little. There is some good news about what works (and what does not) for students with disabilities. What we can say with certainty about what students with disabilities need is contrary to what many regular (and special) educators believe. For example, many classroom teachers operate under the assumption that only specialized training in fields like learning disabilities, mental retardation, and speech and language disorders will allow them to work effectively with disabled students in their classrooms. Similarly, many special educators believe that they are somehow uniquely qualified (by virtue of their training) to work with children with disabilities. Many assume that the magic bullet for working with students with disabilities is finding the right placements and particular academic or behavioral curricula that match the disability in question. We now know, from a variety of research, that all these assumptions are false. In fact, Ysseldyke and Algozzine (1995) have summarized these findings by noting that research in special education has been unable to demonstrate that:

- specific instructional practices and techniques match or work better with specific learner characteristics;

- research has not supported the view that children with mental retardation need X, whereas children with learning disabilities need Y;

- certain placements result in improved academic achievement; or that

- special educators are more effective in working with students with disabilities than are regular educators.

A CLOSER LOOK AT TODAY'S CLASSROOMS

On average, public school districts formally identify between 10%–12% of their students with disabilities, and about 2%–5% of their students as gifted and talented if IQ scores are used as the sole criterion, and 15%–20% if a *talent pool* model is employed (Renzulli, 1999; Turnbull A. P., Turnbull, H. R., Shank, & Smith, 2004). At the national level, Table 6.1 provides a brief overview of who these students are and how their learning differences manifest themselves in today's classrooms.

Table 6.1 Brief Overview of Categories of Disabilities

Term	Definitions	% of AH Students With Disabilities
Specific Learning Disabilities	*Students of average intellectual ability or higher with significant difficulty in one or more academic domain (e.g., reading)*	*50.5*

(Continued)

Table 6.1 (Continued)

Term	Definitions	% of AH Students With Disabilities
Speech or Language Impairment	*Students with significant difficulty in either producing language (e.g., articulation difficulty) or understanding language (e.g., following directions).*	*19*
Mental Retardation	*Students with significantly below average measured intellectual ability* **and** *age-appropriate social skills (e.g., communication, independent living).*	*10.8*
Emotional Disabilities	*Students with chronic emotional, behavioral, or interpersonal difficulties extreme enough to interfere with learning.*	*8.2*
Other Health Impairments	*Students with chronic conditions that limit strength, vitality, alertness (e.g., epilepsy, arthritis, asthma).*	*4.5*
Multiple Disabilities	*Students with more than one disability.*	*2*
Orthopedic Impairments	*Students who have limited functional use of legs, feet, arms, hands, or other body parts.*	*1.3*
Hearing Impairments	*Students with significant hearing loss in one or both ears.*	*1.3*
Visual Impairments	*Students with low vision, even when corrected.*	*0.46*
Traumatic Brain Injury	*Students who have had brain injury as the result of external force (e.g., car accident) or internal occurrence (e.g., stroke).*	*0.24*
Deaf-blindness	*Students with both significant hearing loss and low vision.*	*0.03*
Giftedness	*(% of total population)*	*15–20*

Despite the progressive nature of special education legislation, individuals with identified disabilities, as a group, continue, as noted above, to fare quite poorly both in our schools and in their transition to adulthood. Here is some of what we know:

- Although the overall national graduation rate is approximately 88%, only about 27% of all students with disabilities leave high school with a diploma (Turnbull et al., 2004).

- The employment rates of people with disabilities is only about 32%, compared to an 81% employment rate for people without disabilities; the employment rate either full or part time for individuals with severe disabilities is only 19% (National Center on Education Statistics, 2003).

- Approximately two-thirds of individuals without disabilities report that they are *very satisfied* with life; only one-third of individuals with disabilities report the same level of satisfaction (Turnbull et al., 2004).

- One in five school-aged children is estimated to have reading disabilities. Eighty percent of these students who fail to make significant reading progress by the age of nine will continue to be unskilled readers in the 12th grade, if they even stay in school that long (Shaywitz, 1995).

- Juel (1988) found that about 40% of unskilled readers in the fourth grade would prefer cleaning their rooms to reading.

- Seventy-five to eighty percent of the prison population is estimated to have specific learning disabilities and/or serious emotional disturbance.

Although clearly beyond the scope of this chapter, the most recent data on independent living, wage earning, and rates of incarceration are equally bleak for individuals with disabilities. We must ask to what extent teaching approaches that focus on the transmission of information contribute to student failure, disengagement, and disenfranchisement.

TOUGH QUESTIONS:

Why is the dropout rate so high for students with disabilities?

Why is academic underachievement so prevalent?

Why have behavioral problems increased so dramatically?

Why do students prefer cleaning their rooms to reading?

Is it plausible in all (or even most) cases of student failure that students and/or their families are to blame for weak academic skills and/or behavioral problems? Goodlad (1984) and Cuban (1990) found that students spend a little more than 10% of their time in school asking questions, reading, writing, or engaged in some other form of active learning. Is there something wrong with our children, or are schools and teachers contributing to this state of affairs?

CONSIDER:

Could 5,000 reports be right in finding that no student difficulty was related to shortcomings in school practice? Or would Carnine's (1994) question about this finding ring more true:

"If 5,000 medical files of patients who failed to respond to treatment were analyzed, would there be an absence of professional shortcomings in all 5,000 cases?" (Carnine, 1994, p. 341)

Consider how this plays out for Sam, a 10th-grade student who was described simply as a *behavior problem* when we met him some years ago. Sam's school struggles began in the first grade. Since that time, he had been labeled as learning disabled, mentally retarded, emotionally disturbed, and language impaired, depending on the year he was tested and the person who did the testing. By the time Sam had reached the 10th grade, he refused to go to school and began receiving home tutoring from a man named Mr. Smith.

Mr. Smith reported that Sam was able to do a great deal more than he was led to believe by school personnel. He spoke at length about Sam's knack for fixing virtually anything mechanical (including car engines, grandfather clocks, and electric kitchen ranges), his strong ability to draw, and his memory for exactly how things looked long after he had seen them. Mr. Smith noted that Sam had difficulty expressing himself, read and wrote at about the sixth-grade level, and was extremely anxious and self-conscious about his weak academic skills. Although the primary focus of Mr. Smith's work was on helping Sam to obtain his driver's license, he indicated that he had successfully introduced academics *through the back door.* For example, Mr. Smith had structured math and physics lessons around ice fishing trips and other outdoor activities, brought car manuals to Sam's house that they read together, and communicated in writing on the computer, frequently sending e-mail messages to one another about interesting engineering and mechanically oriented Web sites.

When we met Sam at one of our homes for an evaluation, we found him to be an extremely polite, personable, and engaging adolescent. Although Sam was somewhat slow to warm up, after a brief walk outdoors and some tinkering with an old car, Sam initiated conversation easily, and rapport was established quickly. Sam struggled markedly on tests of reading and writing and on virtually all the evaluation measures that required fluent speaking skill, but he performed extremely well on measures that demanded mechanical problem solving, such as jigsaw puzzles and block designs. Sam shared with us his love of cars, information about his collection of small engines, and a small portfolio of sketches he had made of various sorts of machinery. When asked about school, Sam became sullen. He noted that teachers only asked him to do "stuff I can't." He said that students frequently teased him; that he often became so frustrated that he got involved in fights; and that he hated school and would never return.

The teachers at school were happy that Sam was receiving home tutoring—they were happy that he was no longer their problem. Most believed he was headed for the criminal justice system; others noted that it was just as well. Sam, after all, was not bright, and he had an attitude problem to boot.

Do you know Sam? What is so sad about this story is that it is not fiction, not for Sam and not for others like him whose gifts lie outside what we for too long have considered to be intelligence. What is most striking about Sam, and about so many students in our schools, is what powerful learners they can be and what enormous talents they possess. To recognize these talents, we must look beyond our limited conception that to be intelligent and to learn, one must have strong verbal and/or logical mathematical ability. Let's look more closely at an alternative way of thinking about intelligence, the return to Sam at the end of this section.

A TABLE: EXPANDING OUR COGNITIVE HORIZONS

Howard Gardner's *Frames of Mind: The Theory of Multiple Intelligences* (1983) indicates that there are at least seven, perhaps more, distinct types of human intelligences. Although he was not the first to theorize that intelligence comes in many forms, Gardner has written extensively on the ways in which an understanding of multiple intelligences, or MI, can be applied in educational settings. See Table 6.2 below.

Table 6.2 Types of Human Intelligences

Intelligence	Learner's Strengths
Intrapersonal	Ability to know self; ability to understand one's own strengths/weaknesses and motivations
Interpersonal	Ability to know others; ability to "read" social and /or political situations; ability to influence others; ability to lead and/or care for others–to be sensitive to needs of others
Bodily-kinesthetic	Ability to control the movement of one's body; ability to move in a graceful, highly coordinated fashion
Musical	Ability to produce, write, and/or appreciate music
Spatial	Ability to shape, perceive, design, and/or conceive visual-spatial information; ability to remember visual information
Logical-mathematical	Ability to manipulate numbers and symbolic information; ability to draw logical conclusions; ability to think abstractly
Verbal-linguistic	Ability to manipulate, create, and appreciate the rhythms of language; ability to speak, read, and/or write fluently

EXTENDING YOUR LEARNING:

Since *1983* Gardner has proposed additional types of human intelligence. What are they? How can they be explored in your classroom?

When we think of students who are doing poorly in our classrooms, we typically focus on the things they cannot do, or we speculate about the kinds of difficulty we believe may account for their weak school performance. The MI theory allows us to reframe our thinking about student performance. It calls on us to consider what our students do well, how they learn. and what they find intrinsically interesting so that we may label their strengths, as opposed to their weaknesses.

Let's return for a minute to Sam, who has always done poorly in school. Given what we know about him, would you say it is because he lacks intelligence? Are there things Sam does well? Could you think of a way that Sam could shine in your classroom? Or do you think simply that school should not be for kids like Sam? How do we want to label students like Sam—by what they can do or what they cannot do?

WHY STUDENTS WITH DISABILITIES NEED CONSTRUCTIVIST CLASSROOMS

Clearly, disabilities make learning and classrooms more challenging. Some disabilities may even make the learning of some things impossible. As teachers, we must create opportunities for learning that are more exciting, more enriching, and more rewarding—in short, more appealing—than the desire to clean one's room, leave school, get involved in criminal activity, or become a ward of the state.

> **TOUGH QUESTIONS:**
>
> How do students with disabilities learn? Is it really different from the learning of other students?
>
> Perhaps more important, shouldn't we instead be asking how can we spark their curiosity, facilitate their learning, and, perhaps most important, get out of their way as Suchman suggests above?

These questions are extremely important for students with disabilities, as they are at increased risk of school failure and difficult transitions to adulthood. As noted above, the high school dropout rate for students with disabilities is unacceptably high. Without a compelling reason to stay, and with little academic success and a great deal of frustration, this should come as no surprise. For many students with disabilities, school is deadly boring; it is irrelevant to their lives, needs, and interests; and for many others, it is extremely punishing as well. But the tough questions posed above are virtually never asked. Instead, teachers often assume that students with disabilities are so different, so impaired, so damaged that it is a waste of time to pursue inquiry with them. As Golfus remarks in "When Billy Broke his Head and Other Tales of Wonder" (Simpson & Golfus, 1995), many believe individuals with disabilities are just " . . . too gimped out to work."

In fact, students with disabilities, although in much more urgent need of constructivist approaches, are far less likely to receive them. The most recent research indicates that students with disabilities spend much of their day on tasks requiring little more cognitive energy than rote memorization. Worse still, many advocate for just such an approach. Consider the following, which neatly summarizes not only a very popular view of inclusion, but one about constructivism as well:

> There are several reasons for opposing a policy of full inclusion. One reason is because full inclusion . . . makes direct, systematic instruction nearly impossible. In addition, once full inclusion is implemented, teachers are forced to change their teaching methods to more child-directed, discovery-oriented, project-based learning activities in which every student works at his or her own pace. (Crawford, 2001)

What is shocking about Crawford's position is only his candor. Assuming, as we do, that there is nothing wrong, and everything right, with changing one's teaching so that it *is* "more child-centered, discovery-oriented, project based," how does one begin to develop an inquiry-based learning environment knowing that students with an enormous range of abilities and interests may populate a single classroom? With earlier caveats about following a lock-step, prescribed sequence of instructional activities in mind, we propose instead a series of *infrequently* asked questions, or IAQs, as a point of departure for setting up constructivist approaches in mixed ability classrooms. These IAQs are not simply designed to be provocative; rather, it is our hope that they will lead to careful teacher self-reflection about the importance of constructivist approaches, about the pitfalls of sham inquiry, and about the true conditions necessary for students to get excited about learning.

IAQS

1. How are constructivism and rigid, lock-step, standards-based education incompatible for students with learning differences?

The short answer to this IAQ is that rigid application of standards and constructivism can be incompatible in many, many ways—particularly for students with disabilities. Students with disabilities and/or giftedness are, by definition, different academically, emotionally, physically, or cognitively than their age peers. Thus, in some sense, they are the paradigmatic case of how standards and inquiry are often incompatible, as such students are in a nonstandard place at a nonstandard time, and will by necessity have questions that may differ from those of their peers. But this raises an even larger question: Does it make sense to assume that there is a *standard* time and place in which students are ready (to say nothing of eager) for particular kinds of content learning? Despite overwhelming evidence to the contrary, an increasing number of states seem to be making precisely this assumption as an ever-growing number of them prepare to roll out detailed sets of grade-level expectations. Yet, in a recent study by Peterson and colleagues (2002) when teachers were asked about the range of abilities of students in their class *every* teacher in the sample stated that students crossed at least five grade levels, with some teachers assessing even larger grade-level differences. Clearly, student difference is not merely a special education issue. In a very succinct summary of this problem Tomlinson (2000) notes that:

> Students who are the same age differ in their readiness to learn, their interests, their styles of learning, their experiences, and their life circumstances. The differences in students are significant enough to make a major impact on what students need to learn, the pace at which they need to learn it, and the support they need from teachers and others to learn it well. (p. 6)

As every alert teacher knows, what Tomlinson says is true whether one's classroom contains students with disabilities or not. What is important is that teachers think flexibly about standards and avoid the same rigid expectations for all of their students.

2. Don't students with learning differences need to learn basic skills before they engage in real inquiry?

The value of special education can be summed up as follows: What's good for the goose is necessary for the gander. That is, although all students benefit from good teachers, students with a history of academic and/or behavioral challenges (for whatever reason) need good teachers and the kind of classroom experiences supported and driven by constructivist propositions, including the proposition that student talent and ability can be key to developing knowledge. If a teacher is simply delivering information, he cannot ever deal with the infinite variety of ways of knowing and learning that students with disabilities present. To remain interested and engaged in learning, students need opportunities to discover, create, and problem solve. But, what if problem-solving skill is precisely what they lack?

Many teachers treat students with disabilities as if they have a defect that needs correcting. To fix the disability, some professionals believe that students need high levels of teacher-directed information transmission. At the other extreme, some advocate fostering student strengths (wherever they may be), following the students' leads in learning, and letting students choose whether or not to attempt to improve the academic skill areas in which they may struggle. The first approach often results in the temporary memorization of increased content knowledge. The second approach is also inappropriate because most students with disabilities demonstrate weak ability to approach tasks strategically and often have difficulty carefully monitoring their own progress. The majority of students with disabilities also do not spontaneously initiate problem-solving behaviors, and they demonstrate difficulty sustaining attention (even in areas of their interest), inhibiting impulsive responding, and remaining cognitively flexible. Many students with disabilities, therefore, need a bridge from traditional special education to inquiry-based learning experiences.

Learning in constructivist terms is simply not possible until students possess some fundamental skills; however, this does not mean students need to earn the right to engage in inquiry by demonstrating minimum competencies in reading, writing, or mathematics. The skills referred to here are not academic skills, per se. Rather, they are thinking tools based largely on the work of Meichenbaum's (1977) cognitive behavioral approach to problem solving. These tools were initially developed to help students initiate their own learning; sustain attention for complex, multistep tasks; form hypotheses; and evaluate their own performance. Although there are many kinds of learning strategy models that have grown from this work, perhaps the easiest and most practical of these approaches is Bonnie Camp's *Think Aloud Program* (1987; 1996). The *Think Aloud Program* is designed to increase student self-control by the explicit teaching of self-talk strategies for solving a range of problems. Because many students with disabilities lack verbal mediation skills, teaching them to *think aloud* provides a bridge to help them move toward self-directed, inquiry-based learning. You can also easily incorporate this into whole-class instruction. Camp (1996) suggests that teachers introduce specific questions students can ask themselves as they set about to learn. They involve:

- identifying problems ("What am I to do? How can I find out?");
- choosing a plan or strategy ("How can I do it? What are some plans?");
- self-monitoring ("Am I using my plan?); and
- self-evaluating ("Is my plan working? How did I do? Do I need a new plan?").

When students use these questions in the context of the curriculum (and not separate from it), together with a menu of problem-solving strategies (such as brainstorming, means/ends analysis, mnemonic memory strategies, and so on), they quickly acquire a wide repertoire of powerful learning tools that can be used for real inquiry.

3. Isn't "I differentiate my instruction for students with disabilities" just a more politically palatable way to say "I use tracking within my classroom"?

In practice this is, unfortunately, almost always the case. As Peterson, Hittie, and Tamor (2002b) have noted, most of what is referred to as differentiated instruction is simply tracking within a classroom under a different name. Even well-intentioned teachers traditionally think of differentiation this way and will often group students by a single, global measure of their perceived ability; require less of students they view as below average; and create more challenging assignments for those who are facile verbally and/or mathematically. What distinguishes true differentiation from such ability grouping is largely dispositional. That is, in classrooms where instruction is truly differentiated so that all learners may engage in real inquiry, teachers believe that all learners have strengths, that a uniform lesson format for the whole class is doomed to fail, that flexible grouping strategies (see, for example, Aronson's Jigsaw Model [Aronson & Bridgeman, 1979]) are critical for every student to succeed, and that the collaborative problem solving of authentic (i.e., student created) problems is essential to learning. Such teachers believe further that are many ways students might obtain information and demonstrate their learning.

Gardner's (1983; 1993) MI theory is one way in which teachers can adapt and modify their instruction for heterogeneous grouping. Gardner reminds us that to recognize student talents and interests, to give value to *their questions,* we must look beyond our limited conception that to be intelligent and to learn, one must have strong verbal and/or logical-mathematical ability. Indeed, failure to perform well in one of these two ways is how virtually all students with disabilities come to be identified, labeled, and ultimately thought of as *not able.* When we think of students who are doing poorly in our classrooms, we typically focus on the things they cannot do, or we speculate about the kinds of difficulty we believe may account for their weak school performance. The MI theory allows us to reframe our thinking about student performance. It calls on us to consider what our students do well, how they learn, and what they find intrinsically interesting so that we can label their strengths, as opposed to their weaknesses, and validate the types of inquiry they are most likely to pursue.

4. How can I demonstrate to my students, colleagues, and administrators that having different behavioral and academic expectations is not only necessary but also fair?

For most students who are eligible for special education service, disabilities are life-span issues. The ways in which they approach material, the challenges they face, and the compensatory strategies they use—all these things are unlikely to change over time. Many years ago, one of us was involved in a consultation with a 10th-grade chemistry teacher who complained that a hyperactive student in her class continually tapped his pencil on the lab table, disrupting her and other students. The teacher shared with us that most days ended with arguments (because the student would continue tapping moments after he was asked to stop) and an occasional angry exchange. From the teacher's point of view, it was unclear whether the tapping was a willful attempt to continually disrupt the classroom or a manifestation of a behavior out of the boy's control Either way, the behavior had to stop. Thinking about this behavior as something that must be changed (i.e., thinking that the student must be changed) is a mindset that guarantees teacher frustration and anger, student resentment, and often feelings of inferiority and impotence in both. One way to frame this dilemma is the following: The student needs to tap, and the teacher needs a distraction-free environment. Accepting for a moment that both are in fact true needs (and that the student is not simply trying to be difficult), are these needs mutually exclusive? Of course not. Readers who already have begun to think about how we can change the environment and not the student already know this. For the rest of you, one solution to this dilemma can be found at the end of the chapter.

Unfortunately, many teachers believe that accommodating an individual student need is somehow unfair to other students.

CONSIDER:

As Richard Lavoie has elegantly pointed out on his well-known video about the F.A.T. city workshop (1989), it is not about the other students! Lavoie points out that a teacher who fails to accommodate a student with a disability (because she feels this is unfair to others students) uses the same logic as a teacher skilled in CPR who refuses to resuscitate a student who collapses after heart failure because there isn't time to administer CPR to all the students in her room. Obviously, all the students do not need CPR. Fairness is about need, not about ensuring all students receive the same things at the same time.

In practical terms, this may mean that some students will need note-takers, others will need books on tape, and still others will need extended time to take tests, complete assignments, and so on. Some students will need to demonstrate their learning in writing, whereas others may demonstrate comprehension orally, in song, or through some other form of creative expression. What is important is that we remember our goal: to facilitate real learning. For some students getting out of their way is not enough; they will need support.

5. How can students with disabilities teach each other?

Ironically, perhaps one of the most powerful learning approaches for students with disabilities is to prepare, and encourage, them to teach others. We observed this (and it was dramatic) in Jan Carpenter's classroom, a teacher in a multi-age elementary school. Steve, a student with severe attentional and organizational difficulties, typically arrived unprepared for school—he rarely arrived with his books or writing utensils, had difficulty settling down for class work, and often appeared confused shortly after directions had been given. Many special educators and proponents of collaborative groups emphasize the importance of pairing students like Steve with academically advanced students who can model appropriate classroom and social behaviors. Jan chose a seemingly counterintuitive approach and paired Steve with a student whose organizational skills were weaker than his own. After a variety of interventions that often resulted in Steve becoming upset and Jan becoming frustrated, she asked Steve if he could help a student with mild autism named Maria to get organized in the morning, to keep her materials tidy, and to remember to bring her books home for homework assignments. On the first day of Steve's teaching, Steve approached Maria at the end of the school day and asked the following questions: "Maria, what do you need to do to make sure you have everything you need? How can you remember to bring these materials home? What will you do tomorrow morning to remember to bring your homework to school?" Jan's strategy worked brilliantly. Steve began to rehearse verbally the strategies and questions he needed to ask himself to become more focused, responsible, and engaged with school assignments. For the first time, Steve began to feel empowered, as if learning was something within his control. For the first time, Steve saw at first hand the value of self-questioning, of teaching, and of collaborating with another. Finally, Steve became a model for Maria, and slowly she began to learn. Who might she teach next?

TOUGH QUESTIONS:

Should all students, regardless of the severity of disability, be educated in regular classrooms? Why? Why not?

At what age, if ever, should a decision be made that a student should pursue vocational preparation instead of a more academically based education? Who should be involved in such a decision?

Is there a value to labeling students? Why? Why not?

Are certain intelligences more important for students to develop than others?

The Pen-Tapping Dilemma

A rubber pad was placed on the lab table, allowing the student to tap to his heart's content without disturbing his classmates or the teacher.

FOR FURTHER EXPLORATION

Marlowe, B. A. (July 27, 2011). *This I believe.* Providence, RI: Rhode Island Public Radio.

Marlowe, B. A., & Canestrari, A. S. (2006). *Educational psychology: Readings for future teachers.* Thousand Oaks, CA: Sage.

Marlowe, B. A., & Page, M. L. (2004). The good news about teacher personality disorder. *Encounter: Education for Meaning and Social Justice, 17*(4), 28–30.

Marlowe, B. A., & Page, M. L. (2005). *Creating and sustaining the constructivist classroom.* Thousand Oaks, CA: Corwin.

7

Lesbian, Gay, Bisexual, and Transgender Students

Perceived Social Support in the High School Environment

Corrine Munoz-Plaza, Sandra C. Quinn, and Kathleen A. Rounds

L esbian, gay, bisexual, and transgender youth (LGBT) continue to face extreme discrimination within the school environment. Existing literature suggests that LGBT youth are at high risk for a number of health problems, including suicide ideation and attempts, harassment, substance abuse, homelessness, and declining school performance. This exploratory study consists of face-to-face interviews with 12 male and female participants, 18–21 years old, who identify as gay, lesbian, bisexual, or transgender. The purpose of the study is to determine the types of social support (emotional, appraisal, instrumental, and informational) available to these young adults in high school. In addition, the study examines the connection between social support and sexual identity development. Participants found non-family members, which included peers and non-family adults, to be more supportive than

NOTE: From *The High School Journal*, vol. 85, number 4. Copyright © 2002 by the University of North Carolina Press. Used by permission of the publisher. www.uncpress.edu

family members. More specifically, participants perceived heterosexual and LGBT-identified friends and non-family adults as providing emotional and instrumental support. However, participants perceived limitations to the emotional support they received from heterosexual peers to whom they disclosed their orientation. In addition to providing emotional support, peers and adults who also identified as LGBT provided valuable informational and appraisal support. Finally, most participants did not disclose to their parents during high school and perceived their parents and family members as offering limited emotional, appraisal and informational support. Confronted with their own sense of alienation and confusion, as well as the overwhelmingly negative messages about homosexuality in their home and school environments, respondents described their sexual identity formation as a process characterized by varying degrees of denial and acceptance. The need for multiple resources emerged as a major theme from participant responses to questions about what types of services and support they would have valued from their high school.

LESBIAN, GAY, BISEXUAL, AND TRANSGENDER YOUTH

Despite increasing visibility, persons who are lesbian, gay, bisexual, or transgender (LGBT) continue to face extreme social, legal, and institutional discrimination within the United States. LGBT youth are an extremely vulnerable subset of the larger gay, lesbian, bisexual, and transgender population. Given the degree of homophobia in our society, adolescents who are struggling with issues of sexual orientation face incredible challenges and lack many of the fundamental support systems available to their heterosexual peers (Gonsiorek, 1988). While estimates of the number of gays and lesbians range anywhere from 3% to 10% of the population, the latter figure is more widely accepted (Fontaine, 1998; Robinson, 1994; Marinoble, 1998; Omizo, Omizo, & Okamoto, 1998). Given these estimates, one can safely assume that a significant minority of adolescents in primary and secondary schools either self-identify as LGBT or are questioning their sexuality.

The widespread social stigmatization of homosexuality has been blamed for a myriad of social and health problems that can disproportionately impact LGBT youth (Hetrick & Martin, 1987; Robinson, 1994; Remafedi, 1987; Savin-Williams, 1994; Center for Population Options, 1992). Many researchers have particularly focused on the lack of social support systems for lesbian and gay youth within our schools, identifying the classroom as the most homophobic of all social institutions (Elia, 1993; Unks, 1994; Governors' Task Force on Bias-Related Violence, 1988; Remafedi, 1987).

This article seeks to understand lesbian, gay, bisexual, and transgender youth and available support systems in the high school environment. Overall, the literature on issues facing LGBT youth is rather limited (Radkowsky & Siegel, 1997; Fontaine, 1998) and much of the past research on this population has come from sources other than the youth themselves (Robinson, 1994). Therefore, additional research in this area is necessary to both raise awareness to the issues LGBT youth face in our schools and help guide and inform future interventions aimed at promoting health within this population. This article presents results from a qualitative study that describes the personal experiences of LGBT youth in high school. The research questions guiding this study are: (1) What types of school-based social support (*emotional, appraisal, informational,* and/or *instrumental*) are available to lesbian, gay, bisexual, and transgender youth during their high school years; and (2) How does the available support system influence identity?

HEALTH STATUS OF LESBIAN, GAY, BISEXUAL, AND TRANSGENDER YOUTH

Research has consistently shown that LGBT youth are particularly at risk for suicide, as well as verbal and physical harassment, substance abuse, sexually transmitted diseases, homelessness and prostitution, and declining school performance (Hetrick & Martin, 1987; Robinson, 1994; Remafedi, 1987; Savin-Williams, 1994; Center for Population Options, 1992). A 1989 U.S. Department of Health and Human Services study cited suicide as the number one cause of death of LGBT youth. Lesbian and gay youth were 2–6 times more likely to attempt suicide than heterosexual youth and accounted for more than 30% of all teen suicides. Radkowsky and Siegel (1997) assert that the literature not only consistently provides evidence that LGBT youth are at high risk for suicide ideation and attempts, but that the studies in this area have linked such an outcome with stressors resulting from the issue of sexual orientation. Saunders and Valente (1987) point out that general research on the topic suggests people with reduced social support and broken ties with peers, partners, and families have a higher risk for suicide than those persons whose social networks are more intact.

In addition to suicide, LGBT youth are at risk for other social and health problems. One study focusing on 131 young gay and bisexual males found 76% used alcohol and 25% used cocaine (Rotheram-Borus, Rosario, Meyer-Bahlburg, Koopman, Dopkins, & Davies, 1994). Rotheram-Borus et al. compared their findings to alcohol use by 49% and cocaine use by 2% of heterosexual male youth found in other studies. While the National Network of Runaway and Youth Services reported in 1991 that 6% of the runaways they surveyed self-identified as LGBT, other investigations have found rates as high as 42% (Victim Services, 1991). Recognizing the connection between runaway youth and prostitution, Coleman (1989) reviewed research on male prostitution among adolescents and found that empirical evidence across studies suggest approximately two out of three prostitutes self-identify as gay or bisexual. Furthermore, youth who identify as lesbian, gay, bisexual, or transgender are especially susceptible to high levels of verbal and physical harassment. In a review of research on violence against LGBT junior high and high school students, 33%–49% of youth had reported experiencing harassment, threats, or violence (Herek & Berrill, 1992). Of another 2,000 LGBT teenagers interviewed nationwide, approximately 50% of males and 20% of females reported experiencing harassment or physical violence in junior high or high school (National Gay and Lesbian Task Force, 1985).

LACK OF SOCIAL SUPPORT FOR LGBT YOUTH

Research on major life changes, such as the loss of a spouse or loved one, suggests that social support and social networks can act as buffers against stress and aid the coping abilities of individuals faced with a variety of stressors (Hirsch & DuBois, 1992; Rhodes, Contreras, & Mangelsdorf, 1994). Furthermore, numerous authors have reviewed the literature linking social support and social networks to morbidity and mortality (Berkman, 1984; House, Umberson, & Landis, 1988; Israel & Rounds, 1987).

House (1981) described social support as consisting of four types of behaviors, which include: 1) **emotional support** in the form of love, caring, trust, listening, and other similar affective behaviors; 2) **appraisal support** in the form of positive feedback or affirmation; 3) **instrumental support** in the form of a tangible resource or aid, including money, labor, time, and barter; and 4) **informational support** in the form of advice or suggestions. Mercier and Berger (1989) point to the lack of readily available support systems—at home, in the community, and in the educational system—as the cause of the social isolation that many LGBT youth experience. Elia (1993) argues that the literature consistently associates isolation as one of the major contributors to the high-risk status of many LGBT youth.

SAMPLE

Study participants included lesbian, gay, and bisexual young adults, 18–21 years old. A total of 12 young adults, seven female and five male, participated in the study. While transgender youth were recruited for the study, none chose to participate. Nine participants are Caucasian, with two African-American males and one Asian-American male. Of the females, three identified as lesbian, three as bisexual, and one as undecided. Of the males, four identified as gay and one identified as bisexual. Eleven participants were undergraduates in public universities in the Triangle and Triad areas of North Carolina.

Given the sensitive nature of the subject matter and concerns regarding potential risks of LGBT youth obtaining parental consent to participate in the study, adolescents under the age of 18 were excluded. Campus and community organizations targeting LGBT young adults in North Carolina assisted in identifying and recruiting participants. Inclusion criteria for study participants included self-identification as gay, lesbian, bisexual, or transgender and a desire to participate in the interview process. The University of North Carolina School of Public Health Institutional Review Board approved the study activities and informed consent procedures on January 12, 1999.

Participants met with the principal investigator in a confidential setting to take part in a recorded interview, approximately 1½ hours in length. A review of the literature on both LGBT adolescents and social support informed the development of a standardized interview guide that consisted of a series of open-ended questions about the types of social support available to participants during high school. Specific questions within the interview guide asked respondents to both describe the types of social support available in their school environment—instrumental, appraisal, emotional, and informational—and the people who provided such support. Once transcription of all the interviews was complete, the data were content analyzed for emerging patterns and themes (Patton, 1990). Using cross-case analysis, participants' answers were grouped by topic area and then coded and labeled in order to create an "index" of themes from the transcripts. Once the data were analyzed in this deductive manner, they were processed using NUID*IST, a qualitative data-processing software program.

RESULTS

One area of inquiry was the type of support available to LGBT youth in the high school environment. Participants found non-family members, which included peers and non-family adults, to be more supportive than family members. More specifically, participants perceived heterosexual and LGBT-identified friends and non-family adults as providing *emotional* and *instrumental* support. However, participants perceived limitations to the emotional support they received from heterosexual peers to whom they disclosed their orientation. In addition to providing emotional support, peers and adults who also identified as LGBT provided valuable *informational* and *appraisal* support. Finally, most participants did not disclose to their parents during high school and therefore described their parents as offering minimal support of any type related to their sexual orientation.

Participants cited "close" friends as the members of their network that they relied on most for emotional support. These were people in their network that they felt they could talk to most easily about personal issues in general, depend on in a crisis, and spend quality time with on a day-to-day basis. When asked who at school he would talk to about something personal, a gay participant said, "It would never have been a teacher . . . it would have been a friend." However, participants perceived limitations to the emotional support they received from heterosexual peers to whom they disclosed their sexual orientation. Specifically, while respondents said they could share feelings, resources, affection, and time with their friends, many could not admit to their true sexual feelings. A bisexual women said she could talk to one of her closest friends about, "Pretty much anything . . . ," but added in the next breath, "not my sexual orientation at that point at all." A gay male said that he would go to close friends about a lot of personal issues, but that with regards to his sexuality, "there were lines that weren't crossed with them . . . Like we talked to each other a lot, you know, we were good friends and buddies, but . . . I had a lot on my mind that I just didn't speak of."

Some respondents described the emotional price they paid in high school for the perceived limitations many of their close friends placed on their support. One gay male described this impact:

Very few friends could I talk very candidly with about the details of my sexual relationships . . . generally, you tell them and you get this reaction like that was uncomfortable or awkward . . . if those barriers weren't there . . . that sort of unconscious trust and just total comfort that you can feel with people might be there. I like to be open. Especially with people that are very open with me and people that I consider my best of friends . . .

LGBT-identified peers and adults provided valuable *informational* and *appraisal* support. One lesbian talked about how an LGBT-identified friend at her school was a role model:

Julie was a big role model and [not just] because she was a lesbian . . . [she's] just an amazing person . . . she was like someone who I went to a lot . . . I mean, [her sexuality] probably had something to do with it. I remember before I came to the school, [my friend] saying there'll be this girl, Julie . . . she's a lesbian. I remember like going ooh! Wow!

A bisexual woman talked about how an LGBT-identified peer provided her with information and advice:

. . . she was the one I could turn to my age that was at the same school with me that, you know, would have advice or, you know, knew what I . . . what I felt . . . So, she was definitely an inspiration and also like a really good person to talk to with my own questions and stuff like that. Like Sonya and I could talk about girls, but I couldn't talk about them with anybody else really.

Participants perceived their parents and family members as offering limited emotional, appraisal, and informational support. A gay interviewee explained his primary fear of telling his parents about his sexuality in high school was being disowned, " . . . having the doors changed, having the locks changed literally." Only three of the respondents' parents knew anything about their children's sexuality. These participants overwhelmingly felt a lack of support from their families. The only participant to share her sexuality with a parent directly described her mother's reaction:

. . . She was one of those people that like was very—like as long as it wasn't anybody connected to her, she was very pro LGBT . . . till I came out to her and then she flipped, you know, like she was a Baptist minister or something, you know . . . the first time I told her that I thought I was a lesbian she told me to un-think it.

EMERGING IDENTITY AND SUPPORT

Another major theme throughout participants' responses was their emerging identity during high school and the interplay between sexual identity development and social support. Troiden (1989, p. A.6) defines the concept of identity as "perceptions of self that are thought to represent the self in specific social settings" (such as, a "doctor" identity at work, a "spouse" identity at home, or a heterosexual/homosexual identity within amorous settings).

Uribe and Harbeck (1992) argued that a central role of our high schools is to assist adolescents in developing a sense of personal identity via the adoption of social norms. The teachers, counselors, coaches, and administrators described by participants in this study generally strove to uphold the heterosexual model as normative, a perspective that was in direct conflict with the participants' emerging sense of sexual identity. Subsequently, participants explained how an increasing awareness of their sexual identity represented both an internal and external struggle for them throughout high school. Confronted with their own sense of alienation and confusion, as well as the overwhelmingly negative messages about homosexuality in their home and school environments, respondents described their sexual identity formation as a process characterized by varying degrees of denial and acceptance.

Growing up, many felt a sense that they were different in some way from their peers. One gay-identified male said, " . . . I always knew that the way I felt about guys or opposite sex or whatever, was always different from my friends." This difference was often associated with a reported inability to "fit in" with their peer groups and feelings of alienation. For example, one lesbian said, " . . . I never really . . . since I guess freshman year of high school, I didn't feel like I fit in, exactly . . . I felt alienated most of the time."

During their burgeoning awareness of their sexuality, respondents often relayed a sense of confusion about what they were feeling. A lesbian woman said, "It was like we were both sort of in this process of like not really knowing what was going on, but knowing that we weren't straight." When asked when they first became aware that their sexual orientation was different from the heterosexual norm, respondents pinpointed fairly specific time frames in their adolescence and young adulthood. On the whole, males reported having some awareness of their sexual status in their elementary or middle school years. On the other hand, the women came to grips with their sexuality issues during their high school years.

During the interview, all respondents were given an opportunity to define, in their own words, how they identified with regards to their sexual orientation. While some of the respondents stated that they only partner with members of the same sex, others (both bisexual and gay/lesbian) suggested a more fluid approach to sexuality. Slightly under half of the participants identified themselves as partnering exclusively with members of the same sex. However, while still identifying as lesbian or gay (as opposed to bisexual), several respondents felt that attraction to members of the opposite sex is possible. A lesbian respondent put it this way:

> I identify more as a lesbian . . . I am very much more into women, like I am very much more, like I think my life partner is going to be a woman, but it might be a man . . . but I don't know if I would want to be in a relationship with one—on a continuum? I would be way over to women.

Of those persons that identified as bisexual in the sample, only one expressed an equal likelihood that they would partner with a woman or a man. Overall, there was a theme of fluid sexuality, but identifying more with one sex than the other. One bisexual identified female said, " . . . it's simple in the sense that I guess I would call myself bisexual. But if I—my roommate asked me about percentages once and I told her ninety-ten. Ninety percent gay, ten-percent straight."

The following two female respondents felt a strong identification with the word "dyke" as opposed to being labeled lesbian. Among these women, there seemed to be a conscious "taking back" of a term that has historically been used pejoratively against lesbians. While one woman said, "I am a dyke," another explained:

> Well, I guess that I'm lesbian . . . like before I'd say I was a lesbian, I'd say I was a dyke, like in terms of word choices. Just because it seems like . . . a more politicized choice, and like I'm more like visible and out there. I just think you should have to be at least 35 to be a lesbian.

Respondents explained the degree to which they told other peers, family, and school personnel about their sexuality in high school. In addition, they spoke to those factors that impeded and facilitated their "coming out" process in the school environment. Respondents rarely described disclosure as occurring in a linear fashion, but rather working through a repeating pattern of disclosure and reinforcement.

By far, the major barrier to disclosing their sexual orientation to friends, family, and teachers was fear. Interviewees said they were afraid of losing support, as exemplified by the following comment:

> . . . I guess being rejected by someone you care about and seeing the change. Even if you are not totally rejected, just knowing that there is a change would be enough to really like, keep you [from disclosing] . . . a change in support. A change in how they interact with you and all of a sudden they are still your friend, but they don't talk to you as much or they stop calling you or that sort of thing.

A number of respondents stated that they were particularly concerned about teachers at school finding out about their sexuality for fear of unfair treatment. One respondent stated, "I think part of me would think that teachers may talk and I wouldn't want to have to deal with being singled out because I was gay . . . I would be afraid of being harassed or being given bad grades or something."

Finally, other respondents reported they were afraid of being thought of as a sexual predator by friends. Interestingly, while four of the seven women mentioned this concern, none of the men cited it as a concern. One bisexual woman stated:

> . . . I was pretty much scared to tell her [a friend] because she just seemed like one of those types that would—she doesn't have a problem with it, but if it was me she might think that there was something ulterior going on in our friendship. She would be the one that would freak out and think that I was, you know, like, thinking back to all the slumber parties and stuff.

Participants expressed that their fear was fueled by the negative messages they received about homosexuality in the school environment. This gay male spoke about how witnessing the treatment of openly gay peers influenced him:

> The people who were out, I kind of envied them because I was thinking it would be so much easier if I was just out, but then hearing what the other people would say about them behind their back made me not want to come out.

Other interviewees shared observations on the experience of other LGBT people, namely faculty and school personnel: A lesbian respondent said:

I was more scared. I mean, I thought—[my teacher] was—he still is the coolest person. But at the time it scared me more than anything. People didn't react to him that well.

People would say, you know, he is a brilliant musician, but he is gay. Like gay equals bad. One gay male illustrated a theme present in the majority of the interviews—that they learned that being gay is "bad" or "wrong":

> . . . because it seems like that is what society makes you think . . . it is bad to be gay, it is bad to be LGBT and so you assume, well, they [people at school] are part of society, so they are going to take society's opinion even though they really didn't, but you just assumed that because you are trying to cover yourself.

Several respondents spoke of their own internalized homophobia, suggesting that their own experience with anti-homosexual feelings in the past added to their apprehension about coming out. When asked why she wasn't out at school, one bisexual woman said:

> . . . definitely also because of the hometown. I mean, like with these people, they would sit around and be like, you know—it was—I mean, everyone was homophobic there, you know. I mean, in fact, I was at one point in my life just because that was the only attitude I had ever heard . . .

Many participants suggested that they were simply not far enough along in their identity development during high school to be able to share their homosexual or bisexual feelings with anyone else. Feelings of uncertainty and living up to their old self-image ripple through the following quotes:

(1) I wasn't ready for it yet. There was still sort of a self-denial thing. And part of it is, it's just—I really fought my feelings because, I mean, it's not easy being a lesbian.

(2) I really wasn't sure . . . how I wanted to go about verbalizing it to everyone. So, I just figured, you know, why create this whole new image of myself . . . last semester of high school . . . just to myself I thought I'd be more comfortable being in the environment where I didn't have to re-invent myself at all, and just come in there [college] as this type of individual and that'd be it . . .

(3) I thought I had to be super girl. Super girl—oh my God— she's gay?

Other respondents either shied away from other people who were identified or perceived as LGBT or went along with anti-homosexual remarks to avoid disclosure.

The degree to which participants confided in other people about their sexual orientation ranged from those who never came out to anyone in high school to those who reported their sexual preferences were common knowledge at school. When asked about the degree to which she was out, one lesbian woman said, "Ah . . . I don't really think that people knew. Only because I was so uncomfortable with myself. I was very, very depressed all through high school." While some did not disclose at all in high school, other respondents stated that a larger number of people were aware of their sexuality:

> . . . I told, yeah, like the first beginnings of it all, I told Maria because she was around. And eventually just started—but once I started telling people I just couldn't stop. So, by the time I graduated, everybody knew.

Most interviewees came out to at least a few select peers, with a smaller number disclosing to teachers and school personnel. One gay man describes his experience coming out to a female friend:

> So we ended up just spending a lot of time. And then when we weren't together we'd be on the phone talking. So trust was developed after a certain point. It became clear that I could share anything with her. I kept having crushes on guys and I just had to unload. And then she was just like, have you told your—maybe she asked first and made it easier for me even.

Another gay male talked about why he only disclosed to peers when he said, "Yeah, well there was support from my friends, ya know, and that was good. That is all I really needed. But like in the larger way, I didn't want to make it too big of a deal, that would have just caused conflict." On the other hand, one lesbian woman talked about why she tended to confide in teachers, "Or like a lot of times it was teachers, especially those that I knew were feminists, so I assumed they would be comfortable. I would say—like especially at the beginning, I told more teachers than other people."

Participants outlined methods they employed to disclose their sexual orientation to other people at school. In some situations, respondents described just telling people in a very direct way. One gay man described his matter-of-fact approach:

. . . I would say, probably, most of them [peers] I just told outright, and then there was one guy, who suspected and he was gay himself and so he actually approached me, but most people I just told. They were just told.

Another gay male described a different, yet just as direct, approach—by disclosing his sexuality to a teacher in a term paper:

Actually, because during the class we had the opportunity to read all the different authors—Sappho, Whitman—people like that . . . And during the semester we had to write maybe two or three papers analyzing the material it had in it and also trying to incorporate it with our own opinions and things like that. And so one of the papers . . . I just figured a better way of getting my point across was just saying how it related to me. So that was basically how I came out and told him . . . I wrote it [my sexual orientation] in the paper.

A common theme was the strategy of putting out "feelers" with other people to both determine the safety of disclosing, as well as to actually assist the participant in disclosing in a slightly more indirect way. One bisexual female said that if she weren't positive about how receptive someone would be, she wouldn't tell them. She explained her method for making this assessment: " . . . I definitely, you know, ask a couple of questions and stuff like that just to kind of get an idea of what they would say . . . like testing the waters with people." This quote from a lesbian respondent provided insight into her strategies for assessment and disclosure:

Well, if I didn't know them, I'd probably use like gender-less pronouns, which I started—that's how I usually started talking to people, and then once I know them a little bit, I'll like tell them like . . . I'll say like, "she" and see how they react—if it was fairly positive, I would just keep on going.

Although not all respondents knew people who were LGBT, those that did spoke of how their relationships with these people helped them feel more comfortable with their sexuality and moved them along in the disclosure process. Speaking about a teacher, one gay male said:

But I was just happy that he seemed so happy, even though he was clearly so different . . . I looked at him and thought . . . if I get to a place where I can come out and face up to the—you know, and be in a place where being gay is okay, then maybe I'll be happier.

One lesbian participant agreed, " . . . it was the first time that I had actually met other like young lesbians and it—I was like, ahhh, oh my god, they're talking about girls! I like girls too!" A bisexual woman described her experience relating to other LGBT people:

> . . . like I had a lot—or not a lot but a couple of friends . . . who were openly gay and that I knew about . . . So, I definitely started seeing it a lot and, you know, it was a period of a lot of just discovering there was a community surrounding it, you know? And they weren't isolated, you know, there was something there that, you know, there was a community.

Given that the majority of respondents who did disclose suggested they were very selective about whom they told, reactions to their "coming out" were often described as fairly positive. One gay youth described the reaction of the only other person to whom he disclosed at school, an instructor who was teaching a class on sexual orientation: "Well, actually, he was—he was, I guess you'd say, grateful for me telling him, I guess you would say." A bisexual female participant talked about how her best friend reacted:

> Well, Joanna was . . . my best friend and she was—she's very straight. And I don't know, I don't remember particularly like an event of telling her. But I remember just kind of hinting at an interest . . . I think I remember I just said something like, you know, I think I could be bi. And she was like, really? And I was like, yeah, I think it could happen. And she was just like, okay.

While positive reactions did occur among peers and school personnel, some respondents experienced more negative outcomes from disclosing their sexuality. One lesbian described being crushed by the response from a teacher she had greatly admired:

> And there was this incredible history teacher . . . and he had been so important to me . . . But his response was just horrible. And I expected him to be completely supportive . . . I had to deal with this man who was like pretty hostile to the whole idea, who had been—like who I revered . . . He just completely . . . rejected me, like rejected the fact that I was a lesbian . . . He said that he like, one, didn't believe that I was a lesbian, that I really need to think carefully—like I love this whole thing, like you really need to think carefully. Like you haven't, you know!

DISCUSSION

Findings from this study highlight significant gaps in the social support available to participants from peers, school personnel, and family. Overall, the participants' accounts about the types of social support available to them in high school concur with the three main categories Martin and Hetrick (1988) use to describe the social isolation of LGBT youth—cognitive, social, and emotional. Following this framework, respondents experienced *cognitive isolation* because they had extremely limited access to accurate information on issues related to sexual orientation; *emotional isolation* as a result of constant negative messages about homosexuality from peers, school personnel, and family, which made their feelings seem "bad" or "wrong"; and *social isolation*, not only from peers and family that they could not tell about their sexuality to begin with, but also with many of the friends they did tell. Participants shared some critical experiences related to their sexual identity development during high school. While they described the process of coming to grips with their homosexual or bisexual identity as taking significant time and reflection, very few respondents described moving through this period in a linear fashion. Instead, they described cycling back and forth between feelings of denial, fear, alienation, confusion, and acceptance during their high school years. Participants' descriptions of this process mirror Troiden's (1988; 1989) characterization of homosexual identity formation as a process characterized by fits and starts, with individuals moving back and forth between various stages—*sensitization, identity confusion, identity assumption,* and *commitment.* Participants' descriptions of feeling different and not "fitting in" with peers early on in adolescence parallel Troiden's *sensitization* stage.

In addition, interviewees reported periods of confusion and denial as they came to acknowledge their sexual orientation. These experiences mirror the stage of *identity confusion,* because they began to acknowledge that their feelings were possibly attributable to homosexuality. Often in direct conflict with their previous self-image, participants suggested that admitting this to themselves was difficult and characterized by periods of inner turmoil and confusion. In order to cope with this turmoil, many participants talked about trying to deny or avoid their feelings as much as possible. Negative messages and a lack of information in the school climate about homosexuality contributed to the internal conflict many participants experienced as a result of their homosexual or bisexual feelings.

Troiden characterized the stage of *identity assumption* as generally occurring during late adolescence, with the individual self-identifying as gay or lesbian. Again, discussions about when respondents self-identified appear to follow similar stages or patterns identified within the existing literature. Male respondents generally labeled their feelings as gay or bisexual slightly earlier than women in the sample. While males said they labeled these feelings in elementary or middle school, females said they self-identified as lesbian or bisexual during high school. At that time, interviewees said they often wanted to share their secret with loved ones. In fact, some respondents began telling select peers or other LGBT students about their sexual orientation.

Based on the interviews, it appears that most participants, at the time of the interviews, were cycling between identity assumption and the final stage, *commitment*. While they reported increasing comfort and acceptance of their sexuality, many were still working toward complete acceptance. This suggests that resources for LGBT students are necessary beyond high school into our post-secondary institutions as well. Increased institutional support in schools will ensure that LGBT students continue to develop positive self-images into adulthood. Furthermore, both male and female respondents expressed their discomfort with current categorizations of homosexuality and bisexuality. Whether they ultimately chose to identify as gay, lesbian, or bisexual, many respondents expressed a sense that their own sexuality was not adequately conveyed using commonly accepted terms. On the whole, participants described a more fluid sexuality than that which is implied by contemporary definitions of sexual orientation.

LIMITATIONS

The primary limitation of this study is the fact that the young adults interviewed are fairly homogeneous across several important demographics, including the fact that all but one of the participants was enrolled in a public university in North Carolina. Therefore, this investigation failed to recruit young adults outside the university setting who may have had very different life experiences. In addition, the study did not include any transgender youth. For these reasons, data obtained in this study are in no way intended for generalization to the larger population of LGBT youth.

A second limitation of this study is that it is retrospective. Because they were asked questions about their experiences several years prior to the study, participants may have had difficulty recounting these experiences with absolute accuracy. Additional studies in this area should ideally survey LGBT youth who are currently enrolled in high school.

IMPLICATIONS

The need for multiple resources emerged as a major theme from participant responses to questions about what types of services and support they would have valued from their high school. Table 7.1 provides several recommendations for specific ways in which

Table 7.1   Recommendations for Supporting LGBT High School Students

Increase Awareness and Sensitivity

- Display LGBT info throughout the school campus (stickers, posters, books, etc.)
- Show "no tolerance" for anti-LGBT harassment
- Include sexual orientation in school non-discrimination policy
- Celebrate "diversity" via assemblies, speakers, etc.
- Support LGBT teachers so they can be visible role models and mentors

Professional Training for Educators and School Personnel

- Include training on LGBT issues in education and counseling college curriculum
- Require sensitivity training for all school personnel, including administrators, teachers and aides, guidance counselors, nurses and health educators, coaches, librarians, etc.

Services

- Sponsor a gay/straight club or alliance at school
- Offer confidential, sensitive counseling
- Make sure health services and information address concerns of LGBT youth

Curriculum Development

- Expand sex-ed curriculum to include LGBT issues (*beyond* discussion of *HIV/AIDS*)
- Include LGBT topics in class (i.e., history of LGBT civil rights movement in history class or LGBT authors in English class, etc.)

education professionals can address the social support needs of LGBT youth within the high school setting.

While it is certainly important to highlight the problems LGBT youth face in our society, this approach can tend to overlook the strengths, talents, and skills available to this population. While the literature strongly suggests LGBT youth are at increased risk for many health problems due to intense stigmatization and discrimination, the majority of these young adults manage to develop positive and productive coping strategies to assist them through adolescence and into adulthood. Finding ways to tap into already existing supports, while fostering new ones, is critical for the health and welfare of LGBT students in our schools.

CONCLUSION

Schools can no longer ignore the presence of adolescents and young adults who identify as gay, lesbian, bisexual, or transgender or who are questioning their sexuality. Teachers, administrators, guidance counselors, nurses, and other education professionals are in a unique position to assist young adults who are questioning their sexuality because they come into contact with adolescents in a number of settings and under varying circumstances. Simply by taking the time to recognize the presence of LGBT and questioning youth, educators and health professionals can refuse to participate in the promotion of "compulsory heterosexuality" and help ensure that these youth are afforded the same advantages and opportunities provided to their heterosexual peers. Maintaining sensitivity to the words we use and messages we convey, as well as testing our own assumptions as professionals, can ensure that future LGBT youth can be open about their sexuality. In doing so, we will go far in improving the health of LGBT and questioning youth in our schools.

REFERENCES

Berkman, L. (1984). Assessing the physical health effects of social networks and social support. *Annual Review of Public Health, 5,* 413–432.

Center for Population Options. (1992). *Lesbian, gay and bisexual youth: At risk and underserved.* Washington, DC: Author.

Coleman, E. (1989). The development of male prostitution activity among gay male and bisexual adolescents. *Journal of Homosexuality, 17,* 131–149.

Elia, J. (1993). Homophobia in the high school: A problem in need of a resolution. *The High School Journal, 77*(1–2), 177–185.

Fontaine, J. (1998). Evidencing a need: School counselors' experiences with gay and lesbian students. *Professional School Counseling, 1*(3), 8–14.

Gonsiorek, J. (1988). Mental health issues of gay and lesbian adolescents. *Journal of Adolescent Health Care, 9,* 114–122.

Governor's Task Force on Biased-Related Violence. (1988). *Final Report, 2*(1), 77–89. Division of Human Rights, 55 West 125th Street, New York, NY 10027.

Herek, G., & Berrill, K. (Eds.). (1992). *Hate crimes: Confronting violence against lesbians and gay men.* Newbury Park & London: Sage.

Hetrick, E., & Martin, D. (1987). Developmental issues and the irresolution for gay and lesbian adolescents. *Journal of Homosexuality, 14,* 13–24.

Hirsch, B., & DuBois, D. (1992). The relation of peer social support and psychological symptomatology during the transition to junior high school: A two-year longitudinal analysis. *American Journal of Community Psychology, 20,* 333–347.

House, J. S. (1981). *Work stress & social support.* Reading, MA: Addison-Wesley.

House, J., Umberson, D., and Landis, K.R. (1988). Structures and processes of social support. *Annual Review of Sociology, 14,* 293–318.

Israel, B., and Rounds, K. (1987). Social networks and social support: A synthesis for health educators. *Advances in Health Education and Promotion, 2,* 311–351.

Marinoble, R. (1998). Homosexuality: A blind spot in the school mirror. *Professional School Counseling, 1*(3), 4–7.

Martin, A., & Hetrick, E. (1988). The stigmatization of the gay and lesbian adolescent. *Journal of Homosexuality, 15,* 163–183.

Mercier, L., & Berger, R. (1989). Social service needs of lesbian and gay adolescents: Telling it their way. *Adolescent sexuality: New challenges for social work.* New York: The Haworth Press.

National Gay and Lesbian Task Force and Institute for the Protection of Gay and Lesbian Youth, Inc. (1985). *Testimony presented to the Governor's Task Force on Lesbian and Gay Issues on January 17–18.*

National Network of Runaway and Youth Services. (1991). *To whom do they belong? Runaway, homeless and other youth in high-risk situations in the 1990's.* Washington, DC: Author.

Omizo, M., Sharon, A., & Okamoto, C. (1998). Gay and lesbian adolescents: A phenomenological study. *Professional School Counseling, 1*(3), 35–37.

Patton, M. (1990). *Qualitative evaluation and research methods.* Newbury Park: Sage.

Radkowsky, M., & Siegel, L. (1997). The gay adolescent: Stressors, adaptations, and psychological interventions. *Clinical Psychology Review, 17,* 191–216.

Remafedi, G. (1987). Adolescent homosexuality: Psychosocial and medical implications. *Pediatrics, 79,* 331–337.

Rhodes, J., Contreras, J., & Mangelsdorf, S. (1994). Natural mentors relationships among Latina adolescent mothers: Psychological adjustment, moderating processes, and the role of early parental acceptance. *American Journal of Community Psychology, 22*, 211–227.

Robinson, K. (1994). Addressing the needs of gay and lesbian students: The school counselors' role. *The School Counselor, 41*, 326–332.

Rotheram-Borus, M., Rosario, M., Meyer-Bahlburg, H., Koopman, C., Dopkins, S., & Davies, M. (1994). Sexual and substance use acts of gay and bisexual male adolescents in New York City. *Journal of Sex Research, 31*, 47–57.

Saunders, J., & Valente, S. (1987). Suicide risk among gay men and lesbians: A review. *Death Studies, 11*, 1–23.

Savin-Williams, R. (1994). Verbal and physical abuse as stressors in the lives of lesbian, gay male, and bisexual youths: Associations with school problems, running away, substance abuse, prostitution, and suicide. *Journal of Consulting and Clinical Psychology, 62*, 261–269.

Troiden, R. (1988). Homosexual identity development. *Journal of Adolescent Health Care, 9*, 105–113.

Troiden, R. (1989). The formation of homosexual identities. *Journal of Homosexuality, 17*(1–2), 43–73.

Unks, G. (1994). Thinking about the homosexual adolescent. *The High School Journal, 77* (1–2), 1–6.

Uribe, V., & Harbeck, J. (1992). Addressing the needs of lesbian, gay, and bisexual youth: The origins of Project 10 and school-based intervention. In K. M. Harbeck (Ed.), *Coming out of the classroom closet: Gay and lesbian students, teachers and curricula* (pp. 9–20). Binghamton, NY: Harrington Park Press.

U.S. Department of Health and Human Services (1989). *Report of the Secretary's Task Force on Youth Suicide.* Washington, DC; U.S. Government Printing Office.

Victim Services/Traveler's Aid. (1991). Streetwork Project Study. New York: Victim Services.

FOR FURTHER EXPLORATION

Griffin, P., & Ouellett, M.L. (2002, March). Going beyond gay-straight alliances to make schools safe for lesbian, gay, bisexual, and transgender students. *Angles: The Policy Journal of the Institute for Gay and Lesbian Strategic Studies, 6*(1), 1–7.

Talburt, S. (2004). Constructions of LGBT youth: Opening up subject positions. *Theory Into Practice, 43*(2), 116–121

PART III

What Makes
a Good Teacher?

VIGNETTE 1

Cathy Johnson is charged with teaching her tenth-grade biology class about the digestive system of sheep, their eating habits, and their grazing preferences. Here is her plan: From Monday to Wednesday, she will present a forty-minute lecture, fielding questions as they arise; Thursday is scheduled for review; and on Friday she'll give a multiple-choice test based on the information that she covered during the week.

Let's take a glimpse at a typical exchange between Cathy and her students.

On Tuesday, after twenty-five minutes of lecture, Billy raises his hand and, after being acknowledged by Ms. Johnson, says, "I still don't understand. How come sheep can digest grass but people can't?"

"We covered this yesterday. Can someone help Billy out? Who knows why sheep can digest grass? Come on, people. Anyone? Anyone?"

Jessica dutifully raises her hand. When called on, she says, "Sheep are ruminants. They have three extra specialized stomach sections and humans have one stomach section."

"Thank you, Jessica. At least I know one person is listening."

On Friday, Cathy administers her multiple-choice test. A few students fail, but most earn passing grades. Even though she will not return to the subject of sheep for the remainder of the year, Cathy feels confident that the generally strong test scores indicate that she has adequately covered the content and that her students have learned the material.

VIGNETTE 2

Monday through Thursday, Frankie Stevens, an elder Navajo sheep herder, spends forty minutes each afternoon with tribal children, listening to their questions about sheep's eating habits and grazing preferences. When a child asks a question, the elder often replies, "What do *you* think?" and continues to encourage further observation and inquiry. On Friday, Mr. Stevens asks the students to herd the sheep without him, to rely on one another, and to return prepared to demonstrate what they have learned.

Is Cathy Johnson a good teacher? Is Frankie Stevens teaching? How might Mr. Stevens answer Billy's question to Ms. Johnson in the first vignette?

8

The Banking
Concept of Education

Paulo Freire

A careful analysis of the teacher-student relationship at any level, inside or outside the school, reveals its fundamentally *narrative* character. This relationship involves a narrating Subject (the teacher) and patient listening objects (the students). The contents, whether values or empirical dimensions of reality, tend in the process of being narrated to become lifeless and petrified. Education is suffering from narration sickness.

The teacher talks about reality as if it were motionless, static, compartmentalized, and predictable. Or else he expounds on a topic completely alien to the existential experience of the students. His task is to "fill" the students with the contents of his narration— contents which are detached from reality, disconnected from the totality that engendered them and could give them significance. Words are emptied of their concreteness and become a hollow, alienated, and alienating verbosity.

The outstanding characteristic of this narrative education, then, is the sonority of words, not their transforming power. "Four times four is sixteen; the capital of Para is Belem." The student records, memorizes, and repeats these phrases without perceiving what four times four really means, or realizing the true significance of "capital" in the affirmation "the capital of Para is Belem," that is, what Belem means for Para and what Para means for Brazil.

NOTE: Printed with permission from the Continuum International Publishing Group. Paulo Freire ©1973.

Narration (with the teacher as narrator) leads the students to memorize mechanically the narrated account. Worse yet, it turns them into "containers," into "receptacles" to be "filled" by the teachers. The more completely she fills the receptacles, the better a teacher she is. The more meekly the receptacles permit themselves to be filled, the better students they are.

Education thus becomes an act of depositing, in which the students are the depositories and the teacher is the depositor. Instead of communicating, the teacher issues communiques and makes deposits which the students patiently receive, memorize, and repeat. This is the "banking" concept of education, in which the scope of action allowed to the students extends only as far as receiving, filing, and storing the deposits. They do, it is true, have the opportunity to become collectors or cataloguers of the things they store. But in the last analysis, it is the people themselves who are filed away through the lack of creativity, transformation, and knowledge in this (at best) misguided system. For apart from inquiry, apart from the praxis, individuals cannot be truly human. Knowledge emerges only through invention and re-invention, through the restless, impatient continuing, hopeful inquiry human beings pursue in the world, with the world, and with each other.

In the banking concept of education, knowledge is a gift bestowed by those who consider themselves knowledgeable upon those whom they consider to know nothing. Projecting an absolute ignorance onto others, a characteristic of the ideology of oppression, negates education and knowledge as processes of inquiry. The teacher presents himself to his students as their necessary opposite; by considering their ignorance absolute, he justifies his own existence. The students, alienated like the slave in the Hegelian dialectic, accept their ignorance as justifying the teacher's existence—but unlike the slave, they never discover that they educate the teacher.

The *raison d'etre* of libertarian education, on the other hand, lies in its drive towards reconciliation. Education must begin with the solution of the teacher-student contradiction, by reconciling the poles of the contradiction so that both are simultaneously teachers *and* students.

This solution is not (nor can it be) found in the banking concept. On the contrary, banking education maintains and even stimulates the contradiction through the following attitudes and practices, which mirror oppressive society as a whole:

a. the teacher teaches and the students are taught;

b. the teacher knows everything and the students know nothing;

c. the teacher thinks and the students are thought about;

d. the teacher talks and the students listen—meekly;

e. the teacher disciplines and the students are disciplined;

f. the teacher chooses and enforces his choice, and the students comply;

g. the teacher acts and the students have the illusion of acting through the action of the teacher;

h. the teacher chooses the program content, and the students (who were not consulted) adapt to it;

i. the teacher confuses the authority of knowledge with his or her own professional authority, which she and he sets in opposition to the freedom of the students;

j. the teacher is the Subject of the learning process, while the pupils are mere objects.

It is not surprising that the banking concept of education regards men as adaptable, manageable beings. The more students work at storing the deposits entrusted to them, the less they develop the critical consciousness which would result from their intervention in the world as transformers of that world. The more completely they accept the passive role imposed on them, the more they tend simply to adapt to the world as it is and to the fragmented view of reality deposited in them.

The capability of banking education to minimize or annul the student's creative power and to stimulate their credulity serves the interests of the oppressors, who care neither to have the world revealed nor to see it transformed. The oppressors use their "humanitarianism" to preserve a profitable situation. Thus they react almost instinctively against any experiment in education which stimulates the critical faculties and is not content with a partial view of reality but always seeks out the ties which link one point to another and one problem to another.

Indeed, the interests of the oppressors lie in "changing the consciousness of the oppressed, not the situation which oppresses them,"[1] for the more the oppressed can be led to adapt to that situation, the more easily they can be dominated. To achieve this, the oppressors use the banking concept of education in conjunction with a paternalistic social action apparatus, within which the oppressed receive the euphemistic title of "welfare recipients." They are treated as individual cases, as marginal persons who deviate from the general configuration of a "good, organized and just" society. The oppressed are regarded as the pathology of the healthy society which must therefore adjust these "incompetent and lazy" folk to its own patterns by changing their mentality. These marginals need to be "integrated," "incorporated" into the healthy society that they have "forsaken."

The truth is, however, that the oppressed are not "marginals," are not living "outside" society. They have always been "inside" the structure which made them "beings for others." The solution is not to "integrate" them into the structure of oppression, but to transform that structure so that they can become "beings for themselves." Such transformation, of course, would undermine the oppressors' purposes; hence their utilization of the banking concept of education to avoid the threat of student *conscientização*.

The banking approach to adult education, for example, will never propose to students that they critically consider reality. It will deal instead with such vital questions as whether Roger gave green grass to the goat, and insist upon the importance of learning that, on the contrary, Roger gave green grass to the rabbit. The "humanism" of the banking approach masks the effort to turn women and men into automatons—the very negation of their ontological vocation to be more fully human.

Those who use the banking approach, knowingly or unknowingly (for there are innumerable well-intentioned bank-clerk teachers who do not realize that they are serving only to dehumanize), fail to perceive that the deposits themselves contain contradictions about reality. But sooner or later, these contradictions may lead formerly passive students to turn against their domestication and the attempt to domesticate reality. They may discover through existential experience that their present way of life is irreconcilable with their vocation to become fully human. They may perceive through their relations with reality that reality is really a *process*, undergoing constant transformation. If men and women are searchers and their ontological vocation is humanization, sooner or later they may perceive the contradiction in which banking education seeks to maintain them, and then engage themselves in the struggle for their liberation.

But the humanist revolutionary educator cannot wait for this possibility to materialize. From the outset, her efforts must coincide with those of the students to engage in critical thinking and the quest for mutual humanization. His efforts must be imbued with a profound trust in people and their creative power. To achieve this, they must be partners of the students in their relations with them.

The banking concept does not admit to such partnership—and necessarily so. To resolve the teacher-student contradiction, to exchange the role of depositor, prescriber, domesticator, for the role of student among students would be to undermine the power of oppression and serve the cause of liberation.

Implicit in the banking concept is the assumption of a dichotomy between human beings and the world: a person is merely *in* the world, not *with* the world or with others; the individual is spectator, not re-creator. In this view, the person is not a conscious being (*corpo consciente*); he or she is rather the possessor of *a* consciousness: an empty "mind" passively open to the reception of deposits of reality from the world outside. For example, my desk, my books, my coffee cup, all the objects before me—as bits of the world which surround me—would be "inside" me, exactly as I am inside my study right now. This view makes no distinction between being accessible to consciousness and entering consciousness. The distinction, however, is essential: the objects which surround me are simply accessible to my consciousness, not located within it. I am aware of them, but they are not inside me.

It follows logically from the banking notion of consciousness that the educator's role is to regulate the way the world "enters into" the students. The teacher's task is to organize a process which already occurs spontaneously, to "fill" the students by making deposits of information which he or she considers to constitute true knowledge.[2] And since people "receive" the world as passive entities, education should make them more passive still, and adapt them to the world. The educated individual is the adapted person, because she or he is better "fit" for the world. Translated into practice, this concept is well suited for the purposes of the oppressors, whose tranquility rests on how well people fit the world the oppressors have created and how little they question it.

The more completely the majority adapt to the purposes which the dominant majority prescribe for them (thereby depriving them of the right to their own purposes), the more easily the minority can continue to prescribe. The theory and practice of banking education serve this end quite efficiently. Verbalistic lessons, reading requirements,[3] the methods for evaluating "knowledge," the distance between the teacher and the taught, the criteria for promotion: everything in this ready-to-wear approach serves to obviate thinking.

The bank-clerk educator does not realize that there is no true security in his hypertrophied role, that one must seek to live *with* others in solidarity. One cannot impose oneself, nor even merely co-exist with one's students. Solidarity requires true communication, and the concept by which such an educator is guided fears and proscribes communication.

Yet only through communication can human life hold meaning. The teacher's thinking is authenticated only by the authenticity of the students' thinking. The teacher cannot think for her students, nor can she impose her thought on them. Authentic thinking, thinking that is concerned about *reality*, does not take place in ivory tower isolation, but only in communication. If it is true that thought has meaning only when generated by action upon the world, the subordination of students to teachers becomes impossible.

Because banking education begins with a false understanding of men and women as objects, it cannot promote the development of what Fromm calls "biophily," but instead produces its opposite: "necrophily."

> While life is characterized by growth in a structured functional manner, the necrophilous person loves all that does not grow, all that is mechanical. The necrophilous person is driven by the desire to transform the organic into the inorganic, to approach life mechanically, as if all living persons were things . . . Memory, rather than experience; having, rather than being, is what counts. The necrophilous person can relate to an object—a flower or a person—only if he possesses it; hence a threat to his possession is a threat to himself, if he loses possession he loses contact with the world . . . He loves control, and in the act of controlling he kills life.[4]

Oppression—overwhelming control—is necrophilic; it is nourished by love of death, not life. The banking concept of education, which serves the interests of oppression, is also necrophilic. Based on a mechanistic, static, naturalistic, spatialized view of consciousness, it transforms students into receiving objects. It attempts to control thinking and action, leads women and men to adjust to the world, and inhibits their creative power.

When their efforts to act responsibly are frustrated, when they find themselves unable to use their faculties, people suffer. "This suffering due to impotence is rooted in the very fact that the human has been disturbed."[5] But the inability to act which causes men's anguish also causes them to reject their impotence, by attempting

> . . . to restore [their] capacity to act. But can [they], and how? One way is to submit to and identify with a person or group having power. By this symbolic participation in another person's life, [men have] the illusion of acting, when in reality [they] only submit to and become a part of those who act.[6]

Populist manifestations perhaps best exemplify this type of behavior by the oppressed, who, by identifying with charismatic leaders, come to feel that they themselves are active and effective. The rebellion they express as they emerge in the historical process is motivated by that desire to act effectively. The dominant elites consider the remedy to be more domination and repression, carried out in the name of freedom, order, and social peace (that is, the peace of the elites). Thus they can condemn—logically, from their point of view—"the violence of a strike by workers and [can] call upon the state in the same breath to use violence in putting down the strike."[7]

Education as the exercise of domination stimulates the credulity of students, with the ideological intent (often not perceived by educators) of indoctrinating them to adapt to the world of oppression. This accusation is not made in the naive hope that the dominant elites will thereby simply abandon the practice. Its objective is to call the attention of true humanists to the fact that they cannot use banking educational methods in the pursuit of liberation, for they would only negate that very pursuit. Nor may a revolutionary society inherit these methods from an oppressor society. The revolutionary society which practices banking education is either misguided or mistrusting of people. In either event, it is threatened by the specter of reaction.

Unfortunately, those who espouse the cause of liberation are themselves surrounded and influenced by the climate which generates the banking concept, and often do not perceive its true significance or its dehumanizing power. Paradoxically, then, they utilize this same instrument of alienation in what they consider an effort to liberate. Indeed, some "revolutionaries" brand as "innocents," "dreamers," or even "reactionaries" those who would challenge this educational practice. But one does not liberate people by alienating them. Authentic liberation—the process of humanization—is not another deposit to be made in men. Liberation is a praxis: the action and reflection of men and women upon their world in order to transform it.

Those truly committed to liberation must reject the banking concept in its entirety, adopting instead a concept of women and men as conscious beings, and consciousness as consciousness intent upon the world. They must abandon the educational goal of deposit-making and replace it with the posing of the problems of human beings in their relations with the world. "Problem-posing" education, responding to the essence of consciousness—*intentionality*—rejects communiques and embodies communication. It epitomizes the special characteristic of consciousness: being *conscious* of, not only as intent on objects but as turned in upon itself in a "Jasperian split"—consciousness as consciousness *of* consciousness.

Liberating education consists in acts of cognition, not transferals of information. It is a learning situation in which the cognizable object (far from being the end of the cognitive act) intermediates the cognitive actors—teacher on the one hand and students on the other. Accordingly, the practice of problem-posing education entails at the outset that the teacher-student contradiction be resolved. Dialogical relations—indispensable to the capacity of cognitive actors to cooperate in perceiving the same cognizable object—are otherwise impossible.

Indeed, problem-posing education, which breaks with the vertical characteristic of banking education, can fulfill its function of freedom only if it can overcome the above contradiction. Through dialogue, the teacher-of-the-students and the students-of-the-teacher cease to exist and a new term emerges: teacher-student with students-teachers. The teacher is no longer merely the-one-who-teaches, but one who is himself taught in dialogue with the students, who in turn while being taught also teach. They become jointly responsible for a process in which all grow. In this process, arguments based on "authority" are no longer valid; in order to function authority must be *on the side* of freedom, not *against* it. Here, no one teaches another, nor is anyone self-taught. People teach each other, mediated by the world, by the cognizable objects which in banking education are "owned" by the teacher.

The banking concept (with its tendency to dichotomize everything) distinguishes two stages in the action of the educator. During the first he cognizes a cognizable object while he prepares his lessons in his study or his laboratory; during the second, he expounds to his students about that object. The students are not called upon to know, but to memorize the contents narrated by the teacher. Nor do the students practice any act of cognition, since the object towards which that act should be directed is the property of the teacher rather than a medium evoking the critical reflection of both teacher and students. Hence in the name of the "preservation of culture and knowledge" we have a system which achieves neither true knowledge nor true culture.

The problem-posing method does not dichotomize the activity of teacher-student: she is not "cognitive" at one point and "narrative" at another. He is always "cognitive," whether preparing a projector or engaging in dialogue with the students. He does not regard objects as his private property, but as the object of reflection by himself and his students. In this way, the problem-posing educator constantly re-forms his reflections in the reflection of the students.

The students—no longer docile listeners—are now critical co-investigators in dialogue with the teacher. The teacher presents the material to the students for their consideration, and re-considers her earlier considerations as the students express their own. The role of the problem-posing educator is to create, together with the students, the conditions under which knowledge at the level of the *doxa* is superseded by true knowledge at the level of the *logos*.

Whereas banking education anesthetizes and inhibits creative power, problem-posing education involves a constant unveiling of reality. The former attempts to maintain the *submersion* of consciousness; the latter strives for the *emergence* of consciousness and *critical intervention* in reality.

Students, as they are increasingly posed with problems relating to themselves in the world and with the world, will feel increasingly challenged and obliged to respond to that challenge. Because they apprehend the challenge as interrelated to other problems within a total context not as a theoretical question, the resulting comprehension tends to be increasingly critical and thus constantly less alienated. Their response to the challenge evokes new challenges, followed by new understandings; and gradually the students come to regard themselves as committed.

Education as the practice of freedom—as opposed to education as the practice of domination—denies that man is abstract, isolated, independent and unattached to the world; it also denies that the world exists as a reality apart from people. Authentic reflection considers neither abstract man nor the world without people, but people in their relations with the world. In these relations consciousness and world are simultaneous: consciousness neither precedes the world nor follows it.

> La conscience et le monde sont dormes d'un meme coup: exterieur par essence a la conscience, le monde est, par essence relatif a elle.[8]

In one of our culture circles in Chile, the group was discussing (based on a codification) the anthropological concept of culture. In the midst of the discussion, a peasant who by banking standards was completely ignorant said: "Now I see that without man there is no world." When the educator responded: "Let's say, for the sake of argument, that all the men on earth were to die, but that the earth remained, together with trees, birds, animals, rivers, seas, the stars . . . wouldn't all this be a world?" "Oh no," the peasant replied. "There would be no one to say: 'This is a world.'"

The peasant wished to express the idea that there would be lacking the consciousness of the world which necessarily implies the world of consciousness. I cannot exist without a *non-I*. In turn, the *non-I* depends on that existence. The world which brings consciousness into existence becomes the world of that consciousness. Hence, the previously cited affirmation of Sartre: "*La conscience et le monde sont dormes d'un meme coup.*"

As men, simultaneously reflecting on themselves and on the world, increase the scope of their perception, they begin to direct their observations towards previously inconspicuous phenomena:

> In perception properly so-called, as an explicit awareness [*Gewahren*], I am turned towards the object, to the paper, for instance. I apprehend it as being this here and now. The apprehension is a singling out, every object having a background inexperience. Around and about the paper lie books, pencils, inkwell and so forth, and these in a certain sense are also "perceived" perceptually there, in the "field of intuition"; but whilst I was turned towards the paper there was no turning in their direction, nor any apprehending of them, not even in a secondary sense. They appeared and yet were not singled out, were posited on their own account. Every perception of a thing has such a zone of background intuitions or background awareness, if "intuiting" already includes the state of being turned towards, and this also is a "conscious experience," or more briefly a "consciousness of" all indeed that in point of fact lies in the co-perceived objective background.[9]

That which had existed objectively but had not been perceived in its deeper implications (if indeed it was perceived at all) begins to "stand out," assuming the character of a problem and therefore of challenge. Thus, men and women begin to single out elements from their "background awareness" and to reflect upon them. These elements are now objects of their consideration, and, as such, objects of their action and cognition.

In problem-posing education, people develop their power to perceive critically *the way they exist* in the world *with which* and *in which* they find themselves; they come to see the world not as a static reality, but as a reality in process, in transformation. Although the dialectical relations of women and men with the world exist independently of how these relations are perceived (or whether or not they are perceived at all), it is also true that the form of action they adopt is to a large extent a function of how they perceive themselves in the world. Hence, the teacher-student and the students-teachers reflect simultaneously on themselves and the world without dichotomizing this reflection from action, and thus establish an authentic form of thought and action.

Once again, the two educational concepts and practices under analysis come into conflict. Banking education (for obvious reasons) attempts, by mythicizing reality, to conceal certain facts which explain the way human beings exist in the world; problem-posing education sets itself the task of demythologizing. Banking education resists dialogue; problem-posing education regards dialogue as indispensable to the act of cognition which unveils reality. Banking education treats students as objects of assistance; problem-posing education makes them critical thinkers. Banking education inhibits creativity and domesticates (although it cannot completely destroy) the *intentionality* of consciousness by isolating consciousness from the world, thereby denying people their ontological and historical vocation of becoming more fully human. Problem-posing education bases itself on creativity and stimulates true reflection and action upon reality, thereby responding to the vocation of persons as beings only when engaged in inquiry and creative transformation. In sum: banking theory and practice, as immobilizing and fixating forces, fail to acknowledge men and women as historical beings; problem-posing theory and practice take the people's historicity as their starting point.

Problem-posing education affirms men as beings in the process of *becoming*—as unfinished, uncompleted beings in and with a likewise unfinished reality. Indeed, in contrast to other animals who are unfinished, but not historical, people know themselves to be unfinished; they are aware of their incompletion. In this incompletion and this awareness lie the very roots of education as an exclusively human manifestation. The unfinished character of human beings and the transformational character of reality necessitate that education be an ongoing activity.

Education is thus constantly remade in the praxis. In order to be, it must *become*. Its "duration" (in the Bergsonian meaning of the word) is found in the interplay of the opposites *permanence* and *change*. The banking method emphasizes permanence and becomes reactionary; problem-posing education—which accepts neither a "well-behaved" present nor a predetermined future— roots itself in the dynamic present and becomes revolutionary.

Problem-posing education is revolutionary futurity. Hence it is prophetic (and as such, hopeful). Hence, it corresponds to the historical nature of humankind. Hence, it affirms men as beings who transcend themselves, who move forward and look ahead, for whom immobility represents a fatal threat for whom looking at the past must only be a means of understanding more clearly what and who they are so that they can more wisely build the future. Hence, it identifies with the movement which engages people as beings aware of their incompletion—an historical movement which has its point of departure, its Subjects and its objective.

The point of departure of the movement lies in the men themselves. But since men do not exist apart from the world, apart from reality, the movement must begin with the men-world relationship. Accordingly, the point of departure must always be with men and women in the "here and now," which constitutes the situation within which they are submerged, from which they emerge, and in which they intervene. Only by starting from this situation—which determines their perception of it—can they begin to move. To do this authentically they must perceive their state not as fated and unalterable, but merely as limiting—and therefore challenging.

Whereas the banking method directly or indirectly reinforces men's fatalistic perception of their situation, the problem-posing method presents this very situation to them as a problem. As the situation becomes the object of their cognition, the naive or magical perception which produced their fatalism gives way to perception which is able to perceive itself even as it perceives reality, and can thus be critically objective about that reality.

A deepened consciousness of their situation leads people to apprehend that situation as an historical reality susceptible of transformation. Resignation gives way to the drive for transformation and inquiry, over which men feel themselves to be in control. If people, as historical beings necessarily engaged with other people in a movement of inquiry, did not control that movement, it would be (and is) a violation of their humanity. Any situation in which some individuals prevent others from engaging in the process of inquiry is one of violence. The means used are not important; to alienate human beings from their own decision-making is to change them into objects.

This movement of inquiry must be directed towards humanization— the people's historical vocation. The pursuit of full humanity, however, cannot be carried out in isolation or individualism, but only in fellowship and solidarity; therefore it cannot unfold in the antagonistic relations between oppressors and oppressed. No one can be authentically human while he prevents others from being so. Attempting *to be more* human, individualistically, leads to *having more,* egotistically, a form of dehumanization. Not that it is not fundamental to *have* in order *to be* human. Precisely because it *is* necessary, some men's *having* must not be allowed to constitute an obstacle to others' *having,* must not consolidate the power of the former to crush the latter.

Problem-posing education, as a humanist and liberating praxis, posits as fundamental that the people subjected to domination must fight for their emancipation. To that end, it enables teachers and students to become Subjects of the educational process by overcoming authoritarianism and an alienating intellectualism; it also enables people to overcome their false perception of reality. The world—no longer something to be described with deceptive words—becomes the object of that transforming action by men and women which results in their humanization.

Problem-posing education does not and cannot serve the interests of the oppressor. No oppressive order could permit the oppressed to begin to question: Why? While only a revolutionary society can carry out this education in systematic terms, the revolutionary leaders need not take full power before they can employ the method. In the revolutionary process, the leaders cannot utilize the banking method as an interim measure, justified on grounds of expediency, with intention of *later* behaving in a genuinely revolutionary fashion. They must be revolutionary—that is to say, dialogical—from the outset.

NOTES

1. Simon de Beauvoir. *La Pensee de Droite, Aujord'hui* (Paris); ST, *El Pensamiento politico de la Derecha* (Buenos Aires, 1963), p. 34.

2. This concept corresponds to what Sartre calls the "digestive" or "nutritive" in which knowledge is "fed" by the teacher to the students to "fill them out." See Jean-Paul Sartre, "Une idee fundamentals de la phenomenologie de Husserl: L'intentionalite," *Situations I* (Paris, 1947).

3. For example, some professors specify in their reading lists that a book should be read from pages 10 to 15—and do this to "help" their students!

4. Fromm, op. cit. p. 41.

5. Ibid. p. 31.

6. Ibid. p. 7.

7. Reinhold Niebuhr, *Moral Man and Immoral Society* (New York, 1960), p. 130.

8. Sartre, op. cit., p. 32.

9. Edmund Husserl, *Ideas: General Introduction to Pure Phenomenology* (London, 1969), pp. 105–106.

FOR FURTHER EXPLORATION

Freire, P. (1970). *Pedagogy of the oppressed*. New York, NY: Penguin.
Freire, P. (2004). *Pedagogy of indignation*. Boulder, CO: Paradigm Publishing.
Freire, P. (2008). *Critical pedagogy primer* (2nd ed.). New York: Peter Lang.
Mclaren, P. (2000). *Che Guevara, Paolo Friere and the pedagogy of revolution*. Lanham, MD: The Rowman and Littlefield Publishing Group.

Paulo Freire (deceased) was an author and social activist.

9

On Stir-and-Serve Recipes for Teaching

Susan Ohanian

The notion that just about any Joe Blow can walk in off the street and take over a classroom is gaining ground. It makes me nervous. No, more than that: it infuriates me. We should squash once and for all the idea that schools can be adequately staffed by 32 bookkeepers and a plumber. The right teacher-proof curriculum is not sufficient; children need real teachers, and real teachers must be trained.

Nor am I charmed by the idea of signing up out-of-work computer programmers and retired professors to teach math and science. The mass media like to scoff that current certification requirements would keep Albert Einstein from teaching in the public schools. That news is not all bad. Is there any evidence that Einstein worked particularly well with young children? A Nobel Prize does not guarantee excellence in the classroom.

Having sat through more stupid education courses than I wish to recall, I am not altogether comfortable defending schools of education. But I suspect that the blame for worthless courses lies as much with the teachers who take them as with the professors who teach them. As a group, we teachers are intransigently anti-intellectual. We demand from our professors carry-out formulae, materials with the immediate applicability of scratch-and-sniff stickers. We are indignant when they try instead to offer ideas to grow on, seeds that we have to nurture in our own gardens.

We teachers frequently complain that education courses do not prepare us for the rigorous, confusing work ahead—that they do not show us how to run our classrooms. We refuse to admit that no course or manual can give us all the help we crave. We should not expect professors to set up our classroom systems, as though each of us were heading out to operate a fast-food franchise. There is no instant, stir-and-serve recipe for running a classroom.

Too often, teachers judge the success of education courses by the weight of the materials they cart away—cute cutouts or "story starters," all ready for immediate use. One popular journal for teachers promises 100 new ideas in every issue. "You can use them on Monday" is the promise. No one gets rich admitting that genuinely good ideas are hard to come by.

I understand only too well this yearning for the tangible, the usable. We are, after all, members of a profession ruled by pragmatism. People who sit in judgment on us don't ask about our students, "Are they happy? Are they creative? Are they helpful, sensitive, loving? Will they want to read a book next year?" Instead, these people demand, "What are their test scores?" as if those numbers, though they passeth understanding, will somehow prove that we're doing a good job.

During my first 12 years of teaching I was desperate for new ideas, constantly foraging for schemes with which to engage the children. My frenetic activity was due, in part, to the fact that I was given a different teaching assignment every two years. I figured, "Different children require different methods, different materials." So I would race off to the library or to the arts-and-crafts store. I'd buy another filing cabinet and join another book club for teachers.

But even when I settled in with the same assignment for a six-year stretch, my frenzy did not abate. My classroom became a veritable curriculum warehouse, stuffed with every innovative whiz-bang gizmo I could buy, borrow, or invent. I spent hundreds of hours reading, constructing, laminating. My husband gave up reminding me that I had promised to put the cut-and-paste factory in our living room out of business, once I figured out what to teach. When I wasn't inventing projects, I was taking courses: cardboard carpentry, architectural awareness, science process, Cuisenaire rods, Chinese art, test construction and evaluation, curriculum development, and so on. I even took two courses in the computer language, BASIC. (I thought maybe I'd missed the point in the first course, so I took another—just to be sure.)

I didn't take those courses on whim, any more than I invented curriculum because I had nothing better to do. I chose my courses deliberately, tying to inform my work as a reading teacher. Although

I now look back on much of my frenzied search for methods and media as rather naïve, I don't see it as time wasted. I learned a lot. Mostly I learned to simplify. And then to simplify some more.

But the path to simplicity is littered with complexities. And I suspect that it is hard to figure out how to simplify our lives if we haven't cluttered them in the first place. Sure, we teachers clutter up our classrooms with too much claptrap. The fribble is often alluring at first, and it is hard to recognize that the more gadgets we rely on, the poorer we are—at home as well as at school.

People probably always yearn for gadgets, especially if they haven't had much chance to fool around with them. A university research project makes this point rather nicely. The researcher decided to investigate the effects of computer-assisted instruction in English-as-a-second-language (ESL) classes. He set up a computer-taught group and a control group. Both were instructed in ESL for one year. And guess which group had the more positive attitude about computer-assisted instruction at the end of that year? The youngsters who didn't get to use the computers.

Not surprisingly, we teachers are compulsive pack rats. Fearing the vagaries of future school budgets, we hoard construction paper until it is old and brittle and unusable. We worry that we may need that paper more next year than we need it today. Have you ever known a teacher who could throw away a set of ditto masters? Or half a game of Scrabble? For years I had a gross of tiny, childproof, left-handed scissors. Childproof scissors are a horror in the first place. Those designed for left-handers are beyond description. Why did I keep them? Hey, they were mine, weren't they?

Most of us never use 80% of the materials jammed into our classrooms, but we cling to them "just in case." Because our job is hectic, pressured, stressful, we seldom have a reflective moment to clear our minds, let alone our cupboards. Maybe every teacher should change schools every three years and be allowed to take along only what he or she can carry. However, I must add to this suggestion my own statement of full disclosure: the last time I changed classrooms, after 13 years in the district, it took six strong men and a truck to transfer my belongings. And that was after I had filled two dumpsters.

The good professors must stop yielding to our acquisitive pressures; they must refuse to hand out their 100—or even 10—snazzy new ideas for the well-stocked classroom. They must offer fewer methods, fewer recipes. We teachers need less practicality, not more. We need to have our lives informed by Tolstoy, Jane Addams, Suzanne Langer, Rudolf Arnheim, and their ilk—not by folks who promise the keys to classroom control and creative bulletin boards, along with 100 steps to reading success.

We need a sense of purpose from our professors, not a timetable. Better that they show us a way to find our own ways than that they hand out their own detailed maps of the territory. A map isn't of much use to people who don't know where they're headed. The only way to become familiar with the terrain is to explore a little. I nominate the professors to scout ahead, chart the waters, post the quicksand. I know that I still have to climb my own mountain, but I would welcome scholarly advice about the climbing conditions.

Critics of schools of education insist that prospective teachers would profit more from observing good teachers at work than from taking impractical courses on pedagogy. Maybe so, but what are those novices going to see? Is one observation as good as another? After all, a person can look at "Guernica" and not see it, listen to the "Eroica" and not hear it. E. H. Gombrich says that every observation we make is the result of the questions we ask. And where do novices get the questions? How can they ask intelligent questions without knowing something about the subject? Can anyone really see a classroom without some theoretical, historical, developmental savvy?

No one enters a classroom as a *tabula rasa*, of course. We all know something about schools because we have, for better or for worse, been there. We know how schools are supposed to be. At least we think we do. So we judge schools, as we judge anything, with a notion—or schema—of reality in our heads. Most of us don't just look *at* something; we look *for* something, because we have a hypothesis, a hidden agenda. We observe and evaluate with our minds, our memories, our experiences, our linguistic habits. Obviously, the more we know, the more we see.

But teachers cannot walk into classrooms and simply teach what they know. First, they don't know enough. Second, even this seemingly restrictive world—constrained by bells, desks, and textbooks—contains a rich stock of themes from which teachers must choose their own motifs. They must be flexible and inventive enough to modify the schema they carried into their classrooms.

I was one of those people almost literally picked up off a street corner and allowed to teach in New York City under an emergency credential. I walked into the middle of someone else's lesson plan, and, though it didn't take me 10 minutes to realize that a round-robin reading of "Paul Revere's Ride" was not going to work, it took me quite a while to come up with something much better.

All I could manage at first was to teach as I had been taught. But as I learned more about the students and about ways to get around the assigned curriculum, a more ideal classroom began to emerge in my head. It remains a shadowy image—one I glimpse and even touch occasionally, but one I have long since stopped trying to file neatly in my planbook. That's okay. The bird seen through the window is more provocative than the one in the cage.

Teaching, like art, is born of a schema. That's why we need the professors with their satchels of theory, as well as our own observations and practice. Those who hope to be effective teachers must recognize that teaching is a craft of careful artifice; the profession requires more than a spontaneous overflow of good intentions or the simple cataloguing and distribution of information. It is possible, I suppose, to have an inborn talent for teaching, but I am sure that those teachers who endure and triumph are *made*—rigorously trained—and not born.

Much of the training must be self-initiated. People who have some nagging notion of the ideal classroom tickling their psyches probably look more for patterns that appeal than for practices that are guaranteed to produce higher standardized test scores. Such teachers probably have a capacity for ambiguity; they look for snippets of familiarity but do not insist on sameness. Such teachers have a greater need for aesthetic and psychological satisfaction than for a neat and tidy cupboard. But they also have a willingness to practice the craft, to try out new brushstrokes, to discard dried-out palettes.

Most of us, children and adults alike, have a strong need to make sense of the disparate elements in our lives, to bring them together, to find patterns, to make meaning. This desire for meaning is so strong that some teachers, tired and defeated by the system, rely on ritual to get them through the day, the week, the year. External order and ritual are the only things they have left to give. And these things usually satisfy the casual observer, who believes that teachers who provide clean and orderly classrooms are providing enough.

This is one reason I want the professors in on the act—out of their ivory towers and into our dusty school corridors. Maybe well-informed people, good observers who are not bogged down by school minutiae, could convince us that a tidy desk is far from enough. The professors need to promote the search for a different order, a subtler pattern—one that lies not in behavioral checklists but rather, to use Chia Yi's words, in constant "combining, scattering, waning, waxing."

It was my own search for pattern that led me to try using science as a way to inform, enhance, and give order to my work as a reading teacher. The children and I were far too familiar with the rituals of remedial reading for those routines to fall much short of torture. I've never understood why students who have trouble with a certain system of decoding should be made to rehearse that system over and over again. A few times over the course of a few years, maybe. But surely there comes a time to try a different approach. Reading had already been ruined for my students by the time they came to me. I needed to see how they approached pedagogic puzzlement, and such puzzlement would never occur if I persisted in making them circle blends on worksheets. That's why I learned how to mess around in science.

Tell a poor reader that it's time to read, and watch the impenetrable curtain of defeat and despair descend. So my students and I spent our time on science. All year. We made cottage cheese, explored surface tension, built bridges, figured out optical illusions. And not once did my students associate experiment cards, books on the theory of sound, or my insistence that observations be recorded in writing with the onerous task that they knew reading to be. Children told me that my room was a good place. Too bad, they added, that I wasn't a real teacher.

That reading room, where children were busily measuring, making—and reading—received full parental support and had its moment in the limelight. There were a lot of visitors. The teachers among them invariably asked, "How did you get this job?" Clearly, they intended to apply for one like it.

Get the job? Only in the first year of my teaching career was I ever handed a job. Ever after, I've made my own. No job of any value can be given out, like a box of chalk. We get the jobs we deserve. Maybe that's why so many teachers are disappointed. They believe all those promises that someone else can do the thinking for them.

I held seven different jobs in my school district, and I earned the right to love every one of them. That's not to say that I didn't have plenty of moments of anger, frustration, rage. But I also experienced deep satisfaction.

Because my seven jobs required some pretty dramatic shifts in grade level, people were always asking me, "Where is it better—high school or the primary grades?" It's a question I have never been able to answer, mainly because the more grade levels I taught, the more similarities I saw. Sure, high school dropouts enrolled in an alternative program are harder to tune in to the beauty of a poem than are seventh-graders. Third-graders cry more, talk more; seventh-graders scale more heights and sink into deeper pits. But a common thread runs throughout, and it was that thread I clung to.

Maybe I see this sameness because my teaching is dominated less by skill than by idea—the secret, elusive form. I have a hard time reading other people's prescriptions, let alone writing my own. I always figure that, if you can get the idea right, the specific skill will come. Teaching is too personal, even too metaphysical, to be charted like the daily temperature. Teaching is like a Chinese lyric painting, not a bus schedule.

We need to look very closely at just who is calling for "the upgrading of teacher skills," lest this turn out to be the clarion call of those folks with something to sell. The world does not come to us in neat little packages. Even if we could identify just what a *skill* is, does *more* definitely denote *better?* What profiteth a child whose teacher has gathered up an immense pile of pishposh? We must take care, lest the examiners who claim they can dissect and label the educational process leave us holding a bag of gizzards.

We teachers must recognize that we do not need the behaviorist-competency thugs to chart our course. For us, reality is a feeling state, details of daily routine fade, and what remains is atmosphere, tone, emotion. The ages and the talents of the children become irrelevant. What counts is attitude and endeavor. That's why, even when we try, we often can't pass on a terrific lesson plan to a friend; we probably can't even save it for ourselves to use again next year. It's virtually impossible to teach the same lesson twice.

I'm afraid that all of this sounds rather dim, maybe even dubious. But this is where the professors might step in. There are so many outrageous examples of bad pedagogy that it's easy to overlook the good—easy, but not excusable. The professors need to shape up their own schools of education first—getting rid of Papercutting 306, even if it's the most profitable course in the summer school catalogue. Then they need to get out in the field to work with student teachers, principals, and children.

Is it outrageous to think that the professors might even pop into the classrooms of veteran teachers now and then? Wouldn't it be something if their research occasionally involved real children and real teachers (and if they had to face bells, mandated tests, bake sales, and field trips to mess up their carefully laid plans), instead of four children in a lab staffed by 63 graduate students? That's probably a scary thought for some professors.

I know of one school of education that relegates the observation and direction of student teachers to the local school district. The district, in turn, passes this responsibility on to an administrator who has never taught. In such a situation, pedagogy gets turned upside down and inside out. The outcome is empty platitudes, not effective classroom practice. The student teacher, who is paying for expert training, is being defrauded. The children are being cheated. The system is stupid and immoral. We need teacher trainers who know educational theory and who are savvy about children. Those professors who won't help us should be replaced by ones who will.

But aspiring teachers have a responsibility, too. They must heed the advice of Confucius:

> If a man won't try, I will teach him; if a man makes no effort, I will not help him. I show one corner, and if a man cannot find the other three, I am not going to repeat myself.

We teachers must stop asking the education professors for the whole house. I know plenty of teachers who are disappointed, indignant, and eventually destroyed by the fact that nobody has handed them all four corners. But the best we can expect from any program of courses or training is the jagged edge of one corner. Then it is up to us to read the research and to collaborate with the children to find the other three corners. And, because teaching must be a renewable contract, if we don't keep seeking new understanding, we'll find that the corners we thought we knew very well will keep slipping away. There are constant, subtle shifts in the schoolroom. One can never be sure of knowing the floorplan forever and ever.

In trying to renew my faith in myself as a teacher, I find little help in the "how to" books, those nasty little tomes that define learning in 87 steps. I like to think of learning as a wave that washes over the learner, rather than as a series of incremental hurdles to be pre- and posttested. I reject *How to Teach Reading in 100 Lessons,* relying instead on *The Mustard Seed Garden Manual of Painting,* which advises that "neither complexity in itself nor simplicity is enough"—nor dexterity alone nor conscientiousness. "To be without method is worse."

What can we do? What is the solution? In painting, there is an answer: "Study 10,000 volumes and walk 10,000 miles." One more thing is required of teachers. We must also work with 10,000 children.

FOR FURTHER EXPLORATION

Ohanian, S. (1999). *One size fits few: The folly of educational standards.* Portsmouth, NH: Heinemann.

Ohanian, S. (2001). *Caught in the middle: Nonstandard kids and a killing curriculum.* Portsmouth, NH: Heinemann.

Ohanian, S. (2002). *What happened to recess and why are our children struggling in kindergarten?* New York, NY: McGraw-Hill.

Ohanian, S. (2004). *Why is corporate America bashing our public schools?* Portsmouth, NH: Heinemann.

Susan Ohanian is a freelance writer and former teacher.

10

Psst . . . It Ain't About the Tests

It's Still About Great Teaching

Robert DiGiulio

I f you are planning to become a teacher, welcome, and prepare to be overwhelmed. If you are already teaching, you know this already. After a seminar I gave for teachers recently, we were standing by the coffee: "My head is spinning! There's too much to think about: Portfolios, standards-based lessons, differentiated instruction, IEPs, ESTs, continuous assessment, making sure the kids pass those standardized tests, fundraisers, getting the computers to work, inclusion, trying to keep discipline in a classroom where some can't even sit still for a minute!" As I drove home from that seminar, I thought about how right they were. There seemed to be two huge but connected problems here: First, teachers today have been swamped by tasks—often, trivial and unconnected to students—that demand compliance, to the point where it is difficult for teachers to balance or to discern what was really important. Second, teachers have a vague (or all-too-clear) uneasiness, based on a hazy sense of how well they were doing. There was a lack of useful information that ought to help teachers connect what they were doing to how well students were learning. A common form of data—students' standardized test scores, now all the rage—provide little guidance for teachers, and are among the most useless (and harmful) pieces of data, in terms of helping teachers and future teachers, to say nothing of useless in helping students actually be successful.

Since I began teaching in the inner-city public schools of New York City in 1970, I have been absorbed by the question of good teaching. Along with the New York State and City teacher licensing boards, Al Shanker and the teachers' union defined good teaching in terms of qualifications, years teaching, seniority, number of advanced degrees, and so on. But my firsthand observation of some great teachers contradicted that—I saw no connection between these paper qualifications and how excellent teachers actually were in the classroom. The skills and qualities of great teachers seemed to be increasingly marginalized; crowded out by administrative, compliance paperwork (I call it "ditto worksheets for teachers"), somebody's Great New Idea, and other time killers imposed on teachers. Later, as a school principal, my awareness grew of even darker reasons for the downplaying of good teaching, and I suppose money has a lot to do with it. Simply stated, when one acknowledges someone as being good (or great), there is a corresponding expectation to pay those people well. So while I have heard a lot over thirty years about teacher competency and merit pay, I have yet to hear a sincere effort to acknowledge what is the essence of great teaching. For once that is done, it forces the question of how we should expect it, recognize it, and maybe, pay great teachers well for what they do. I am still waiting for that discussion.

In a sense, I am writing this piece as a historical document. Great teaching has existed since one of the first humans—generously and competently—showed another how to make a fire and how to cook food. Great teaching has been great because it placed the learner's needs and interests first. Today, however, I see a tendency to marginalize great teaching by redefining it as teaching that emphasizes interests other than the needs of students. These other interests include those of special interest groups that often hide their interests behind the cloak of reform and of school improvement. They address alleged defects of teachers and/or public schools, and provide solutions to problems that only they have identified, and narrowly so at that. In these cases, neither the public's best interests nor students' best interests are at the heart of their "solutions." Some groups insist, for example, that standardized testing is essential to accountability. I am not opposed to accountability, and I can agree that under some circumstances standardized tests can provide useful information. But they don't inform teaching; standardized tests are beside the point of great teaching because they are too narrow in scope. While data from well-designed tests can help inform teachers as to their students' mastery of content, those tests cannot provide help for teachers seeking to improve their teaching skills and qualities. No standardized test for students can ever inform us of a teacher's enthusiasm, caring, or belief that students can be successful—three factors that have an enormous effect on student achievement and self-esteem. We simply have to use other means to focus on these important traits.

And focus we must. We see great teachers, and we see the undeniably powerful effect great teachers have on students. Yet, I worry that special-interest agendas are distorting (or submerging) the traditional, commonsense notion of what great teaching is. As proof, think about what we know works in schools. After thousands of studies (some better than others), we know a lot about high-quality teaching. We know that there are good and better things that teachers do with and for students, and we know there are not-so-good things that teachers do. Yet despite the research data, and despite our commonsense perceptions, how often do we hear about teachers who do the right things? How often do we see what and how they do those good things? I am not simply calling for mere praise for the great, even heroic teacher, although that is long overdue. I am calling for simply naming, noting, identifying what these teachers do, teachers whose students are succeeding—academically and socially—despite unfortunate conditions in their schools and communities. How often do we hear about students who do not bring weapons to school, students who are not violent? Students who don't hurt others; students who have learned how civilized human beings behave, learning much of this, in large part, from a good teacher? I am only asking for "the facts," not for a massive public relations campaign promoting teachers and schools.

When well-organized and well-funded anti-public education voices and special interest group voices have reached a fever pitch so that the acts of great teachers and great teaching are marginalized or disregarded, it is time to speak out. When the elements comprising great teaching are minimized, it is time to speak out. Again, I am concerned not so much that great teachers and their successes are being ignored (which they are), but that the qualities and skills that great teachers bring to great teaching are in danger of vanishing, disappearing from both the public eye and from the curriculum of teacher preparation. I speak out not as a cheerleader of great teachers, but as a curator who seeks to keep alive the awareness of the qualities and skills that comprise great teaching. These qualities and skills apply to all levels of education, from preschool through graduate school, private school as well as public school. They apply to teaching throughout the world, because they go directly to the heart of how teachers teach so that students learn most effectively.

As we get to the heart of what really matters in fostering student achievement, we realize more and more how important the individual teacher is. We know this; we have known this since the time of the wise Buddha, but we still seem to dance around focusing on the essence of the great teacher. Teacher education college programs are just as guilty as corporate interests: When was the last time you heard an education professor talk about great teaching? Is there anything in any syllabus that refers to great teaching? Yet we know—or *should know*—that this issue should not be summarily ignored. Probably the strongest voice is that of University of Tennessee professor William Sanders (2003), whose research shows how the effective teacher is more important—as a predictor of student success—than any of the other traditional social indicators usually blamed for student failure:

> . . . we've been able to get a very fair measure of the school district, the school, and the individual classroom. And we've been able to demonstrate that ethnicity, poverty, and affluence can no longer be used as justifications for the failure [of students] to make academic progress. The single biggest factor affecting academic growth of any population of youngsters is the effectiveness of the individual classroom teacher. [Furthermore,] [t]he teacher's effect on academic growth dwarfs and nearly renders trivial all these other factors that people have historically worried about.

Fine. But the devil is in the details, and how we define the "effectiveness" of that teacher is the heart of the problem. Shall we use standardized test scores? I think not. What shall we do instead? Richard B. Traina, former President of Clark University, is a research historian who asked, "What makes a good teacher?" (1999, 34). He looked through the biographies and autobiographies of prominent 19th and 20th century Americans, focusing on what they had to say about the traits their best teachers possessed. Traina saw a thread that ran through their stories: The best teachers—the memorable ones—were remembered as being skillful and enthusiastic, having such a solid command of the subject matter that students could "pick up on their excitement" for the subject. Second, these teachers were *caring*—they cared "deeply about each student and about that student's accomplishment and growth." Third, Traina said that these teachers had "distinctive character . . . there was a palpable energy that suffused the competent and caring teacher, some mark-making quality." In short, the memorable teachers were skillful, enthusiastic, caring, and perhaps even idiosyncratic. Dr. Traina's third trait—"distinctive character"—is indeed the most elusive category. Although we can't *teach* teachers to "acquire distinctive character," we certainly can work to not destroy it, by demanding conformity and narrow definitions of what successful teachers are. Distinctive character is a fragile naturally occurring resource. Like a gemstone, the distinctive character of each teacher is revealed as she or he teaches. Our job is to guard it, and not allow it to be shattered.

Aside from this *je ne sais quoi* of distinctive character, what else do great teachers do that helps kids learn? Knowledge and "distinctive character" are part of it, but it is also about efficacy, a teacher's belief that she or he will be successful, because his or her students will be successful. And, to achieve student success, great teachers help move their students via three paths: producing, empowering, and connecting.

Great teachers know that to actually be successful, a student must first do something of value. Simply telling kids they are good won't wash. Student success is fostered by the work students do, by what they produce. This can include participating, performing, creating, practicing, designing, producing, carrying out an experiment, finishing an assignment, or any of hundreds of other activities. Worksheets, on the other hand, are all too often mindless, and require little thinking (input). The quality and value of the output, then, is quite low. Some worksheets may be okay for practicing, or passing time with puzzles, but not for producing. In the final analysis, what the student does will have a greater impact on how successful the student is (and feels he or she is) than what the teacher knows, says, or believes.

Student success is also fostered by empowering students (and students are automatically empowered when they are producing!). Empowering means actively teaching students how to help themselves, how to take responsibility for their work; how to get help: How to ask for help, whom to ask for help, and when to seek help. This is a real-world skill that starts and grows in class and in school. Students must also be weaned from depending on the teachers to provide direction at every step.

The third path to student success lies in helping students make connections. Success is fostered by activities/assignments that draw on—connect with—what students already know, and/or what they do well. Perhaps it is too obvious to state that what I learn best and fastest is that which is closest to what I already know; I learn best what builds on what I already know. What I do not learn well is when I try to make sense of material that is alien to what I presently know. Making connections is a core tenet of constructivism, and classrooms with a constructivist orientation are not only the most productive, but are happier places than classrooms with reward-and-punishment teachers, and far, far better than classrooms with laissez-faire (uninvolved) teachers.

Among its other provisions, the "No Child Left Behind" Act includes a provision that all public schools have a highly qualified teacher in each classroom. Unfortunately, there is nothing promising in that goal, especially when we have created so many alternative routes to licensure that even a measurable pulse may not any longer be a consistent requirement to teach (the poorest school districts in America tend to qualify almost anyone to teach).

Every classroom should have not merely a qualified teacher, but a great teacher. But for this to happen, we must move the definition of "qualified" back from *quantity indicators* (test scores, teachers' college degrees, number of years teaching, and other items easily tallied) and onto *quality*, by teaching teachers about efficacy and caring, about the ways one can empower and engage students, while allowing teachers to retain their "distinctive character." What matters at every turn is the teacher, and all kids deserve great teachers. This need has never before been so pressing.

FOR FURTHER EXPLORATION

DiGiulio, R. (2000). *Educate, medicate, or litigate: What teachers, parents and administrators must do about student behavior.* Thousand Oaks, CA: Corwin.

DiGiulio, R. (2004). *Great teaching: What matters most in helping students succeed.* Thousand Oaks, CA: Corwin.

DiGiulio, R., & benShea, N. (2004). *A compass for the classroom: How teachers (and students) can find their way & keep from getting lost.* Thousand Oaks, CA: Corwin.

DiGiulio, R. (2006). *Positive classroom management: A step-by-step guide to successfully running the show without destroying student dignity.* Thousand Oaks, CA: Corwin.

Robert DiGiulio (deceased) was an author and a professor of Education at Johnson State College in Johnson, Vermont.

PART IV

What Do Good Schools Look Like?

Though a K–8 facility, Thayer is a small school with fewer than four hundred students attending this tasteful stone and brick building situated in a lovely, bucolic setting. As a bedroom community to one of the nation's largest cities, students at Thayer generally hail from homes of considerable affluence. Thayer boasts strong music and art programs, numerous after-school activities, including drama and the usual sports teams, computers with video streaming capabilities in every classroom, and an abundance of actively involved parent volunteers. The teachers at Thayer tend to be happy too. The average class size is under twenty students, and there is so little turnover in the staff that Thayer hasn't advertised a teaching position in years.

This year, like most years before it, students at Thayer Elementary School earned the distinction of having the highest test scores in the state. Tom Rogers, the principal at Thayer for the last six years, takes special pleasure in announcing this fact every year at the June Parent's Night meeting. He states, "Student performance on reading, writing, and math has been consistent enough for the State Department of Education to label the school 'high performing' and 'a model school' where exemplary teaching and learning are the norm."

The Johnsons were thrilled to move to the Thayer district over the summer. And, when they arrived for their first Parent-Teacher Night in early September, they were brimming with anticipation when their daughter's teacher began her introduction.

"We've purchased a new basal reader for all sixth grade students," the teacher began. "We like this series because each reading is short and the text is accompanied by a teacher's edition that contains plenty of discussion questions, quizzes, and worksheets."

As their daughter's new teacher continued, the Johnsons thumbed through the basal readers. The Johnsons were crestfallen. Between the hard covers of the basal reader were no fewer than 25 great novels, each abridged into 5–10 page versions of the originals. More depressing, their daughter had already read most of the novels in their original form. The teacher continued and encouraged parents to walk around the room and examine student work from the previous year. The Johnsons wondered about the geography worksheets that required, for example, students to identify country names based upon longitude and latitude coordinates, the "A–Z List" which asked students to match Egypt-related vocabulary words with their definitions, and reams of math dittos. By the end of the evening, the Johnsons had serious questions about whether Thayer was the right place for their daughter.

Is Thayer a good school? What are the defining characteristics of a good school?

11

The Idea of Summerhill

A. S. Neill

This is a story of a modern school—Summerhill.

Summerhill was founded in the year 1921. The school is situated within the village of Leiston, in Suffolk, England, and is about one hundred miles from London.

Just a word about Summerhill pupils. Some children come to Summerhill at the age of five years, and others as late as fifteen. The children generally remain at the school until they are sixteen years old. We generally have about twenty-five boys and twenty girls.

The children are divided into three age groups: The youngest range from five to seven, the intermediates from eight to ten, and the oldest from eleven to fifteen.

Generally, we have a fairly large sprinkling of children from foreign countries. At the present time (1960) we have five Scandinavians, one Hollander, one German and one American.

The children are housed by age groups with a house mother for each group. The intermediates sleep in a stone building, the seniors sleep in huts. Only one or two older pupils have rooms for themselves. The boys live two or three or four to a room, and so do the girls. The pupils do not have to stand room inspection and no one picks up after them. They are left free. No one tells them what to wear: they put on any kind of costume they want to at any time.

Newspapers call it a *Go-as-you-please* School and imply that it is a gathering of wild primitives who know no law and have no manners.

It seems necessary, therefore, for me to write the story of Summerhill as honestly as I can. That I write with a bias is natural; yet I shall try to show the demerits of Summerhill as well as its merits. Its merits will be the merits of healthy, free children whose lives are unspoiled by fear and hate.

Obviously, a school that makes active children sit at desks studying mostly useless subjects is a bad school. It is a good school only for those who believe in such a school, for those uncreative citizens who want docile, uncreative children who will fit into a civilization whose standard of success is money.

Summerhill began as an experimental school. It is no longer such; it is now a demonstration school, for it demonstrates that freedom works.

When my first wife and I began the school, we had one main idea: *to make the school fit the child*—instead of making the child fit the school.

I had taught in ordinary schools for many years. I knew the other way well. I knew it was all wrong. It was wrong because it was based on an adult conception of what a child should be and of how a child should learn. The other way dated from the days when psychology was still an unknown science.

Well, we set out to make a school in which we should allow children freedom to be themselves. In order to do this, we had to renounce all discipline, all direction, all suggestion, all moral training, all religious instruction. We have been called brave, but it did not require courage. All it required was what we had—a complete belief in the child as a good, not an evil, being. For almost forty years, this belief in the goodness of the child has never wavered; it rather has become a final faith.

My view is that a child is innately wise and realistic. If left to himself without adult suggestion of any kind, he will develop as far as he is capable of developing. Logically, Summerhill is a place in which people who have the innate ability and wish to be scholars will be scholars; while those who are only fit to sweep the streets will sweep the streets. But we have not produced a street cleaner so far. Nor do I write this snobbishly, for I would rather see a school produce a happy street cleaner than a neurotic scholar.

What is Summerhill like? Well, for one thing, lessons are optional. Children can go to them or stay away from them—for years if they want to. There is a timetable—but only for the teachers.

The children have classes usually according to their age, but sometimes according to their interests. We have no new methods of teaching, because we do not consider that teaching in itself matters very much. Whether a school has or has not a special method for teaching long division is of no significance, for long division is of no importance except to those who want to learn it. And the child who wants to learn long division will learn it no matter how it is taught.

Children who come to Summerhill as kindergartners attend lessons from the beginning of their stay; but pupils from other schools vow that they will never attend any beastly lessons again at any time. They play and cycle and get in people's way, but they fight shy of lessons. This sometimes goes on for months. The recovery time is proportionate to the hatred their last school gave them. Our record case was a girl from a convent. She loafed for three years. The average period of recovery from lesson aversion is three months.

Strangers to this idea of freedom will be wondering what sort of madhouse it is where children play all day if they want to. Many an adult says, "If I had been sent to a school like that, I'd never have done a thing." Others say, "Such children will feel themselves heavily handicapped when they have to compete against children who have been made to learn."

I think of Jack who left us at the age of seventeen to go into an engineering factory. One day, the managing director sent for him.

"You are the lad from Summerhill," he said. "I'm curious to know how such an education appears to you now that you are mixing with lads from the old schools. Suppose you had to choose again, would you go to Eton or Summerhill?"

"Oh, Summerhill, of course," replied Jack.

"But what does it offer that the other schools don't offer?"

Jack scratched his head. "I dunno," he said slowly; "I think it gives you a feeling of complete self-confidence."

"Yes," said the manager dryly, "I noticed it when you came into the room."

"Lord," laughed Jack. "I'm sorry if I gave you that impression."

"I liked it," said the director. "Most men when I call them into the office fidget about and look uncomfortable. You came in as my equal. By the way, what department did you say you would like to transfer to?"

This story shows that learning in itself is not as important as personality and character. Jack failed in his university exams because he hated book learning. But his lack of knowledge about *Lamb's Essays* or the French language did not handicap him in life. He is now a successful engineer.

All the same, there is a lot of learning in Summerhill. Perhaps a group of our twelve-year-olds could not compete with a class of equal age in handwriting or spelling or fractions. But in an examination requiring originality, our lot would beat the others hollow.

We have no class examinations in the school, but sometimes I set an exam for fun. The following questions appeared in one such paper:

Where are the following:—Madrid, Thursday Island, yesterday, love, democracy, hate, my pocket screwdriver (alas, there was no helpful answer to that one).

Give meanings for the following: (the number shows how many are expected for each)—Hand (3) . . . only two got the third right—the standard of measure for a horse. Brass (4) . . . metal, cheek, top army officers, department of an orchestra. Translate Hamlet's To-be-or-not-to-be speech into Summerhillese.

These questions are obviously not intended to be serious, and the children enjoy them thoroughly. Newcomers, on the whole, do not rise to the answering standard of pupils who have become acclimatized to the school. Not that they have less brain power, but rather because they have become so accustomed to work in a serious groove that any light touch puzzles them.

This is the play side of our teaching. In all classes much work is done. If, for some reason, a teacher cannot take his class on the appointed day, there is usually much disappointment for the pupils.

David, aged nine, had to be isolated for whooping cough. He cried bitterly. "I'll miss Roger's lesson in geography," he protested. David had been in the school practically from birth, and he had definite and final ideas about the necessity of having his lessons given to him. David is now a lecturer in mathematics at London University.

A few years ago someone at a General School Meeting (at which all school rules are voted by the entire school, each pupil and each staff member having one vote) proposed that a certain culprit should be punished by being banished from lessons for a week. The other children protested on the ground that the punishment was too severe.

My staff and I have a hearty hatred of all examinations. To us, the university exams are anathema. But we cannot refuse to teach children the required subjects. Obviously, as long as the exams are in existence, they are our master. Hence, the Summerhill staff is always qualified to teach to the set standard.

Not that many children want to take these exams; only those going to the university do so. And such children do not seem to find it especially hard to tackle these exams. They generally begin to work for them seriously at the age of fourteen, and they do the work in about three years. Of course they don't always pass at the first try. The more important fact is that they try again.

Summerhill is possibly the happiest school in the world. We have no truants and seldom a case of homesickness. We very rarely have fights—quarrels, of course, but seldom have I seen a stand-up fight like the ones we used to have as boys. I seldom hear a child cry, because children when free have much less hate to express than children who are downtrodden. Hate breeds hate, and love breeds love. Love means approving of children, and that is essential in any school. You can't be on the side of children if you punish them and storm at them. Summerhill is a school in which the child knows that he is approved of.

Mind you, we are not above and beyond human foibles. I spent weeks planting potatoes one spring, and when I found eight plants pulled up in June, I made a big fuss. Yet there was a difference between my fuss and that of an authoritarian. My fuss was about potatoes, but the fuss an authoritarian would have made would have dragged in the question of morality—right and wrong. I did not say that it was wrong to steal my spuds; I did not make it a matter of good and evil—I made it a matter of my spuds. They were *my spuds* and they should have been left alone. I hope I am making the distinction clear.

Let me put it another way. To the children, I am no authority to be feared. I am their equal, and the row I kick up about my spuds has no more significance to them than the row a boy may kick up about his punctured bicycle tire. It is quite safe to have a row with a child when you are equals.

Now some will say: "That's all bunk. There can't be equality. Neill is the boss; he is bigger and wiser." That is indeed true. I am the boss, and if the house caught fire the children would run to me. They know that I am bigger and more knowledgeable, but that does not matter when I meet them on their own ground, the potato patch, so to speak.

When Billy, aged five, told me to get out of his birthday party because I hadn't been invited, I went at once without hesitation—just as Billy gets out of my room when I don't want his company. It is not easy to describe this relationship between teacher and child, but every visitor to Summerhill knows what I mean when I say that the relationship is ideal. One sees it in the attitude to the staff in general. Rudd, the chemistry man, is Derek. Other members of the staff are known as Harry, and Ulla, and Pam. I am Neill, and the cook is Esther.

In Summerhill, everyone has equal rights. No one is allowed to walk on my grand piano, and I am not allowed to borrow a boy's cycle without his permission. At a General School Meeting, the vote of a child of six counts for as much as my vote does.

But, says the knowing one, in practice of course the voices of the grownups count. Doesn't the child of six wait to see how you vote before he raises his hand? I wish he sometimes would, for too many of my proposals are beaten. Free children are not easily influenced; the absence of fear accounts for this phenomenon. Indeed, the absence of fear is the finest thing that can happen to a child.

Our children do not fear our staff. One of the school rules is that after ten o'clock at night there shall be quietness on the upper corridor. One night, about eleven, a pillow fight was going on, and I left my desk, where I was writing, to protest against the row. As I got upstairs, there was a scurrying of feet and the corridor was empty and quiet. Suddenly I heard a disappointed voice say, "Humph, it's only Neill," and the fun began again at once. When I explained that I was trying to write a book downstairs, they showed concern and at once agreed to chuck the noise. Their scurrying came from the suspicion that their bedtime officer (one of their own age) was on their track.

I emphasize the importance of this absence of fear of adults. A child of nine will come and tell me he has broken a window with a ball. He tells me, because he isn't afraid of arousing wrath or moral indignation. He may have to pay for the window, but he doesn't have to fear being lectured or being punished.

There was a time some years back when the School Government resigned, and no one would stand for election. I seized the opportunity of putting up a notice. "In the absence of a government, I herewith declare myself Dictator. Heil Neill!" Soon there were mutterings. In the afternoon Vivien, aged six, came to me and said, "Neill, I've broken a window in the gym."

I waved him away. "Don't bother me with little things like that," I said, and he went.

A little later he came back and said he had broken two windows. By this time I was curious, and asked him what the great idea was.

"I don't like dictators," he said, "and I don't like going without my grub." (I discovered later that the opposition to dictatorship had tried to take itself out on the cook, who promptly shut up the kitchen and went home.)

"Well," I asked, "what are you going to do about it?"

"Break more windows," he said doggedly.

"Carry on," I said, and he carried on.

When he returned, he announced that he had broken seventeen windows. "But mind," he said earnestly, "I'm going to pay for them."

"How?"

"Out of my pocket money. How long will it take me?"

I did a rapid calculation. "About ten years," I said.

He looked glum for a minute; then I saw his face light up. "Gee," he cried, "I don't have to pay for them at all."

"But what about the private property rule?" I asked. "The windows are my private property."

"I know that but there isn't any private property rule now. There isn't any government, and the government makes the rules."

It may have been my expression that made him add, "But all the same I'll pay for them."

But he didn't have to pay for them. Lecturing in London shortly afterward, I told the story; and at the end of my talk, a young man came up and handed me a pound note "to pay for the young devil's windows." Two years later, Vivien was still telling people of his windows and of the man who paid for them. "He must have been a terrible fool, because he never even saw me."

Children make contact with strangers more easily when fear is unknown to them. English reserve is, at bottom, really fear; and that is why the most reserved are those who have the most wealth. The fact that Summerhill children are so exceptionally friendly to visitors and strangers is a source of pride to me and my staff.

We must confess, however, that many of our visitors are people of interest to the children. The kind of visitor most unwelcome to them is the teacher, especially the earnest teacher, who wants to see their drawing and written work. The most welcome visitor is the one who has good tales to tell—of adventure and travel or, best of all, of aviation. A boxer or a good tennis player is surrounded at once, but visitors who spout theory are left severely alone.

The most frequent remark that visitors make is that they cannot tell who is staff and who is pupil. It is true: the feeling of unity is that strong when children are approved of. There is no deference to a teacher as a teacher. Staff and pupils have the same food and have to obey the same community laws. The children would resent any special privileges given to the staff.

When I used to give the staff a talk on psychology every week, there was a muttering that it wasn't fair. I changed the plan and made the talks open to everyone over twelve. Every Tuesday night, my room is filled with eager youngsters who not only listen but give their opinions freely. Among the subjects the children have asked me to talk about have been these: The Inferiority Complex, The Psychology of Stealing, The Psychology of the Gangster, The Psychology of Humor,

Why Did Man Become a Moralist?, Masturbation, Crowd Psychology. It is obvious that such children will go out into life with a broad clear knowledge of themselves and others.

The most frequent question asked by Summerhill visitors is, "Won't the child turn round and blame the school for not making him learn arithmetic or music?" The answer is that young Freddy Beethoven and young Tommy Einstein will refuse to be kept away from their respective spheres.

The function of the child is to live his own life—not the life that his anxious parents think he should live, nor a life according to the purpose of the educator who thinks he knows what is best. All this interference and guidance on the part of adults only produces a generation of robots.

You cannot make children learn music or anything else without to some degree converting them into will-less adults. You fashion them into accepters of the status quo—a good thing for a society that needs obedient sitters at dreary desks, standers in shops, mechanical catchers of the 8:30 suburban train—a society, in short, that is carried on the shabby shoulders of the scared little man—the scared-to-death conformist.

FOR FURTHER EXPLORATION

Neill, A. S. (1939). *The problem teacher*. Madison, CT: International Universities Press.

Neill, A. S. (1945). *Hearts not heads in the school*. H Jenkins Limited.

Neill, A. S. (1953). *The free child*. Grove City, PA: Jenkins, Inc.

Neill, A. S. (1960). *Summerhill: A radical approach to child rearing*. Oxford, UK: Hart Publishing Company.

A. S. Neill (deceased) was the founder of the Summerhill School.

12

Success in East Harlem

How One Group of Teachers Built a School That Works

Deborah Meier

n the spring of 1991, Central Park East will graduate its first high school students. Some of them will have been with us since they were 4 years old. From age 4 to age 18, they will have attended a school—located in East Harlem in the midst of New York City's District 4—that many observers believe is as good as any school in the public or the private sector: A progressive school in the tradition of so many of New York's independent private schools, Central Park East is now firmly fixed within New York's school bureaucracy.

But it wasn't always so. We have had our share of luck, and we owe a great deal to many different people over the years. We know, too, that our success depended on the success of a district wide effort to create a whole network of alternative schools. We are, in fact, just one of nearly 30 "options" that are available to families in District 4, aside from the regular neighborhood-zoned elementary schools.

In the fall of 1974 Anthony Alvarado, the new superintendent of District 4, initiated just two such alternatives: our elementary school and a middle school, the East Harlem School for the Performing Arts. Each year thereafter the district supported the launching of several more alternative schools—generally at the junior high level. These schools were rarely the result of a central plan from the district office,

NOTE: Reprinted with permission from the Fall 1987 issue of *American Educator*, the quarterly journal of the American Federation of Teachers, AFL-CIO.

but rather tended to be the brainchildren of particular individuals or groups of teachers. They were initialed by the people who planned to teach in them.

It was the district's task to make such dreams come true. The details differed in each case. Most of these schools were designed around curricular themes—science, environmental studies, performing arts, marine biology. But they also reflected a style of pedagogy that suited their founders. They were always small, and, for the most part, staff members volunteered for duty in them. Finally, when the alternative schools outnumbered the "regulars," Alvarado announced that henceforth all junior high schools would be schools of "choice." By 1980 all sixth graders in the district chose where they would go for seventh grade. No junior high had a captive population.

On the elementary school level, neighborhood schools remain the norm, though the district handles zoning rather permissively. The only schools of choice on the elementary level are the Central Park East Schools, the East Harlem Block School (founded in the 1960s as a nonpublic, parent-run "free" school), and a network of bilingual elementary schools.

Today, Central Park East is, in fact, not one school but a network of four schools: Central Park East I, Central Park East II, and River East are elementary schools that feed into Central Park East Secondary School, which enrolls students from grades 7 through 12 and is affiliated with Theodore Sizer's* Coalition of Essential Schools.

The Central Park East schools were founded in 1974, during a time of great educational grief in New York City—just before the schools were forced to lay off more than 15,000 teachers and close elementary school libraries and at a time when the spirit of hope was crushed out of the parent movement and out of the struggles for decentralization, for teacher power and for structural change. Progressive educators suffered particularly, both because people began to claim that "openness" was "through" (and discredited) and because many of the young teachers and programs that had carried the progressive message were hardest hit by the layoffs.

In the spring of 1974, when Alvarado invited me to build a school in one wing of PS. 171, it seemed a most unlikely offer. School District 4 served a dismal, bitterly torn, largely Hispanic community. Still, I accepted. Who could refuse such an offer? After struggling for years to make my beliefs "fit" into a system that was organized on quite

---

*Theodore Sizer is the author of *Horace's Compromise* and the founder of the Coalition of Essential Schools.

different principles, after spending considerable energy looking for cracks, operating on the margins, "compromising" at every turn, the prospect that the district bureaucracy would organize itself to support alternative ideas and practices was irresistible. I was being offered a chance to focus not on bureaucratic red tape, but on the intractable issues of education—the ones that really excited me and many of the teachers I knew.

But this was not a time for having large visions, and I didn't want to be disappointed. I met with Alvarado, began to collect some experienced teaches to help launch effort, and gradually began to believe that he meant what he said. He offered to let us build a school just the way we wanted. The total allocation of funds (per-pupil costs) would have to be comparable to what was spent on any other school, and our teachers would have to meet the usual requirements of the city, the state, and the union contract. Nor could we be exempt from any city or state regulations. Beyond that, however, the district would support us in doing things our own way.

We began very small and very carefully. First there was the question of "we." Creating a democratic community was both an operational and an inspirational goal. While we were in part the products of what was called "open" education, our roots went back to early progressive traditions, with their focus on the building of a democratic community, on education for full citizenship and for egalitarian ideals. We looked upon Dewey, perhaps more than Piaget, as our mentor.

Virtually all of us had been educated in part at City College's Workshop Center under Lillian Weber. We came out of a tradition that was increasingly uneasy about the strictly individualistic focus of much of what was being called "open."

We were also unhappy about the focus on skills rather than on content in many of the "modern," innovative schools—even those that did not embrace the "back-to-basics" philosophy. Many "open" classrooms had themselves fallen prey to the contemporary mode of breaking everything down into discrete bits and pieces—skills that children could acquire at their own pace and in their own style. In contrast, we were looking for a way to build a school that could offer youngsters a deep and rich curriculum that would inspire them with the desire to know; that would cause them to fall in love with books and with stories of the past; that would evoke in them a sense of wonder at how much there is to learn. Building such a school required strong and interesting adult models—at home and at school—who could exercise their own curiosity and judgment.

We also saw schools as models of the possibilities of democratic life. Although classroom life could certainly be made more democratic than traditional schools allowed, we saw it as equally important that the school life of *adults* be made more democratic. It seemed unlikely that we could foster democratic values in our classrooms unless the adults in the school also had significant rights over their workplace.

We knew that we were tackling many difficult issues at once. Because of political considerations, planning time was insufficient, but the district tried to make up for this by being extra supportive. Looking back, we were so euphoric that we had the energy of twice our numbers.

We purposely started our school with fewer than a hundred students in kindergarten, first grade, and second grade only. At the superintendent's request, we recruited outside of the usual district channels, in part so that we wouldn't threaten other schools in the district and in part because one of Alvarado's goals was to increase the pupil population of the district and thus guard against school closings.

One of our primary reasons for starting the school—although we didn't often say—was our personal desire for greater autonomy as teachers. We spoke a lot about democracy, but we were also just plain sick and tired of having to negotiate with others, worry about rules and regulations, and so on. We all came together with our own visions—some collective and some individual—of what teaching could be like if only we had control. Ours was to be a teacher-run school. We believed that parents should have a voice in their children's schooling, and we thought that "choice" itself was a form of power. We also believed that we could be professionally responsive to parents and that, since the school would be open to parents at all times and the staff would be receptive, there would be plenty of opportunity to demonstrate our responsiveness.

Good early childhood education, we believed, required collaboration between the school and the family. This was a matter not only of political principle but also of educational principle, and it motivated us from the start to work hard to build a family-oriented school. We wanted a school in which children could feel safe. Intellectual risk-taking requires safety, and children who are suspicious of a school's agenda cannot work up to their potential. To create a safe school, we needed to have the confidence of parents, and children needed to know that their parents trusted us. It was that simple. Hard to create, perhaps, but essential.

We stumbled a lot in those early years. We fought among ourselves. We discovered that remaining committed to staff decision making was not easy. It was hard, too, to engage in arguments among ourselves without frightening parents and raising doubts about our professionalism. We were often exhausted—sometimes by things that mattered least to us.

By the end of the second year, I had made some crucial decisions regarding the organization and structure of Central Park East. These involved my leaving the classroom to become a somewhat more traditional principal. We have never entirely resolved the tensions over who makes which decisions and how. But the staff continues to play a central role in all decisions, big and small. Nothing is "undiscussable," though we have learned not to discuss everything—at least not all the time. This has actually meant more time for discussing those issues that concern us most: how children learn, how our classes really work, what changes we ought to be making, and on what bases. We have also become better observers of our own practice, as well as more open and aware of alternative practices.

Today, we understand better the many, often trivial ways in which schools undermine family support systems, undercut children's faith in their parents as educators, and erode parents' willingness to assume their responsibilities as their children's most important educators. We have become more supportive of parents whose "home instruction" differs from ours. We give less advice on such topics as how not to teach arithmetic or how to be a good parent.

As we became more secure with ourselves and our program, the district was expanding its network of alternative schools. In the fall of 1974 we were one of two. Within a half-dozen years there were about 15 "alternative concept" schools, mostly glaringly broken down.

The district also dispensed with the assumption that one building equals one school. Instead, every building in the district was soon housing several distinct schools—each with its own leadership, parent body, curricular focus, organization, and philosophy. Most of the new junior highs were located in elementary school buildings. Former junior high buildings were gradually turned to multiple uses, as well. Sometimes three or more schools shared a single building. As a result, the schools were all small, and their staffs and parents were associated with them largely by choice.

By the late seventies, Central Park East was so inundated with applicants that the district decided to start a small annex at PS. 109, now known as Central Park East II. The district's decision was probably also motivated by the availability of federal funds for the purpose of school integration. While Central Park East has always had a predominantly black (45%) and Hispanic (30%) student population, it is one of the few district schools that has also maintained a steady white population, as large as about 25%. (The population of District 4 is about 60% Hispanic, 35% black, and 5% white.)

In the beginning, this ratio came about largely by chance, but the 25% white population in the school has been maintained by choice. In general, the school has sought to maintain as much heterogeneity as possible, without having too many fixed rules and complex machinery. The school accepts all siblings, as part of its family orientation. After siblings, priority goes to neighborhood families. In other cases, the school tries to be nonselective, taking in most of its population at age five strictly on the basis of parental choice, with an eye to maintaining a balanced student body. Well over half of the students have always qualified for free or reduced-price lunches and some 15% to 20% meet the state requirements for receiving special education funds.

The demand for spaces still far outstripped available seats, and, a few years later, the district decided to start a third elementary school. This one was named River East.

Thus, by 1984 Central Park East had become three schools, each designed for about 250 students, each with its own individual style and character, yet united in basic ways. Then, in 1984, at the 10th anniversary celebration of our founding, Theodore Sizer congratulated the school for its impressive history and asked, "why not a Central Park East secondary school?" Why not keep the good things going through the 12th grade?

We agreed. Our own study of our sixth-grade graduates persuaded us that starting a secondary school was a good idea. Some of our critics had said that a secure and supportive elementary school would not prepare students to cope with the "real world." Our study of our graduates had proved them wrong. Regardless of race or social class, our graduates had handled the real world well. They had coped. The statistics we compiled amazed even us. Only one of our graduates, who were hardly an academic elite, had left school prior to earning a high school diploma. Furthermore, half of our graduates had gone on to college.

But our graduates had stories to tell. And their stories were not stories about being educated, but about survival. They told us stories that confirmed what Sizer had written about U.S. high schools in *Horace's Compromise*. But the stories our graduates told us were generally far worse than Sizer chronicled, since he was often describing wealthy or middle-class schools.

We began negotiations with the district and with the city. In the fall of 1985 we opened the doors to Central Park East Secondary School, which serves grades 7 through 12. We are now back where we began, starting something entirely new. However, the obstacles that block the path of reforming a high school are harder to budge than those that face elementary schools.

For instance, the idea that an "alternative" high school means a school for "difficult" kids is firmly entrenched in the tradition of New York City high schools, and the anxiety about preparing students for the "real world" is more pressing than in elementary schools. Moreover, the Regents exam, course requirements, college pressures, and the usual panic about dealing with adolescents and their problems combine to make the task even more complex—especially in light of New York's recently adopted Regents Action Plan, which runs counter to everything we and the Coalition of Essential Schools believe. With its increased number of required courses and standardized examinations and its greater specificity about course content, the Regents Action Plan leaves far less room for initiative and innovation at the school level. There is little for us to learn from and not much of a network of teachers or teacher education institutions that can provide us with support, ideas, and examples.

But we have a lot going for us, too. We have our three sister elementary schools to lean on and draw support from. We have the Coalition of Essential Schools and a growing national interest in doing something about the appalling quality of many public secondary schools. And, under its current superintendent, Carlos Medina, the district continues to support the idea of alternative "schools of choice" for all children, all parents, and all staff members. We have also been receiving invaluable support from the citywide high school division and the alternative high school superintendent, who oversees a disparate collection of small high schools throughout New York City.

And we are determined. New York City's high schools are clearly in a state of crisis. The dropout rate is appalling, the fate of many who do not drop out officially is equally devastating, and the decline in college attendance by black and Hispanic students is frightening. Perhaps the time has come for progressive education to tackle the high school again, to demonstrate that giving adolescents and their teachers greater responsibility for the development of educational models is the key ingredient.

The notion of respect, which lies at the heart of democratic practice, runs counter to almost everything in our current high schools. Today's urban high schools express disrespect for teachers and students in myriad ways—in the physical decay of the buildings, in their size, in the anonymity of their students, and in the lack of control over decisions by those who live and work in them.

Although the reasons for the recent national concern over high schools may have little to do with democracy, the current reform mood offers an important opening—if we can resist the desire for a new "one best way." We cannot achieve true reform by fiat. Giving wider choices and more power to those who are closest to the classroom are not the kinds of reforms that appeal to busy legislators, politicians, and central board officials. They cannot be mandated, only facilitated. Such reforms require fewer constraints, fewer rules—not more of them. They require watchfulness and continuous documenting and recording, not a whole slew of accountability schemes tied to a mandated list of measurable outcomes.

Do we have the collective will to take such risks? Only if we recognize that the other paths are actually far riskier and have long failed to lead us out of the woods. Like democratic societies, successful schools can't be guaranteed. The merits of letting schools try to be successful schools can't be guaranteed. The merits of letting schools try to be successful are significant. But allowing them to try requires boldness and patience—not a combination that is politically easy to sustain.

WHAT THEY DO AND HOW THEY DO IT

As teachers at Central Park East overhauled and rebuilt the traditional school structure, they kept one key aim in mind: to give teachers time to get to know each student and time to tailor the instructional program for each individual. Here are some examples of what they've done:

Time for Students

- To get the student load way down, all professional staff—including the librarian and the director—teach. Aside from one director, there are no supervisors.

- The high school is organized into Houses of 80 students, each with a faculty of four. The basic class is 20 students and the student load per teacher is never more than 80. If the teacher teaches two disciplines instead of one, the load is just 40.

- To maximize the personal relationship between students and teachers, students stay with the same teacher (or teachers) two years in a row.

Time for Teachers

- Each fall the staff plans a series of semi-monthly faculty meetings. One year, every other faculty meeting considered various approaches to writing. Sometimes, at a teacher's request, one student's progress or one teacher's curriculum is discussed.

- Once a week, the staff of each House takes an 80-minute lunch and discusses the progress of individual students and the overall work of the House.

- One morning a week, while students work in the community, teachers from each department can spend three uninterrupted hours designing, evaluating, and tinkering with the curriculum.

The Curriculum

The curriculum is designed by those who teach it. Teachers can opt to hire consultants.

- The seventh and eighth grade science sequence includes an interdisciplinary unit on "Light and Sight" that exposes students to both biology (optics) and physics (the properties of light).

- The eighth grade humanities sequence focuses on "power"—who has it, who doesn't, and how different people have gotten it. The first semester focuses on the English, French, and American revolutions; the second, on nonrevolutionary change in America.

Flexible Scheduling

Because the schedule is in the hands of teachers, the time allotted the revolutions could be increased when it was discovered that at least one student still thought Boston was in London.

Resources

Once a topic—such as the revolutions—has been chosen, all faculty haunt used-book shops to build a resource library on the subject. Teachers are thus not text bound, but have access to a variety of materials—some of which will interest every student.

Writing

Working in different settings with different "editors," students get plenty of practice with—and individual attention to—their writing. They write at least once a week in humanities and in a "writing work shop," plus four days a week in regularly reviewed journals.

Parent Conferences

Twice a year, parents must come to the school, review a portfolio of their child's work, and meet with the teacher *and* the student to discuss the student's progress. With everybody in the same room together, parents won't hear one version of events from the student and another from the teacher.

FOR FURTHER EXPLORATION

Meier, D. (1995). *The power of their ideas: Lessons for America from a small school in Harlem.* Boston, MA: Beacon Press.
Meier, D. (2000). *Will standards save public education?* Boston, MA: Beacon Press.
Meier, D. (2002). *In schools we trust: Creating communities of learning in an era of testing and standardization.* Boston, MA: Beacon Press.
Meier, D. (2004). *Many children left behind.* Boston, MA: Beacon Press.

Deborah Meier is the principal and one of the founders of Central Park East School in New York City. She was recently awarded a "Genius Grant" from the MacArthur Foundation in honor of her work in education. This article was adapted with permission from the June 1987 issue of Phi Delta Kappan.

13

Beyond the Deficit Paradigm

An Ecological Orientation to Thriving Urban Schools

Kelly Donnell

I couldn't teach without being who I am as a person. And who I am as a person is going to put myself out there with families. I think that's why I have the [positive] response that I have. Because they see that. My boss, it used to drive her nuts that I would hug my kids at the end of the night before they went home. That's who I am, and my kids know me. You hug me before you go home for the day. That's it. That's how it goes. Because that way they know that no matter what happened during the day, "I'm not mad at you. You know, everything is fine. You made some mistakes. You made some bad choices. But you know what? Tomorrow is a new day."

—First-year urban elementary schoolteacher
referring to her work in the afterschool program

You have to walk into that classroom expecting to change all of them. If you go in saying, "Okay, some of them I'm just not going to reach," I think it's going to make you try less hard. When you get that resistance and a child is, like, putting up a wall, I think that if you are expecting failure, you are that much more likely to

*just be okay with that wall being there. Whereas if you go saying,
"No way, my kids are succeeding by the end of the year," you are
going to work to get over the wall.*

—Student teacher in an urban high school

I magine if everyone who taught in an urban school acted on this deep commitment and asked not whether it can be done, but how! After reading newspaper headlines, watching the nightly news, or seeing too many Hollywood movies, you may have developed a sense that urban schools are in a state of perpetual, even inevitable, crisis. Urban schools have certainly struggled. For too long, dehumanizing bureaucracies; insufficient funding; wave upon wave of new, often arbitrary, reforms and initiatives; and cultural mismatches between teachers and students have dominated the lives of those connected with city schools. These are very real, often daunting concerns. As a beginning teacher recently commented, one feels the "weight of society on your shoulders" when teaching in an urban school.

But focusing intensely, and solely, on the challenges of urban schools ignores the many city schools that are thriving, caring and just, and that seek to help all children—without exception—become successful. Concentrating solely on the very real challenges of urban schools leads inevitably to an even greater danger than failing to acknowledge just how well many urban schools are doing: Such a narrow emphasis reinforces a "deficit paradigm" in which everyone associated with urban schools—city kids, their parents, their teachers—is viewed as damaged goods. You've encountered the deficit paradigm when you hear children labeled as "underprepared" or when you hear complaints about certain groups of parents "just not caring" or when folks talk about "crime-ridden" neighborhoods. The deficit paradigm is an orientation in which children, their families, and the larger communities in which they live are seen as deficient and therefore responsible for their lack of success. This "what you haven't got" approach is based in endogenous theory, which posits that students struggle because of personal deficiencies, like weak motivation or inadequate learning potential. Those who engage in deficit thinking regard student failure as a result of poor student choices or insufficient ability and in so doing pathologize and marginalize children and their families. In short, those who ascribe to the deficit paradigm believe that urban children and their families are responsible for the success or failure of their schools.

The deficit paradigm is highly counterproductive precisely because it fails to acknowledge and capitalize on the positive and powerful resources in families and communities and the myriad opportunities available in urban education. This dominant framework is problematic for a host of reasons: It ignores school and other institutional account-ability. It is based in pseudoscience and a lack of documentable research. It fails to offer solutions to school issues, and it often exacerbates them (Valencia, 1997). Furthermore, as noted urban educator and researcher Lois Weiner (2006) has pointed out, bureaucratic urban school cultures foster "the pervasive assumption that when students misbehave or achieve poorly, they must be 'fixed' because the problem inheres in the students or their families, not in the social ecology of the school, grade, or classroom" (p. 42). Power, in the deficit paradigm, lies exclusively within teachers and schools, while families and communities are seen at best as partners, and at worst as passive recipients and even obstacles.

Rather than trying to determine what is "wrong" with urban students or their families or their communities, could it be that the problem has been in the type of schools we have been providing for them? Rather than "blaming the victim" for school failure, might we look at how some schools are structured to prevent urban students from learning?

Some urban schools are structured to support student learning. One paradigm from which to understand the success of many urban schools is an ecological, asset-based approach. This approach helps educators find new ways of framing and addressing long-standing issues. An ecological, asset-based approach views school life and class-room teaching as occurring within interconnected webs of settings and institutions that transcend classroom and school borders. While most children, families, and communities have their struggles, this affirming approach recognizes that all children, families, and communities have intrinsic worth, strengths, and resources. An asset-based perspective acknowledges, seeks, and utilizes these cultural, linguistic, social, and intellectual resources.

The ecological paradigm acknowledges that schools are embedded in, and therefore influenced by, socially and culturally organized environments. Ecological systems, more than isolated factors such as out-dated textbooks or school violence, affect schooling. Systems (such as the students, the classroom, the family, the school, the community, the society) are nested within one other and have a cascading influence upon each other.

With regard to urban schools, an ecological view acknowledges that urban policy, structure, and customs are integrally related to what happens in urban classrooms. Urban schools function within an eco-logical web of interconnected social entities, beginning with children in classrooms extending out to schools, districts, and communities. These complex, layered contexts influence each other in multidirectional ways. Urban schools are embedded in a much larger context, one that requires multiple sectors of the community acting in concert. The teacher, students and their families, the school, or even the school dis-trict alone cannot bring about meaningful change in urban schools. But together they can create highly successful schools that ensure achieve-ment for all students and that function as a service to the community.

As previously suggested, "loving, highly successful" urban schools may be more common than many citizens and educators alike would believe, given the pervasive nature of the deficit paradigm. Scheurich (1998) has researched schools that have operationalized a model that has become known as HiPass (high performance all student success) schools. Developed at the grassroots level, not by university academics or state bureaucrats, the model encompasses many of the concepts throughout this chapter. The schools in Scheurich's study perform exceptionally well on state-based high stakes tests, and they are deeply caring and child-centered. These schools reveal, support, and empha-size students' assets rather than focus on their perceived deficits.

Focusing on students' strengths is critically important because if we consider the ecology of urban education as a web at its center are the students. A critical thread in this ecological web is utilization of the wealth of diversity and of the cultural and personal resources that stu-dents and their families bring to urban schools. In thriving urban schools, children's cultural backgrounds, including their first language, are highly valued and seen as assets. Students bring essential "funds of knowledge" (González et al., 2005) to school. They bring rich cultural and cognitive resources that teachers use to provide meaningful learn-ing that incorporates students' prior knowledge and experience. One beginning teacher describes how she learned to integrate students' funds of knowledge while teaching a high school poetry unit:

> I wanted to introduce them to traditional poets, the classic, canonical poets. But at the same time, I realized that that has not been working. I could not think of a creative way to engage them with learning about T. S. Eliot! And so, I thought I would start in a place I assumed they were. They all listen to music, but my primary assumption was that they listen to hip-hop or some form of rap. I just thought, how can I make it academic? So I picked rappers

or hip-hop artists who talk about significant things, you know like historical events. And then I picked lyrics that use like metaphors and other things that I talk about on and on, like personification and all these things. Because the first thing we did we read this article about the need for revolution in contemporary hip-hop, the need for like music to change and stop being so materialistic, misogynist, and all this stuff. And just within the text there was so much vocabulary that they hadn't encountered that I realized we needed to do vocab first. And the vocab took a week because so much discussion came out of the kinds of words that we used. . . . You know, it was amazing for me because the last three weeks we were doing my unit was the only time I had good attendance and actual engagement and students talking about what we did in class outside of class, you know, in a positive way. They actually asked me questions, and they would call me. I took some of them to poetry readings.

In thriving urban schools, everyone associated with life in the school fiercely believes that each and every child can succeed at high academic levels. This is common rhetoric but is rarely enacted in practice. This belief is not rooted in the current discourse that high standards will address deficiencies in urban children but in an understanding that children are naturally inclined to high engagement and achievement. Successful schools embrace a strong, shared vision, a commitment to the idea that there are ways to engage in school so that everyone achieves, so long as everyone is willing to find that way. One beginning teacher put it this way:

All children are treated with compassion, care, and respect. This is not to say that successful urban schools are driven by a coddling notion of the primacy of self-esteem. Strengths are not fabricated nor are expectations lowered. Rather, the school focuses on building communities children want to go to in which they feel treasured.

And another had this to say:

I have to be able to say that the reason I'm teaching this class of kids or [am] there every day is because I care about the students. And I want them to reach their fullest potential. . . . And I can always believe that that's right. Like those are very fundamental truths to teaching any classroom of kids. And so as long as I can really apply that to what I'm doing then I can know that at least that much is right.

Here, care and respect for children is viewed as ethical and moral accountability, not sentimentality, and it is a care not just for the individual but for the larger community as well. Indeed, moving from a simple focus on individual students to the community as a whole is a key element that is woven again and again throughout thriving urban schools. Community is emphasized in many capacities: through the perspective of the teacher, through the culture of the school, and through partnerships with other community institutions.

For example, Peter Murrell (2001), from Northeastern University, has developed the concept of "the community teacher." At the core of a community teacher's educational practice is the development of his or her ecological understanding of the urban culture, community, and identity of children and families. The community teacher sees learning as situated in particular contexts and settings and resists the separation of school and the everyday world of students. The community teacher views learning as a process of co-participation and activity with other people and human systems and works to create "communities of practice."

Successful urban schools are integral parts of their communities. There is very little separation between the two. The school is often the nerve center of the community. One teacher observed the following:

> *I think another critical thing about [this urban high school] is that their support services are incredible. They have a health center right in the school. They have a day care center at the high school.*

This nerve center is often built through partnerships with organizations in the community. There are many different types of partnerships. Schools find meaningful relationships with businesses, universities, youth organizations, service agencies, and faith-based organizations. Historically, many organizations in urban communities such as Boys and Girls Clubs, YMCAs, and the Urban League, and Scouting have provided urban students with opportunities to connect with the larger society and have promoted a positive sense of purpose and participation. The roles of these organizations continue to evolve to meet the needs of students in urban schools. Because of their long-standing history, they often have built relationships and cultural knowledge of local communities and their families.

Urban schools, just like their counterparts in other types of communities in our country, can and must be places where children and adults thrive and are cared for. We can develop schools in which every single child achieves meaningful success and is encouraged to capitalize on the strengths and assets inherent in their culture, in their communities, in their homes, and in themselves. It is happening in urban schools across the country. And not only are these schools thriving but they are offering us all a window into how our participation in the ecology of our communities is essential. Scheurich (1998) suggested that the teachers and parents who created HiPass schools have

> given us a gift that is larger than just education, as vitally important as education is to our society. In terms of organizations and life in those organizations, these schools have given us living examples of a kind of organization that is wonderful to work within and that performs at the highest levels . . . the very idea that our work environments could be both loving and high performing is truly startling for most of us, given our typical experiences in organizations. . . . It would be ironic, indeed, if a better kind of organization has emerged from low-SES schools and communities of color. (p. 478)

As a student of education, you may marvel at or, perhaps, feel overwhelmed by the challenges and complexity of teaching and learning; however, beginning teachers just like you are succeeding in urban schools. Successful teaching requires recognition of the social and cultural context of schools and a deep understanding of how these factors influence, shape, and, most importantly, can nurture urban schools. Successful, caring urban schools will require recognition of and commitment to the importance of the entire ecology in which students are embedded. But as the HiPass schools attest, this is not hollow rhetoric or an idealistic dream; it is a thriving reality in many urban schools.

REFERENCES

González, N., Moll, L., Tenery, M. F., Rivera, A., Rendón, P., Gonzales, R., et al. (2005). Funds of knowledge for teaching in Latino households. In N. González, L. C. Moll, & C. Amanti (Eds.), *Funds of knowledge: Theorizing practices in households, communities, and classrooms* (pp. 89–111). Mahwah, NJ: Lawrence Erlbaum.

Murrell, P. C., Jr. (2001). *The community teacher: A new framework for effective urban teaching.* New York: Teachers College Press.

Scheurich, J. J. (1998). Highly successful and loving, public elementary schools populated mainly by low-SES children of color: Core beliefs and cultural characteristics. *Urban Education, 33,* 451–491.

Valencia, R. (1997). Conceptualizing the notion of deficit thinking. In R. Valencia (Ed.), *The evolution of deficit thinking: Educational thought and practice* (pp. 1–12). Washington, DC: Falmer Press.

Weiner, L. (2006). Challenging deficit thinking. *Educational Leadership, 64*(1), 42–45.

FOR FURTHER EXPLORATION

Donnell, K. (2007). Getting to we: Developing a transformative urban teaching practice. *Urban Education, 42*(3), 223–249.

Stairs, A., & Donnell, K. (Eds.). (2010). *Research on urban teacher learning: The role of contextual factors across the professional continuum.* Charlotte, NC: Information Age Publishing.

Stairs, A., Donnell, K., & Dunn, A. H. (2011). *Urban teaching in America: Theory, research, and practice in K–12 classrooms.* Thousand Oaks, CA: Sage.

PART V

How Should We Assess Student Learning?

M rs. Yan is puzzled. Shayla is one of the hardest working, most motivated students in her 11th-grade English class. Shayla participates actively, writes poetry and short fiction, and always offers the most astute insights when class discussion turns to the interpretation of literature.

And yet Shayla struggles on Mrs. Yan's exams and she can't seem to memorize even a simple soliloquy for the oral presentation requirement. In addition, she gets glassy-eyed whenever Mrs. Yan talks about the importance of learning vocabulary as part of SAT preparation.

When reviewing Shayla's performance for the semester, Mrs. Yan noticed that Shayla's poetry and her short fiction, often published in the school's literary magazine, was exemplary, as was her effort and classroom participation. But her performance on exams, research papers, and more formal, oral presentations was, more often than not, deficient.

Struck by these inconsistencies, Mrs. Yan decided that the only fair way to arrive at a final report card grade was to average all Shayla's marks together. However, there was something about this approach that made Mrs. Yan uncomfortable.

For her part, Shayla believes that her grade should reflect her exceptional fiction and poetry, her sophisticated interpretation of literature, and her active class participation. Shayla is not happy with Mrs. Yan's simple solution to the complex problem.

Why assess student learning? What is the purpose of assessment? What does good assessment look like?

14

A Mania for Rubrics

Thomas Newkirk

Near the beginning of the film *Dead Poets Society*, the English teacher played by Robin Williams forces his students to read aloud—from the absurd preface to their anthology. Works of literature, the preface states, can be evaluated by graphing two qualities: importance and execution. Midway through the reading, Mr. Williams' character tells his students to rip out the offending pages. Art can never be so mechanically reduced.

This movie's warning is relevant today because we are now in the middle of a resurgence of mechanical instruction in writing. Driven by state testing, teachers are being pulled toward prompt-and-rubric teaching that bypasses the human act of composing and the human gesture of response.

Proponents of rubrics will claim that they are simply trying to be clear about criteria that are too often tacit and unexplained. By using rubrics, the argument goes, we are giving students more precise and analytic reasons for the evaluations they receive. By placing these criteria in the clear light of day, students will come to see evaluations as less subjective, less what the teacher "likes."

If this were truly the case, who could disagree? The crux of the issue is this: Do rubrics clarify the process of sensitive response? Or do they distort, obscure, or mystify that response? And to answer that question, we need to think carefully about what we do when we read student work (when we are at our best)—and what we want from an evaluator.

NOTE: Previously published in *Education Week*, September 2000. Reprinted with permission.

Personally, I have never been able to use rubrics that establish pre-determined weighting systems. I always cheat. I work backwards, determining the impression or sense I had of the writing, a unitary evaluative reaction. Then I jimmy the categories so that they fit my general reaction, hoping to escape detection. In other words, I am not thinking of multiple criteria (organization, detail, mechanics) as I read, parceling out my attention.

As I read, I feel myself in a magnetized field. I am drawn to—or released from—the text I am reading. Initially, this response is more physical than cognitive or analytic; when the text is working I feel more alert, and a good line or image propels me forward. At other times, I feel slack, unmagnetized, as if nothing is drawing me in, drawing me on. This lack of attraction may come from too little detail (or too much), from a lack of direction, absence of personality or voice, from dialogue that doesn't reveal character, but the immediate sensation is physical. The student's text has let me go.

Rather than reveal processes like the one I have described, rubrics conceal or mystify them. They fail to reveal the narrative, moment-by-moment process of evaluation. Their formal and categorical ratings belie—or worse, short-circuit—the work of the reader. Terms like "organization" fail to clarify (or even locate) the disruption in the reader's sense of continuity. Rubrics fail to provide a *demonstration* of the reading process that can later be internalized by the writer.

The very authoritative language and format of rubrics, their pretense to objectivity, hides the human act of reading. The key qualities of good writing (organization, detail, a central problem) are represented as something the writing *has*—rather than something the writing *does.*

All of this, of course, assumes that the purpose of rubrics is to convey response. More often, however, they are used to enforce uniformity of evaluation—as a preparation to test-taking. A striking example appeared in the February 2000 issue of *Educational Leadership*, describing the way kindergartners were prepped for a drawing test. I will quote from the article so that I might not be accused of exaggeration.

After the teacher explained what elements of the drawing were needed to get a score of 4, she said, "Notice that this drawing shows the ground colored green and brown. There are also a tree, the sky, some clouds, and the sun." She then showed a picture earning a 3, in which the tree, clouds, and sun were not as clearly defined. After this explanation, she asked each student to create "artwork that met the requirement of the level-4 drawing" and rate the artwork of a partner. Children spent the rest of class time "improving their drawings until all the student pictures either met the level-4 rubric or went up at least one level."

This is not *preparation*—it is capitulation. This developmentally inappropriate task is presented not as educational malpractice, but as a "success" for standards-based instruction. Which only goes to prove the education writer Alfie Kohn's point: that the standards movement is going to make satire obsolete.

FOR FURTHER EXPLORATION

Andrade, H.G. (2000). Using rubrics to promote thinking and learning. *Educational Leadership*.

Kohn, Alfie. www.alfiekohn.org/teaching/rubrics.htm

Mabry, L. (1999). Writing to the rubric: Lingering effects of traditional standardized testing on direct writing assessment. *Phi Delta Kappan*.

Wilson M. (2006). *Rethinking rubrics in writing assessment*. Portsmouth, NH: Heineman.

Thomas Newkirk is a professor of English at the University of New Hampshire.

15

Grading

The Issue Is Not How but Why?

Alfie Kohn

W hy are we concerned with evaluating how well students are doing? The question of motive, as opposed to method, can lead us to rethink basic tenets of teaching and learning and to evaluate what students have done in a manner more consistent with our ultimate educational objectives. But not all approaches to the topic result in this sort of thoughtful reflection. In fact, approaches to assessment may be classified according to their depth of analysis and willingness to question fundamental assumptions about how and why we grade. Consider three possible levels of inquiry:

Level 1. These are the most superficial concerns, those limited to the practical issue of how to grade students' work. Here we find articles and books offering elaborate formulas for scoring assignments, computing points, and allocating final grades—thereby taking for granted that what students do must receive *some* grades and, by extension, that students ought to be avidly concerned about the ones they will get.

Level 2. Here educators call the above premises into question, asking whether traditional grading is really necessary or useful for assessing students' performance. Alternative assessments, often designated as "authentic," belong in this category. The idea here is to provide a richer, deeper description of students' achievement. (Portfolios of students' work are sometimes commended to us in this context, but when a portfolio is used merely as a means of arriving at a traditional grade, it might more accurately be grouped under Level 1.)

Level 3. Rather than challenging grades alone, discussions at this level challenge the whole enterprise of assessment—and specifically why we are evaluating students as opposed to how we are doing so. No matter how elaborate or carefully designed an assessment strategy may be, the result will not be constructive if our reason for wanting to know how students are doing is itself objectionable.

GRADING RATIONALE I: SORTING

One reason for evaluating students is to be able to label them on the basis of their performance and thus to sort them like so many potatoes. Sorting, in turn, has been criticized at each of the three levels, but for very different reasons. At Level 1, the concern is merely that we are not correctly dumping individuals into the right piles. The major problem with our high schools and colleges, the argument goes, is that they don't keep enough students off the Excellent pile. (These critics don't put it quite this way, of course; they talk about "grade inflation.") Interestingly, most studies suggest that student performance does not improve when instructors grade more stringently and, conversely, that making it relatively easy to get a good grade does not lead students to do inferior work—even when performance is defined as the number of facts retained temporarily as measured by multiple-choice exams (Vasta & Sarmiento, 1979; Abrami, Dickens, Perry, & Leventhal, 1980).

At Level 2, questions are raised about whether grades are reliable enough to allow students to be sorted effectively. Indeed, studies show that any particular teacher may well give different grades to a single piece of work submitted at two different times. Naturally, the variation is even greater when the work is evaluated by more than one teacher (Kirschenbaum, Napier, & Simon, 1971). What grades offer is spurious precision, a subjective rating masquerading as an objective assessment.

From the perspective of Level 3, this criticism is far too tame. The trouble is not that we are sorting students badly—a problem that logically should be addressed by trying to do it better. The trouble is that we are sorting them at all. Are we doing so in order to segregate students by ability and teach them separately? The harms of this practice have been well established (Oakes, 1985). Are we turning schools into "bargain-basement personnel screening agencies for business"

(Campbell, 1974, p. 145)? Whatever use we make of sorting, the process itself is very different from—and often incompatible with—the goal of helping students to learn.

GRADING RATIONALE II: MOTIVATION

A second rationale for grading—and indeed, one of the major motives behind assessment in general—is to motivate students to work harder so they will receive a favorable evaluation. Unfortunately, this rationale is just as problematic as sorting. Indeed, given the extent to which A's and F's function as rewards and punishments rather than as useful feedback, grades are counterproductive regardless of whether they are intentionally used for this purpose. The trouble lies with the implicit assumption that there exists a single entity called "motivation" that students have to a greater or lesser degree. In reality, a critical and qualitative difference exists between intrinsic and extrinsic motivation—between an interest in what one is learning for its own sake, and a mind-set in which learning is viewed as a means to an end, the end being to escape a punishment or snag a reward. Not only are these two orientations distinct, but they also often pull in opposite directions.

Scores of studies in social psychology and related fields have demonstrated that extrinsic motivators frequently undermine intrinsic motivation. This may not be particularly surprising in the case of sticks, but it is no less true of carrots. People who are promised rewards for doing something tend to lose interest in whatever they had to do to obtain the reward. Studies also show that, contrary to the conventional wisdom in our society, people who have been led to think about what they will receive for engaging in a task (or for doing it well) are apt to do lower quality work than those who are not expecting to get anything at all.

These findings are consistent across a variety of subject populations, rewards, and tasks, with the most destructive effects occurring in activities that require creativity or higher-order thinking. That this effect is produced by the extrinsic motivators known as grades has been documented with students of different ages and from different cultures. Yet the findings are rarely cited by educators.

Studies have shown that the more students are induced to think about what they will get on an assignment, the more their desire to learn evaporates, and, ironically, the less well they do. Consider these findings:

• On tasks requiring varying degrees of creativity, Israeli educational psychologist Ruth Butler has repeatedly found that students perform less well and are less interested in what they are doing when being graded than when they are encouraged to focus on the task itself (Butler & Nissan 1986; Butler, 1987, 1988).

- Even in the case of rote learning, students are more apt to forget what they have learned after a week or so—and are less apt to find it interesting—if they are initially advised that they will be graded on their performance (Grolnick & Ryan, 1987).

- When Japanese students were told that a history test would count toward their final grade, they were less interested in the subject— and less likely to prefer tackling difficult questions than those who were told the test was just for monitoring their progress (Kage, 1991).

- Children told that they would be graded on their solution of anagrams chose easier ones to work on—and seemed to take less pleasure from solving them—than children who were not being graded (Harter, 1978).

As an article in the *Journal of Educational Psychology* concluded, "Grades may encourage an emphasis on quantitative aspects of learning, depress creativity, foster fear of failure, and undermine interest" (Butler & Nissan, 1986, p. 215). This is a particularly ironic result if the rationale for evaluating students in the first place is to encourage them to perform better.

GRADING RATIONALE III: FEEDBACK

Some educators insist that their purpose in evaluating students is neither to sort them nor to motivate them, but simply to provide feedback so they can learn more effectively tomorrow than they did today. From a Level 2 perspective, this is an entirely legitimate goal—and grades are an entirely inadequate means of reaching it. There is nothing wrong with helping students to internalize and work toward meeting high standards, but that is most likely to happen when they experience success and failure not as reward and punishment, but as information (Bruner, 1961, p. 26). Grades make it very difficult to do this. Besides, reducing someone's work to a letter or number simply is not helpful; a B+ on top of a paper tells a student nothing about what was impressive about that paper or how it could be improved.

But from Level 3 comes the following challenge: Why do we want students to improve? This question at first seems as simple and bland as baby food; only after a moment does it reveal a jalapeño kick: It leads us into disconcerting questions about the purpose of education itself.

DEMAND VS. SUPPORT

Eric Schaps (1993), who directs the Developmental Studies Center in Oakland, California, has emphasized "a single powerful distinction: focusing on what students ought to be able to do, that is, what we will demand of them—as contrasted with focusing on what we can do to support students development and help them learn." For lack of better labels, let us call these the "demand" and "support" models.

In the demand model, students are workers who are obligated to do a better job. Blame is leveled by saying students "chose" not to study or "earned" a certain grade—conveniently removing all responsibility from educators and deflecting attention from the curriculum and the context in which it is taught. In their evaluations, teachers report whether students did what they were supposed to do. This mind-set often lurks behind even relatively enlightened programs that emphasize performance assessment and—a common buzzword these days—outcomes. (It also manifests itself in the view of education as an investment, a way of preparing children to become future workers.)

The support model, by contrast, helps children take part in an "adventure in ideas" (Nicholls & Hazzard, 1993), guiding and stimulating their natural inclination to explore what is unfamiliar; to construct meaning; to develop a competence with and a passion for playing with words, numbers, and ideas. This approach meshes with what is sometimes called "learner-centered" learning, in which the point is to help students act on their desire to make sense of the world. In this context, student evaluation is, in part, a way of determining how effective we have been as educators. In sum, improvement is not something we require of students so much as something that follows when we provide them with engaging tasks and a supportive environment.

SUPPORTIVE ASSESSMENT

Here are five principles of assessment that follow from this support model:

1. Assessment of any kind should not be overdone. Getting students to become preoccupied with how they are doing can undermine their interest in what they are doing. An excessive concern with performance can erode curiosity—and, paradoxically, reduce the quality of performance. Performance-obsessed students also tend to avoid difficult tasks so they can escape a negative evaluation.

2. The best evidence we have of whether we are succeeding as educators comes from observing children's behavior rather than from test scores or grades. It comes from watching to see whether they continue arguing animatedly about an issue raised in class after the class is over, whether they come home chattering about something they discovered in school, whether they read on their own time. Where interest is sparked, skills are usually acquired. Of course, interest is difficult to quantify, but the solution is not to return to more conventional measuring methods; it is to acknowledge the limits of measurement.

3. We must transform schools into safe, caring communities. This is critical for helping students to become good learners and good people, but it is also relevant to assessment. Only in a safe place, where there is no fear of humiliation and punitive judgment, will students admit to being confused about what they have read and feel free to acknowledge their mistakes. Only by being able to ask for help will they be likely to improve.

Ironically, the climate created by an emphasis on grades, standardized testing, coercive mechanisms such as pop quizzes and compulsory recitation, and pressure on teachers to cover a prescribed curriculum makes it more difficult to know how well students understand—and thus to help them along.

4. Any responsible conversation about assessment must attend to the quality of the curriculum. The easy question is whether a student has learned something; the far more important—and unsettling—question is whether the student has been given something worth learning. (The answer to the latter question is almost certainly no if the need to evaluate students has determined curriculum content.) Research corroborates what thoughtful teachers know from experience: when students have interesting things to do, artificial inducements to boost achievement are unnecessary (Moeller & Reschke, 1993).

5. Students must be invited to participate in determining the criteria by which their work will be judged, and then play a role in weighing their work against those criteria. Indeed, they should help make decisions about as many elements of their learning as possible (Kohn, 1993). This achieves several things: It gives them more control over their education, makes evaluation feel less punitive, and provides an important learning experience in itself. If there is a movement away from grades, teachers should explain the rationale and solicit students' suggestions for what to do instead and how to manage the transitional period. That transition may be bumpy and slow, but the chance to engage in personal and collective reflection about these issues will be important in its own right.

AND IF YOU MUST GRADE . . .

Finally, *while conventional grades persist, teachers and parents ought to do everything in their power to help students forget about them.* Here are some practical suggestions for reducing their salience.

• *Refrain from giving a letter or number grade for individual assignments,* even if you are compelled to give one at the end of the term. The data suggest that substantive comments should replace, not supplement, grades (Butler, 1988). Make sure the effect of doing this is not to create suspense about what students are going to get on their report cards, which would defeat the whole purpose. Some older students may experience, especially at first, a sense of existential vertigo: a steady supply of grades has defined them. Offer to discuss privately with any such student the grade he or she would probably receive if report cards were handed out that day. With luck and skill, the requests for ratings will decrease as students come to be involved in what is being taught.

• *Never grade students while they are still learning something and, even more important, do not reward them for their performance at that point.* Studies suggest that rewards are most destructive when given for skills still being honed (Condry & Chambers, 1978). If it is unclear whether students feel ready to demonstrate what they know, there is an easy way to find out: ask them.

• *Never grade on a curve.* The number of good grades should not be artificially limited so that one student's success makes another's less likely. Stipulating that only a few individuals can get top marks regardless of how well everyone does is egregiously unfair on its face. It also undermines collaboration and community. Of course, grades of any kind, even when they are not curved to create artificial scarcity—or deliberately publicized—tend to foster comparison and competition, an emphasis on relative standing. This is not only destructive to students' self-esteem and relationships but also counterproductive with respect to the quality of learning (Kohn, 1992). As one book on the subject puts it: "It is not a symbol of rigor to have grades fall into a normal distribution; rather, it is a symbol of failure: failure to teach well, to test well, and to have any influence at all on the intellectual lives of students" (Milton Pollio, & Eison, 1986, p. 225).

- *Never give a separate grade for effort.* When students seem to be indifferent to what they are being asked to learn, educators sometimes respond with the very strategy that precipitated the problem in the first place: grading students' efforts to coerce them to try harder. The fatal paradox is that while coercion can sometimes elicit resentful obedience, it can never create desire. A low grade for effort is more likely to be read as "You're a failure even at trying." On the other hand, a high grade for effort combined with a low grade for achievement says, "You're just too dumb to succeed." Most of all, rewarding or punishing children's efforts allows educators to ignore the possibility that the curriculum or learning environment may have something to do with students' lack of enthusiasm.

REFERENCES

Abrami, P. C., Dickens, W. J., Perry, R. P., & L. Leventhal. (1980). "Do teacher standards for assigning grades affect student evaluations of instruction?" *Journal of Educational Psychology, 72,* 107–118.

Bruner, J. S. (1961). The act of discovery. *Harvard Educational Review, 31,* 21–32.

Butler, R. (1987). Task-involving and ego-involving properties of evaluation. *Journal of Educational Psychology, 79,* 474–482.

Butler, R. (1988). Enhancing and undermining intrinsic motivation. *British Journal of Educational Psychology, 58,* 1–14.

Butler, R., & Nissan, M. (1986). Effects of no feedback, task-related comments, and grades on intrinsic motivation and performance. *Journal of Educational Psychology, 78,* 210–216.

Campbell, D. N. (October 1974). On being number one: Competition in education. *Phi Delta Kappan,* 143–146.

Condry, J., & Chambers, J. (1978). Intrinsic motivation and the process of learning. In *The hidden costs of rewards: New perspectives on the psychology of human motivation,* M. R. Lepper & D. Greene (Eds.). Hillsdale, NJ: Lawrence Erlbaum.

Grolnick, W. S., & Ryan, R. M. (1987). Autonomy in children's learning: An experimental and individual difference investigation. *Journal of Personality and Social Psychology, 52,* 890–898.

Harter, S. (1978). Pleasure derived from challenge and the effects of receiving grades on children's difficulty level choices. *Child Development, 49,* 788–799.

Kage, M. (1991). *The effects of evaluation on intrinsic motivation.* Paper presented at the meeting of the Japan Association of Educational Psychology, Joetsu, Japan.

Kirschenbaum, H., Napier, R. W., & Simon, S. B. (1971). *Wad-Ja-Get?: The grading game in American education.* New York: Hart.

Kohn, A. (1992). *No contest: The case against competition.* Rev. ed. Boston: Houghton Mifflin.

Kohn, A. (September 1993). Choices for children: Why and how to let students decide. *Phi Delta Kappan,* 8–20.

Milton, O., Pollio, H. R., & Eison. J. A. (1986). *Making sense of college grades.* San Francisco: Jossey-Bass.

Moeller, A. J., & Reschke, C. (1993). A second look at grading and classroom performance. *Modern Language Journal, 77,* 163–169.

Nicholls, J. C., & Hazzard, S. P. (1993). *Education as adventure: Lessons from the second grade.* New York: Teachers College Press.

Oakes, J. (1985). *Keeping track: How schools structure inequality.* New Haven: Yale University Press.

Schaps, E. (October 1993). Personal communication.

Vasta, R., & Sarmiento, R. F. (1979). Liberal grading improves evaluations but not performance. *Journal of Educational Psychology, 71,* 207–211.

FOR FURTHER EXPLORATION

Kohn, A. (2004). *What does it mean to be well educated? And more essays on standards, grading and other follies.* Boston: Beacon Press.

Kohn, A. (2005). *Unconditional parenting: Moving from rewards and punishments to love and reason.* New York, NY: Atria Books.

Kohn, A. (2006). *The homework myth: Why our kids get too much of a bad thing.* Cambridge, MA: Da Capo Books.

Kohn, A. (2011). *Feel-bad education . . . And other contrarian essays on children and schooling.* Boston: Beacon Press.

Alfie Kohn is an author, speaker, and social critic.

16

Confessions of a "Bad" Teacher

William Johnson

I AM a special education teacher. My students have learning disabilities ranging from autism and attention-deficit disorder to cerebral palsy and emotional disturbances. I love these kids, but they can be a handful. Almost without exception, they struggle on standardized tests, frustrate their teachers and find it hard to connect with their peers. What's more, these are high school students, so their disabilities are compounded by raging hormones and social pressure.

As you might imagine, my job can be extremely difficult. Beyond the challenges posed by my students, budget cuts and changes to special-education policy have increased my workload drastically even over just the past 18 months. While my class sizes have grown, support staff members have been laid off. Students with increasingly severe disabilities are being pushed into more mainstream classrooms like mine, where they receive less individual attention and struggle to adapt to a curriculum driven by state-designed high-stakes tests.

On top of all that, I'm a bad teacher. That's not my opinion; it's how I'm labeled by the city's Education Department. Last June, my principal at the time rated my teaching "unsatisfactory," checking off a few boxes on an evaluation sheet that placed my career in limbo. That same year, my school received an "A" rating. I was a bad teacher at a good school. It was pretty humiliating.

NOTE: William Johnson. *Confessions of a "Bad" Teacher* from *The New York Times*, 3/4/2012 issue. Used with permission.

Like most teachers, I'm good some days, bad others. The same goes for my students. Last May, my assistant principal at the time observed me teaching in our school's "self-contained" classroom. A self-contained room is a separate classroom for students with extremely severe learning disabilities. In that room, I taught a writing class for students ages 14 to 17, whose reading levels ranged from third through seventh grades.

When the assistant principal walked in, one of these students, a freshman girl classified with an emotional disturbance, began cursing. When the assistant principal ignored her, she started cursing at me. Then she began lobbing pencils across the room. Was this because I was a bad teacher? I don't know.

I know that after she began throwing things, I sent her to the dean's office. I know that a few days later, I received notice that my lesson had been rated unsatisfactory because, among other things, I had sent this student to the dean instead of following our school's "guided discipline" procedure.

I was confused. Earlier last year, this same assistant principal observed me and instructed me to prioritize improving my "assertive voice" in the classroom. But about a month later, my principal observed me and told me to focus entirely on lesson planning, since she had no concerns about my classroom management. A few weeks earlier, she had written on my behalf for a citywide award for "classroom excellence." Was I really a bad teacher?

In my three years with the city schools, I've seen a teacher with 10 years of experience become convinced, after just a few observations, that he was a terrible teacher. A few months later, he quit teaching altogether. I collaborated with another teacher who sought psychiatric care for insomnia after a particularly intense round of observations. I myself transferred to a new school after being rated "unsatisfactory."

Behind all of this is the reality that teachers care a great deal about our work. At the school where I work today, my "bad" teaching has mostly been very successful. Even so, I leave work most days replaying lessons in my mind, wishing I'd done something differently. This isn't because my lessons are bad, but because I want to get better at my job.

In fact, I don't just want to get better; like most teachers I know, I'm a bit of a perfectionist. I have to be. Dozens and dozens of teenagers scrutinize my language, clothing and posture all day long, all week long. If I'm off my game, the students tell me. They comment on my taste in neckties, my facial hair, the quality of my lessons. All of us teachers are evaluated all day long, already. It's one of the most exhausting aspects of our job.

Teaching was a high-pressure job long before No Child Left Behind and the current debates about teacher evaluation. These debates seem to rest on the assumption that, left to our own devices, we teachers would be happy to coast through the school year, let our skills atrophy and collect our pensions.

The truth is, teachers don't need elected officials to motivate us. If our students are not learning, they let us know. They put their heads down or they pass notes. They raise their hands and ask for clarification. Sometimes, they just stare at us like zombies. Few things are more excruciating for a teacher than leading a class that's not learning. Good administrators use the evaluation processes to support teachers and help them avoid those painful classroom moments—not to weed out the teachers who don't produce good test scores or adhere to their pedagogical beliefs.

Worst of all, the more intense the pressure gets, the worse we teach. When I had administrators breathing down my neck, the students became a secondary concern. I simply did whatever my assistant principal asked me to do, even when I thought his ideas were crazy. In all honesty, my teaching probably became close to incoherent. One week, my assistant principal wanted me to focus on arranging the students' desks to fit with class activities, so I moved the desks around every day, just to show that I was a good soldier. I was scared of losing my job, and my students suffered for it.

That said, given all the support in the world, even the best teacher can't force his students to learn. Students aren't simply passive vessels, waiting to absorb information from their teachers and regurgitate it through high-stakes assessments. They make choices about what they will and won't learn. I know I did. When I was a teenager, I often stayed up way too late, talking with friends, listening to music or playing video games. Did this affect my performance on tests? Undoubtedly. Were my teachers responsible for these choices? No.

My best teachers, the ones I still think about today, exposed me to new and exciting ideas. They created classroom environments that welcomed discussion and intellectual risk-taking. Sometimes, these teachers' lessons didn't sink in until years after I'd left their classrooms. I'm thinking about Ms. Leonard, the English teacher who repeatedly instructed me to "write what you know," a lesson I've only recently begun to understand. She wasn't just teaching me about writing, by the way, but about being attentive to the details of my daily existence.

It wasn't Ms. Leonard's fault that 15-year-old me couldn't process this lesson completely. She was planting seeds that wouldn't bear fruit in the short term. That's an important part of what we teachers do, and it's the sort of thing that doesn't show up on high-stakes tests.

How, then, should we measure students and teachers? In ninth grade, my students learn about the scientific method. They learn that in order to collect good data, scientists control for specific variables and test their impact on otherwise identical environments. If you give some students green fields, glossy textbooks and lots of attention, you can't measure them against another group of students who lack all of these things. It's bad science.

Until we provide equal educational resources to all students and teachers, no matter where they come from, we can't say—with any scientific accuracy—how well or poorly they're performing. Perhaps if we start the conversation there, things will start making a bit more sense.

FOR FURTHER EXPLORATION

DiGiulio, R. C. (2004). *Great teaching: What matters most in helping students succeed.* Thousand Oaks, CA: Corwin.

Postman, N., & Weingartner, C. (1969). *Teaching as a subversive activity.* New York, NY: Random House.

Stuart, M. (2006). *The Hobart Shakespeareans.* New York, NY: Docurama.

Traina, R. (1999). What makes a good teacher? *Education Week, 18*(19), p. 34.

William Johnson is a teacher at a public high school in Brooklyn who writes on education for the Web site Gotham Schools. A version of this op-ed appeared in print on March 4, 2012, on page SR6 of the *New York Times* edition with the headline: Confessions of a 'Bad' Teacher.

17

How, and How Not, to Improve the Schools

Diane Ravitch

In his 2012 State of the Union address, President Barack Obama proposed that teachers should "stop teaching to the test" and that the nation should "reward the best ones" and "replace teachers who just aren't helping kids learn." This all sounds sensible, but it is in fact a contradictory message. The president's signature education program, called Race to the Top, encourages states to award bonuses to teachers whose students get higher test scores (they are, presumably "the best ones") and to fire teachers if their students get lower test scores (presumably the teachers "who just aren't helping kids"). If teachers want to stay employed, they must "teach to the test." The president recommends that teachers stop doing what his own policies make necessary and prudent.

Like George W. Bush's No Child Left Behind, Barack Obama's Race to the Top program is part of what Pasi Sahlberg calls "the Global Education Reform Movement," or GERM. GERM demands teaching to the test. GERM assumes that students must be constantly tested, and that the results of these tests are the most important measures and outcomes of education. The scores can be used not only to grade the quality of every school, but to punish or reward students, teachers, principals, and schools. Those at the top of the education system, the elected officials and leaders who make the rules, create the budgets, and allocate resources, are never accountable for the consequences of their decisions. GERM assumes that people who work in schools need carrots and sticks to persuade (or compel) them to do their best.

In Finland, the subject of the first part of this article,[1] teachers work collaboratively with other members of the school staff; they are not "held accountable" by standardized test scores because there are none. Teachers devise their own tests, to inform them about their students' progress and needs. They do their best because it is their professional responsibility. Like other professionals, as Pasi Sahlberg shows in his book *Finnish Lessons*, Finnish teachers are driven by a sense of intrinsic motivation, not by the hope of a bonus or the fear of being fired. Intrinsic motivation is also what they seek to instill in their students. In the absence of standardized testing by which to compare their students and their schools, teachers must develop, appeal to, and rely on their students' interest in learning.

The GERM model seeks to emulate the free market, by treating parents as consumers and students as products, with teachers as compliant workers who are expected to obey orders and follow scripts. Advocates of GERM often are hostile to teachers' unions, which are considered obstacles to the managerial ethos necessary to control the daily life of a school. Unions also make it hard, if not impossible, to carry out cost savings, such as removing the highest-paid teachers and replacing them with low-wage, entry-level teachers.

Finland's success confounds the GERM theorists, because almost every teacher and principal in Finland belongs to the same union. The union works closely with the Ministry of Education to improve the quality of education, and it negotiates for better salaries, benefits, and working conditions for educators.

The American school reform movement—the odd coalition of corporate-friendly Democrats, right-wing Republicans, Tea Party governors, Wall Street executives, and major foundations—proudly advocates the tenets of GERM. More testing, more privately managed schools, more deregulation, more firing of teachers, more school closings, they believe, and eventually every student will go to college and poverty will be eliminated. There is little evidence to support this approach.

The Duke University economist Helen F. Ladd recently delivered a major address titled "Education and Poverty: Confronting the Evidence," in which she demonstrated that poverty drags down academic performance, not only in the United States, but in other nations as well.[2] To argue, as so many of the corporate reformers blithely do, that poverty is used as "an excuse" for bad teachers is either naive or ignorant. Or it may be a way of avoiding the politically difficult subjects of poverty and income inequality, both of which are rising and threaten the well-being of our society.

The corporate reformers believe that entrepreneurship will unleash a new era of innovation and creativity, but it seems mostly to have unleashed canny entrepreneurs who seek higher test scores by any means possible (such as excluding students with disabilities or students learning English as a second language) or who seek maximum profit. One facet of the business plan for reform is reducing the cost of instruction. Many governors tackle this head-on by slashing the budget and laying off teachers. Others, claiming to act in the name of "reform," replace teachers with online instruction. Another way to reduce costs is to rely on inexperienced teachers, who are at the bottom of the salary scale and are likely to leave teaching for more remunerative, less demanding jobs before they are eligible for a pension.

Experienced teachers are fleeing American public education in response to the testing demands of No Child Left Behind, which reduce professional autonomy. According to federal data, the "modal years" of teacher experience in our public schools in 1987–1988 was fifteen, meaning that there were more teachers with fifteen years of experience than any other group. By 2007–2008, the largest number of teachers were in their first year of teaching. In response to the ongoing drumbeat of public opprobrium inspired by corporate-style school reform, we are losing the experienced teachers that students and new teachers need.

Unlike Finland, where entry into teaching is limited and competitive, the United States has low standards for new teachers. In Finland the profession is highly esteemed; in the United States it is not. Some states require master's degrees, some do not. The difference is not compensation but the high degree of professionalism that Finland expects of its teachers. In the United States, some states and districts require teachers to have a degree in the subject they teach or to pass a test to demonstrate their mastery of their subject; some do not.

Schools of education are held in low esteem within the university system. Online universities now award the largest numbers of master's degrees in education. The teaching profession in the United States is a revolving door. It's easy to enter, and many teachers leave—up to 40 to 50 percent—in their first five years as teachers. The turnover is highest in low-scoring urban districts. We do not support new teachers with appropriate training and mentoring, and we have a problem retaining teachers. No other profession in the United States has such a high rate of turnover.

For those who take seriously the need to improve the teaching profession, this would seem to be the right time to raise entry standards and to improve teacher education. If we were to learn from Finland's example, we would select well-educated candidates for entry into teaching, require academic excellence and a master's degree, and make certification as an education professional meaningful. But corporate reformers have shown no interest in raising standards for the teaching profession. They believe that entry-level requirements such as certification, master's degrees, and other credentials are unrelated to "performance," that is, student test scores. They also scorn seniority, experience, tenure, and other perquisites of the profession. Instead, they believe that a steady infusion of smart but barely trained novices will change the face of teaching. In no other field but education would such judgments be tolerated, because they reinforce the low status of education as a profession, one where no prolonged preparation is thought necessary.

The "corporate reformers'" favorite remedy for the ills of the profession is the Teach for America program. By now, everyone in the education field knows the story of how the Princeton student Wendy Kopp developed the idea for Teach for America as her senior thesis in 1989, then raised millions of dollars from corporations and turned her idea into a wildly successful brand. TFA enlists new graduates from the nation's best colleges and universities, who commit themselves to teach in distressed urban and rural schools for two years. In the past decade, Kopp has raised hundreds of millions of dollars for TFA.

Just in the past eighteen months, TFA received $50 million from the U.S. Department of Education, $49.5 million from the ultra-conservative Walton Family Foundation, and $100 million from a consortium of other foundations, as well as additional millions from corporations and other major donors. Each year, TFA selects several thousand idealistic young people, gives them five weeks of training, and sends them out to teach. The school districts pay members of TFA a starting teacher's salary and typically pay TFA $5,000 for each new teacher.

TFA, like the Peace Corps, is an admirable idea. The young people who join TFA are typically among our brightest students from top-tier universities. On some campuses, more students apply to TFA than to any other prospective employer. Like others who become teachers, they want to make a difference in the lives of children, particularly those who are poor.

And yet TFA has aroused the anger of veteran educators because of the organization's arrogance. TFA claims that its young recruits are better than other teachers, presumably because they are carefully selected and therefore smarter than the average teacher. It also claims that its corps members produce remarkable results even in the two or three years that most are likely to teach. But researchers such as Linda Darling-Hammond at Stanford, Barbara Torre Veltri at Northern Arizona University, Philip Kovacs at the University of Alabama, and Julian Vasquez Heilig at the University of Texas have challenged TFA's claims.[3] They maintain that the students of TFA's young recruits have not achieved the remarkable test score gains that the organization boasts about. Critics ask why inexperienced young graduates are permitted to teach the nation's most vulnerable children. Veteran educators resent the suggestion that new college graduates have arrived to save their schools; they know that novices with a few weeks' training, no matter how smart and idealistic, can't be expected to produce dramatic results in two or three years as a teacher.

Teach for America is a worthy idea. It is wonderful to encourage young people to commit themselves to public service for two years. The program would be far more admirable if the organization showed some modesty, humility, and realism in its claims for its inexperienced teachers. Many foundations, corporations, and even the U.S. Department of Education treat TFA as a systemic solution to the critical needs of the teaching profession. But it is foolhardy to expect that a profession of more than three million teachers will be transformed by the annual addition of a few thousand college graduates who agree to stay for only two years.

Teach for America is no substitute for the deep changes needed in the recruitment, support, and retention of career educators. Our nation's schools need professional teachers who have had the kind of intensive preparation and practice that nations like Finland insist upon. The Peace Corps sends out young people to do whatever is required in impoverished communities, not to serve as full-fledged Foreign Service officers for two years. Nor is it realistic to claim that these young people, because they are smart, can fix American schools and end the inequities in American society by teaching for a few years. If only it were that easy!

The current reform movement in education has embraced Teach for America and privately managed charter schools as remedies for the nation's schools. But this combination is unlikely to succeed because one alienates career educators and the other destabilizes our public education system. It is hard to imagine improving the schools without the support and trust of the people who work in them every day.

Under pressure from the Obama administration's Race to the Top program, many state legislatures have recently passed laws to evaluate the effectiveness of teachers in relation to the test scores of their students. This is very questionable, not least because most teachers do not teach subjects that are tested (only reading and mathematics in grades 3–8 are regularly tested, but not history, science, civics, the arts, foreign languages, or other subjects). Many economists are excited about measuring teachers by "results" in this way, but test publishers warn that the tests measure student performance, not teacher quality.

Although many legislatures want student scores to count for as much as 50 percent of a teacher's evaluation, these measures turn out to be inaccurate, unreliable, and unstable. Students are not randomly assigned, and the scores say more about the composition of a class than about the quality of the teacher. A teacher may look highly effective one year but ineffective the next, depending on which students end up in his or her classroom. Research has demonstrated that those who teach students with disabilities, students who are just learning English, and other students with high needs are less likely to get big test score gains and more likely to be rated as "bad" teachers. By imposing such indiscriminate standards, some excellent teachers will be fired, and others of less distinction will get bonuses. No profession worthy of being considered a profession would allow legislatures to determine how to assess the quality of its practitioners. They are not competent to do so. Part of the definition of a profession is that it is self-regulating, not subservient to external mandates. More self-regulation and professionalism is needed in teaching, not less.

The problems of American education are not unsolvable, but the remedies must be rooted in reality. Schools are crucial institutions in our society and teachers can make a huge difference in changing children's lives, but schools and teachers alone cannot cure the ills of an unequal and stratified society. Every testing program—whether the SAT, the ACT, or state and national tests—demonstrates that low scores are strongly correlated to poverty. On the SAT, for example, students from the most affluent families have the highest scores, and children from the poorest families have the lowest scores. Children need better schools, and they also need health clinics, high-quality early childhood education, arts programs, after-school activities, safe neighborhoods, and basic economic security. To the extent that we reduce poverty, we will improve student achievement.

So what does Finland teach us? We need to raise the standards for entry into the teaching profession, and future teachers should have intensive professional and academic preparation. If we were to improve the teaching profession, then perhaps more of the talented young people who now apply to Teach for America would choose to enter teaching as a career, not as a stepping stone to graduate school or another more remunerative line of work. If teaching were to become admired and prestigious, our schools would certainly benefit. But no matter how admired the teaching profession becomes, our society must do much more to reduce poverty and to improve the lives of children and families.

NOTES

1. Diane Ravitch, "Schools We Can Envy," *The New York Review*, March 8, 2012.

2. Working Paper SAN11-01, Sanford School of Public Policy, Duke University, November 4, 2011; forthcoming in *The Journal of Policy Analysis and Management*.

3. See Julian Vasquez Heilig, "Teach for America: A False Promise," National Education Policy Center, June 9, 2010; Philip Kovacs, "Huntsville Takes a Closer Look at Teach for America's 'Research,'" *Living in Dialogue* (blog), *Education Week*, December 11, 2011; Philip Kovacs, "Research Suggests Teach for America Does Not Belong in Huntsville," *Living in Dialogue* (blog), *Education Week* , January 9, 2012; Linda Darling-Hammond, Deborah J. Holtzman, Su Jin Gatlin, and Julian Vasquez Heilig, "Does Teacher Preparation Matter? Evidence About Teacher Certification and Teacher Effectiveness," *Education Policy Analysis Archives*, Vol. 13 (2005); Barbara Torre Veltri, *Learning on Other People's Kids: Becoming a Teach for America Teacher* (Information Age, 2010).

FOR FURTHER EXPLORATION

Ravitch, D. (2001). *Left back: A century of battles over school reform*. New York, NY: Simon & Schuster.

Ravitch, D. (2003). *Making good citizens: Education and civil society*. New Haven, CT: Yale University Press.

Ravitch, D. (2010). *The death and life of the great American school system: How testing and choice are undermining education*. New York, NY: Basic Books.

Ravitch, D., & Viteritti, J. (2000). *City schools: Lessons from New York*. Baltimore, MD: The John Hopkins University Press.

PART VI

How Does One Develop a Critical Voice?

I t's August 26th and, together with my colleagues, I'm gearing up for yet another—in a seemingly endless series—professional development workshop designed to tell me how to "do it right." Every year, usually right before school begins, the district brings in a math consultant, or a behavior specialist, or a literacy coach, or a curriculum expert, or an assessment guru or . . . for goodness sake, who knew there were so many authorities on teaching that don't have their own classrooms, may never have worked with kids?

Dutifully, I attend the scheduled sessions anyway, as I always do. There are no surprises. The other teachers, too, have gotten used to the routine. The district has brought in a consultant for the day to train us to use newly established reading standards. We take our seats and thumb through our resource packages as the consultant makes a PowerPoint presentation on the importance of the standards, exactly how they will be implemented, and how the state assessment will monitor student reading achievement. We listen attentively. There are a few questions and the consultant does her best to answer concerns. Most concerns are deflected with the statement, "This is the direction that everybody is heading." After lunch, small grade-level focus groups meet. The discussions are collegial, cordial; as teachers we are all compliant. Time well spent. Very professional. Everyone agrees. I guess I better start modifying my plans to align with the new district approach.

How should a teacher respond? If a teacher disagrees, then what words should he or she use? What shall be the tone?

18

Teachers as Transformative Intellectuals

Henry Giroux

T he call for educational reform has gained the status of a recurring national event, much like the annual Boston Marathon. There have been more than 30 national reports since the beginning of the 20th century, and more than 300 task forces have been developed by the various states to discover how public schools can improve educational quality in the United States.[1] But unlike many past educational reform movements, the present call for educational change presents both a threat and challenge to public school teachers that appears unprecedented in our nation's history. The threat comes in the form of a series of educational reforms that display little confidence in the ability of public school teachers to provide intellectual and moral leadership for our nation's youth. For instance, many of the recommendations that have emerged in the current debate either ignore the role teachers play in preparing learners to be active and critical citizens, or they suggest reforms that ignore the intelligence, judgment and experience that teachers might offer in such a debate. Where teachers do enter the debate, they are the object of educational reforms that reduce them to the status of high-level technicians carrying out dictates and objectives decided by "experts" far removed from the everyday realities of classroom life.[2] The message appears to

NOTE: "Teachers as Transformative Intellectuals" by Henry Giroux. - *Social Education*, 49(5), 376–379. Reprinted with permission.

be that teachers do not count when it comes to critically examining the nature and process of educational reform.

The political and ideological climate does not look favorable for teachers at the moment. But it does offer them the challenge to join in a public debate with their critics as well as the opportunity to engage in a much-needed self-critique regarding the nature and purpose of teacher preparation, inservice teacher programs and the dominant forms of classroom teaching. Similarly, the debate provides teachers with the opportunity to organize collectively so as to struggle to improve the conditions under which they work and to demonstrate to the public the central role that teachers must play in any viable attempt to reform the public schools.

In order for teachers and others to engage in such a debate, it is necessary that a theoretical perspective be developed that redefines the nature of the educational crisis while simultaneously providing the basis for an alternative view of teacher training and work. In short, recognizing that the current crisis in education largely has to do with the developing trend towards the disempowerment of teachers at all levels of education is a necessary theoretical precondition in order for teachers to organize effectively and establish a collective voice in the current debate. Moreover, such a recognition will have to come to grips not only with a growing loss of power among teachers around the basic conditions of their work, but also with a changing public perception of their role as reflective practitioners.

I want to make a small theoretical contribution to this debate and the challenge it calls forth by examining two major problems that need to be addressed in the interest of improving the quality of teacher work, which includes all the clerical tasks and extra assignments as well as classroom instruction. First, I think it is imperative to examine the ideological and material forces that have contributed to what I want to call the proletarianization of teacher work; that is, the tendency to reduce teachers to the status of specialized technicians within the school bureaucracy, whose function then becomes one of managing and implementing curricula programs rather than developing or critically appropriating curricula to fit specific pedagogical concerns. Second, there is a need to defend schools as institutions essential to maintaining and developing a critical democracy and also to defending teachers as transformative intellectuals who combine scholarly reflection and practice in the service of educating students to be thoughtful, active citizens. In the remainder of this essay, I will develop these points and conclude by examining their implications for providing an alternative view of teacher work.

TOWARD A DEVALUING AND
DESKILLING OF TEACHER WORK

One of the major threats facing prospective and existing teachers within the public schools is the increasing development of instrumental ideologies that emphasize a technocratic approach to both teacher preparation and classroom pedagogy. At the core of the current emphasis on instrumental and pragmatic factors in school life are a number of important pedagogical assumptions. These include: a call for the separation of conception from execution; the standardization of school knowledge in the interest of managing and controlling it; and the devaluation of critical, intellectual work on the part of teachers and students for the primacy of practical considerations.[3]

This type of instrumental rationality finds one of its strongest expressions historically in the training of prospective teachers. That teacher training programs in the United States have long been dominated by a behavioristic orientation and emphasis on mastering subject areas and methods of teaching is well documented.[4] The implications of this approach, made clear by Zeichner, are worth repeating:

> Underlying this orientation to teacher education is a metaphor of "production," a view of teaching as an "applied science" and a view of the teacher as primarily an "executor" of the laws and principles of effective teaching. Prospective teachers may or may not proceed through the curriculum at their own pace and may participate in varied or standardized learning activities, but that which they are to master is limited in scope (e.g., to a body of professional content knowledge and teaching skills) and is fully determined in advance by others often on the basis of research on teacher effectiveness. The prospective teacher is viewed primarily as a passive recipient of this professional knowledge and plays little part in determining the substance and direction of his or her preparation program.[5]

The problems with this approach are evident in John Dewey's argument that teacher training programs that emphasize only technical expertise do a disservice both to the nature of teaching and to their students.[6] Instead of learning to reflect upon the principles that structure classroom life and practice, prospective teachers are taught methodologies that appear to deny the very need for critical thinking. The point is that teacher education programs often lose sight of the need to educate students to examine the underlying nature of school problems. Further, these programs need to substitute for the language of management and efficiency a critical analysis of the less obvious conditions that structure the ideological and material practices of schooling.

Instead of learning to raise questions about the principles underlying different classroom methods, research techniques and theories of education, students are often preoccupied with learning the "how to," with "what works," or with mastering the best way to teach a *given* body of knowledge. For example, the mandatory field-practice seminars often consist of students sharing with each other the techniques they have used in managing and controlling classroom discipline, organizing a day's activities and learning how to work within specific time tables. Examining one such program, Jesse Goodman raises some important questions about the incapacitating silences it embodies. He writes:

> There was no questioning of feelings, assumptions, or definitions in this discussion. For example, the "need" for external rewards and punishments to "make kids learn" was taken for granted; the educational and ethical implications were not addressed. There was no display of concern for stimulating or nurturing a child's intrinsic desire to learn. Definitions of *good kids* as "quiet kids," *workbook work* as "reading," *on task time* as "learning," and *getting through the material on time* as "the goal of teaching"—all went unchallenged. Feelings of pressure and possible guilt about not keeping to time schedules also went unexplored. The real concern in this discussion was that everyone "shared."[7]

Technocratic and instrumental rationalities are also at work within the teaching field itself, and they play an increasing role in reducing teacher autonomy with respect to the development and planning of curricula and the judging and implementation of instruction. This is most evident in the proliferation of what has been called "teacher-proof" curriculum packages.[8] The underlying rationale in many of these packages reserves for teachers the role of simply carrying out predetermined content and instructional procedures. The method and aim of such packages is to legitimate what I call management pedagogies. That is, knowledge is broken down into discrete parts, standardized for easier management and consumption, and measured through predefined forms of assessment. Curricula approaches of this sort are management pedagogies because the central questions regarding learning are reduced to the problem of management, i.e., "how to allocate resources (teachers, students and materials) to produce the maximum number of certified . . . students within a designated time."[9] The underlying theoretical assumption that guides this type of pedagogy is that the behavior of teachers needs to be controlled and made consistent and predictable across different schools and student populations.

What is clear in this approach is that it organizes school life around curricular, instructional and evaluation experts who do the thinking while teachers are reduced to doing the implementing. The effect is not only to deskill teachers, to remove them from the processes of deliberation and reflection, but also to routinize the nature of learning and classroom pedagogy. Needless to say, the principles underlying management pedagogies are at odds with the premise that teachers should be actively involved in producing curricula materials suited to the cultural and social contexts in which they teach. More specifically, the narrowing of curricula choices to a back-to-basics format, and the introduction of lock-step, time-on-task pedagogies operate from the theoretically erroneous assumption that all students can learn from the same materials, classroom instructional techniques and modes of evaluation. The notion that students come from different histories and embody different experiences, linguistic practices, cultures and talents is strategically ignored within the logic and accountability of management pedagogy theory.

TEACHERS AS TRANSFORMATIVE INTELLECTUALS

In what follows, I want to argue that one way to rethink and restructure the nature of teacher work is to view teachers as transformative intellectuals. The category of intellectual is helpful in a number of ways. First, it provides a theoretical basis for examining teacher work as a form of intellectual labor, as opposed to defining it in purely instrumental or technical terms. Second, it clarifies the kinds of ideological and practical conditions necessary for teachers to function as intellectuals. Third, it helps to make clear the role teachers play in producing and legitimating various political, economic and social interests through the pedagogies they endorse and utilize.

By viewing teachers as intellectuals, we can illuminate the important idea that all human activity involves some form of thinking. In other words, no activity, regardless of how routinized it might become, can be abstracted from the functioning of the mind in some capacity. This is a crucial issue because by arguing that the use of the mind is a general part of all human activity we dignify the human capacity for integrating thinking and practice, and in doing so highlight the core of what it means to view teachers as reflective practitioners. Within this discourse, teachers can be seen not merely as "performers profession-ally equipped to realize effectively any goals that may be set for them. Rather [they should] be viewed as free men and women with a special dedication to the values of the intellect and the enhancement of the critical powers of the young."[10]

Viewing teachers as intellectuals also provides a strong theoretical critique of technocratic and instrumental ideologies underlying an educational theory that separates the conceptualization, planning and design of curricula from the processes of implementation and execu-tion. It is important to stress that teachers must take active responsibil-ity for raising various questions about what they teach, how they are to teach, and what the larger goals are for which they are striving. This means that they must take a responsible role in shaping the purposes and conditions of schooling. Such a task is impossible within a division of labor in which teachers have little influence over the ideological and economic conditions of their work. This point has a normative and political dimension that seems especially relevant for teachers. If we believe that the role of teaching cannot he reduced to merely training in the practical skills, but involves, instead, the education of a class of intellectuals vital to the development of a free society, then the category of intellectual becomes a way of linking the purpose of teacher educa-tion, public schooling and inservice training to the very principles necessary for developing a democratic order and society.

I have argued that by viewing teachers as intellectuals those per-sons concerned with education can begin to rethink and reform the traditions and conditions that have prevented schools and teachers from assuming their full potential as active, reflective scholars and practitioners. It is imperative that I qualify this point and extend it further. I believe that it is important not only to view teachers as intel-lectuals, but also to contextualize in political and normative terms the concrete social functions that teachers perform. In this way, we can be more specific about the different relations that teachers have both to their work and to the dominant society.

A fundamental starting point for interrogating the social function of teachers as intellectuals is to view schools as economic, cultural and social sites that are inextricably tied to the issues of power and control. This means that schools do more than pass on in an objective fashion a common set of values and knowledge. On the contrary, schools are places that represent forms of knowledge, language practices, social relations and values that are representative of a particular selection and exclusion from the wider culture. As such, schools serve to introduce and legitimate *particular* forms of social life. Rather than being objective institutions removed from the dynamics of politics and power, schools actually are contested spheres that embody and express a struggle over what forms of authority, types of knowledge, forms of moral regulation and versions of the past and future should be legitimated and transmitted to students. This struggle is most visible in the demands, for example, of right-wing religious groups currently trying to institute school prayer, remove certain books from the school library, and include certain forms of religious teachings in the science curricula. Of course, different demands are made by feminists, ecologists, minorities and other interest groups who believe that the schools should teach women's studies, courses on the environment, or black history. In short, schools are not neutral sites, and teachers cannot assume the posture of being neutral either.

In the broadest sense, teachers as intellectuals have to be seen in terms of the ideological and political interests that structure the nature of the discourse, classroom social relations and values that they legitimate in their teaching. With this perspective in mind, I want to conclude that teachers should become transformative intellectuals if they are to subscribe to a view of pedagogy that believes in educating students to be active, critical citizens.

Central to the category of transformative intellectual is the necessity of making the pedagogical more political and the political more pedagogical. Making the pedagogical more political means inserting schooling directly into the political sphere by arguing that schooling represents both a struggle to define meaning and a struggle over power relations. Within this perspective, critical reflection and action become part of a fundamental social project to help students develop a deep and abiding faith in the struggle to overcome economic, political and social injustices, and to further humanize themselves as part of this struggle. In this case, knowledge and power are inextricably linked to the presupposition that to choose life, to recognize the necessity of improving its democratic and qualitative character for all people, is to understand the preconditions necessary to struggle for it.

Making the political more pedagogical means utilizing forms of pedagogy that embody political interests that are emancipatory in nature; that is, using forms of pedagogy that treat students as critical agents; make knowledge problematic; utilize critical and affirming dialogue; and make the case for struggling for a qualitatively better world for all people. In part, this suggests that transformative intellectuals take seriously the need to give students an active voice in their learning experiences. It also means developing a critical vernacular that is attentive to problems experienced at the level of everyday life, particularly as they are related to pedagogical experiences connected to classroom practice. As such, the pedagogical starting point for such intellectuals is not the isolated student but individuals and groups in their various cultural, class, racial, historical and gender settings, along with the particularity of their diverse problems, hopes and dreams.

Transformative intellectuals need to develop a discourse that unites the language of critique with the language of possibility, so that social educators recognize that they can make changes. In doing so, they must speak out against economic, political and social injustices both within and outside of schools. At the same time, they must work to create the conditions that give students the opportunity to become citizens who have the knowledge and courage to struggle in order to make despair unconvincing and hope practical. As difficult as this tack may seem to social educators, it is a struggle worth waging. To do otherwise is to deny social educators the opportunity to assume the role of transformative intellectuals.

NOTES

1. K. Patricia Cross, "The Rising Tide of School Reform Reports," *Phi Delta Kappan*, 66:3 (November 1984), p. 167.

2. For a more detailed critique of the reforms, see my book with Stanley Aronowitz, *Education Under Siege* (South Hadley, MA: Bergin and Garvey Publishers, 1985); also see the incisive comments on the impositional nature of the various reports in Charles A. Tesconi, Jr., "Additive Reforms and the Retreat from Purpose," *Educational Studies* 15:1 (Spring 1984), pp. 1–11: Terrence E. Deal, "Searching for the Wizard: The Quest for Excellence in Education," *Issues in Education* 2:1 (Summer 1984), pp. 56–67; Svi Shapiro, "Choosing Our Educational Legacy: Disempowerment or Emancipation?" *Issues in Education* 2:1 (Summer 1984), pp. 11–22.

3. For an exceptional commentary on the need to educate teachers to be intellectuals, see John Dewey, "The Relation of Theory to Practice," in John Dewey, *The Middle Words, 1899–1924*, edited by Jo Ann Boydston (Carbondale: Southern Illinois University Press, 1977) [originally published in 1904]. See also, Israel Scheffler, "University Scholarship and the Education of Teachers," *Teachers College Record*, 70:1 (1968), pp. 1–12; Henry A. Giroux, *Ideology, Culture, and the Process of Schooling* (Philadelphia: Temple University Press, 1981).

4. See, for instance, Herbert Kliebard, "The Question of Teacher Education," in D. McCarty (ed.), *New Perspectives on Teacher Education* (San Francisco: Jossey-Bass, 1973).

5. Kenneth M. Zeichner, "Alternative Paradigms on Teacher Education," *Journal of Teacher Education* 34:3 (May–June 1983), p. 4.

6. Dewey, op. cit.

7. Jesse Goodman, "Reflection and Teacher Education: A Case Study and Theoretical Analysis," *Interchange* 15:3 (1984), p. 15.

8. Michael Apple, *Education and Power* (Boston: Routledge & Kegan Paul, Ltd., 1982).

9. Patrick Shannon, "Mastery Learning in Reading and the Control of Teachers and Students," *Language Arts* 61:5 (September 1984), p. 488.

10. Israel Scheffler, op. cit., p. 11.

FOR FURTHER EXPLORATION

Giroux, H. (2011). *Education and the crisis of public values: Challenging the assault on teachers, students, and public education.* New York, NY: Peter Lang Publishing.

Giroux, H. (2011). *Education and public sphere: Ideas of radical pedagogy.* Cracow, Poland: Impuls.

Giroux, H. (2011). *On critical pedagogy.* New York City, NY: Continuum.

Giroux, H. (2011). *Zombie politics in the age of casino capitalism.* New York, NY: Peter Lang Publishing

Henry Giroux is the Global Television Network Chair in English and Cultural Studies at McMaster University.

19

Resistance and Courage

A Conversation With Deborah Meier

Alan Canestrari: What does teaching require these days?

Deborah Meier: First of all, any kind of teaching requires toughness. You have to have firm convictions about a whole lot of stuff that you are not, in fact, always so sure about. But, if a kid asks can he sharpen his pencil or go to the bathroom, you have to exercise a judgment pretty fast and firmly even if more than one good answer might make sense, or even be the right one. You have to be tough on yourself, so that at the end the day you're left with a bunch of unanswered questions of the "Could I have . . . ?" or "Maybe next time . . ." or even, "Did I just blow a great moment for . . . ?" And, you need to carve out of an exceedingly unleisurely profession, time to think . . . enough time to think about these sticky matters over time, realizing that all the odd living and reading you do can help you in finding the answers. And then, you need to be tough enough to stick to it.

Bruce Marlowe: Suppose your way of doing your work, exercising judgment—about those little things you mention like going to the bathroom or the big things about what's worth teaching—is very different than your colleagues' ways? Or very different from what the principal, school district, or state is invested in?

Meier: Now that's tougher still. And, these days, that's what many of us are struggling with—the plethora of external regulation about what our work is and how we do it. But of course in fact with rare exceptions,

---

NOTE: This reading consists of a conversation between the editors and Deborah Meier. Reprinted with permission.

those of us involved all our lives in public education have rarely been in situations where we have had to deal with anything less.

Today, though, we are witnessing something new. And there are some tough choices facing us in the teaching field as a result. After a decade or more of considerable "laissez-faire" between the mid-70s and the early 90s (it varied by locale) we're witnessing a retightening of the screws—with more of the screws coming from higher and more remote places, in a setting in which technology makes it harder to hide. The culture of privacy has been ripped apart—for reasons both good and bad. Thus, the kind of quiet, behind-closed-doors resistance that flourished during my earliest teaching years is more problematic. Today, the standardized curriculums and lesson plans which were always part of the traditional public schools—even when ignored—are being republished and reissued, in even greater detail. The old regime has been reinstalled, plus.

Canestrari: So, what lessons would you offer new teachers?

Meier: Number one is: How to survive. It probably helps to remember that this is not new. The technology to enforce it [teacher compliance] is more brutal, but the intent is old and familiar. And, it has, unfortunately, been accepted by too many men and women of good will as a necessity if all children are to meet "high standards."

When I first arrived in New York City there was a loosely enforced grade-by-grade curriculum, and fairly decent guides for carrying it out step-by-step. We survived in part by figuring out where we had space to deviate and where we didn't. In Head Start I was told teaching the names of numbers, letters, and colors was what we'd be tested on in June; but I figured if we did modestly well at that I could spend 90 percent of my time exploring more important stuff like the properties of real life. I realized I never met a kid of 8 who didn't know his colors—unless he was color blind and then drilling colors at age 4 was worse than useless. And the same would be true of the names of letters unless we persisted in teaching them to read formally too early and insisted that we use the names of the letters as a key way into such early instruction. Survival, in other words, depends on making some decisions about what's important, and living by them—most of the time.

Canestrari: Can teachers be effective in changing their conditions?

Meier: Of course, once they learn to survive. The second strategy is to organize—join with others. It starts with being a good colleague in one's own schools. Not easy work. Another way is through teacher and staff organizations. The power of solidarity among working people is still, or once again, obviously vital. As fewer unions exist nationwide, natural allies among other working people have lessened. But teacher unions also provide us with links to other organized working people.

But it's important to remember that it's not just joining with the teachers. For example, you may also be a parent. Don't hesitate to speak out in that role also, without feeling that somehow it's unfair or unwise. Not at all. We listen to what doctors say about the kind of medicine they want for their own kids. So you are doubly powerful in this dual role. But even if you decide to be just a parent in your child's school, be a loud one on behalf of the things you believe are good for all kids and teachers.

And then work, within both roles—as teacher and parent—for the strongest and loudest alliance between these two self-interested and powerful groups. If parents and teachers were truly able to use their strength in even a semi-united way, they'd overcome. But, we've allowed a rift to exist between us that serves others, but neither parents nor teachers. This is a time in history when we have to put the issues that unite us to the fore, and agree to disagree on others.

Then there's using your voice. I don't just mean your teacherly voice, but your broader professional voice. Find every way you can to hone your skills as a writer and speaker—to little audiences and big ones, letters to the editors included. And, not just on contentious reform issues. Speak out and write out as an expert on reading, or science, or classroom management, or children's aspirations. Insist on the idea that you are a theorist and an expert, not only a practitioner; don't make it easy to be seen as hardworking, dedicated, loving but a wee bit weak in the head and too prone to sentimentality, or likely to only see the faces in front of you, to miss the important systemic problems!

Then comes the last course of action. For those who can't find any of the above individual or group strategies feasible, and begin to find it hard to face themselves each morning in the mirror, it may be best to change schools, move to another less draconian locale, or even, dare I say it, quit teaching. There is other important work to be done in the world, including work on behalf of children. And, if and when you leave, don't miss the opportunity; don't go quietly and don't go blaming your former colleagues, families, or kids.

Marlowe: Any final advice for new teachers?

Meier: In each and every way that you work in the field, bring the best of yourself as a parent, citizen, and passionate learner into your work, and put "getting along" in perspective. Getting along helps smooth the way, no mean goal, and it makes for more allies, and it makes your voice more effective. Assuming that your colleagues (like the families whose kids you teach) want similar things, acting out of their best intentions is the place to begin. But, watch out when getting along starts becoming a way of life, and other people's good intentions begin to undermine your own. The "courage" you need is the courage to not excuse yourself too often for failing to do what needs doing, for pretending that bad practice—including your own—is good practice, or for seeing yourself and your colleagues as the enemy—or the victims. Victims don't make good teachers—because above all we want our kids to see themselves as competent actors who have learned how to be competent citizens from teachers who saw themselves as that— citizens of their schools and communities.

FOR FURTHER EXPLORATION

Capellaro, C. (2006). Conversations on quality: An interview with Deborah Meier. *Rethinking Schools, 20*(2), 23.

Deborah Meier. *Current Biography, 67*(5), 70–75.

Page, M.L. (2010). Speaking in a critical voice. In *Educational Foundations: An Anthology of Critical Readings 2nd Edition* (Eds. Canestrari, A. S. & Marlowe, B. A.).

Page, M. L. & Marlowe, B. A. (2000). Battered teacher syndrome: Using standards implementation as a weapon. *Education Week, 20*(15), 43, 46.

Deborah Meier is the principal of the Mission Hill Elementary School in Boston, Massachusetts.

20

From Silence to Dissent

Fostering Critical Voice in Teachers

Alan S. Canestrari and Bruce A. Marlowe

> In today's top-down school structures, new teachers need to develop capacities for critical reflection during pre-service training.

Despite their sense of expectation, enthusiasm, and energy, new teachers too often become assimilated into school cultures that are characterized by cynicism, resignation, and, ultimately, compliance. As Albert Shanker once famously remarked, it only takes about six weeks for new teachers to look like old ones. The reasons for this sad state of affairs are obviously complex, but we believe that such resignation is, at least in part, due to a lack of pre-service opportunity for potential teachers to think critically about the most salient characteristics of American public education.

Teacher preparation programs seem to cover every conceivable facet of teaching. However, in their breadth and their depoliticized, neutral stand on every question, they perpetuate what Tyack and Cuban (1995) refer to as the "grammar of schooling." That is, there is plenty of expository, rhetorical discourse describing the management of student behavior, methods of instruction, the construction of curricula, and the assessment of students. And, there is narrative too: for example, about what it is like to be a teacher. But there is virtually no critical discourse. As a result, the tone and level of student engagement with such programs rarely moves beyond the prosaic. Worse, when teacher preparation programs take a critical stance about current practices or provide examples of alternative models of teaching and learning, they do so in a way that invariably marginalizes these approaches as radical, impractical, or, at the very least, controversial. In part, this framing of the critical stance as extreme occurs because teachers no longer set the agenda.

In fact, teachers today have lost almost all control over their work. Few are capable of standing up to state-mandated, top-down curricular and instructional mandates. They are tightly constrained by school districts seeking compliance and higher test scores. We need critically literate teachers capable of challenging the technocratic demands of state-mandated curricula. Preparing such teachers must begin at the *pre-service* level; otherwise new teachers will find themselves looking very much like the old ones, mindlessly going through the motions without question or reflection.

But even when new teachers know that the top-down system is wholly inadequate, they lack clear direction as to how to move purposefully in another direction, to ask questions and challenge assumptions. But what questions should teachers ask? What answers should teachers accept? We hope new teachers will consider asking whether their instruction promotes the status quo. New teachers need models of critical reflection (and even dissent) in order to help them develop their *own* critical questions, their *own* voice, by being given the opportunity to engage in serious conversations about learning and teaching in the context of increasing pressures for accountability and uniformity of instruction.

Serious discussions with our students about teaching and learning inevitably begin with what we have begun to call the "Yes, but..." question because this is how the conversation inevitably begins. That is, after introducing commonsense—and-research-based—notions about teaching and learning we frequently hear, for example,

- Yes, but... won't I have to teach to the test if the district demands that scores on statewide assessments improve?

- Yes, but... what if the principal requires that all second grade classrooms work on math at 9:15, regardless of my kids' needs or interests on a particular day?

- Yes, but... what if the school district adopts basal readers and requires that we use them to the exclusion of other approaches and instructional activities?

- Yes, but... what if the schoolwide discipline policy requires that kids stay in for recess if they don't finish their homework?

On several occasions we have used these "Yes, but . . ." questions as a point of departure, and after simply asking what our students thought about all of this, we taped the discussion that ensued. The conversations are invariably thoughtful, reflective, and insightful, and the occasional debate between students addresses exactly the kinds of questions new teachers should be contemplating. These include the kinds of teacher decisions that rise to the level of moral imperatives, about how we got where we are, about whether teachers should even make decisions about curriculum, and about the role teachers can, and should, play in the shaping of broader educational policy and decision making.

Imagine how our schools might be different if in-service teachers engaged in regular discussions like the one below about whether the mandates they face are consistent with their view of what is in the best interest of their students.

Jane: But, what do we do when we are asked to do something we know isn't right, or is contrary to what we've learned in some of our classes here? I just had a class in literacy where we talked about how research indicates that "Round Robin" reading is not best practice. And yet, the classroom I'm in now as a student teacher, that's all they do. It's the whole reading program.

Maya: As a new person, as a first year teacher I wouldn't say anything. I mean you don't have any credibility. You're the new kid on the block and you have to go along at first.

Marlowe: Will it be the same as a tenth year teacher? How long do you wait to do what you see as the right thing?

Ted: One thing we can count on is that what's wrong today will be right tomorrow. School reforms come in waves.

Canestrari: So will you allow yourself to be swept in and out with the tide?

Kate: Yeah, but I agree with Maya. You want the job, right? You're not going to say, "See ya later," because, I mean, good luck finding another job. There aren't that many out there so you do have to swim with the tide.

Alex: Should you risk losing your job by raising questions? Don't you have a larger responsibility to your family?

I mean what do we really know about teaching any-way? We're new. I agree with Maya too. We have to go along at first. After a while, maybe then you can say something. But, definitely not at first.

Marlowe: Is there a point at which you stop saying to yourself, "I'm just going to hold my tongue, and I'm not going to say a thing?" Okay, Jane mentioned round-robin read-ing. The stakes seem relatively low here. But, what about practices that you view as actually harmful? Is there a point at which you will respond to a principal's directive with "No, I won't do that"?

Ronald: I would. I would absolutely refuse if I thought morally or educationally something I was asked to do was wrong.

Kate: You need to be respectful though. Whether you agree or not, you are the rookie. So you can disagree I guess, but be tactful. Something like, "I know the test scores are down, and I realize that you want more seat time to help my students prepare for the tests, but I'm thinking about doing it a little differently. I've looked into the research . . ." Something like that, where you go into the discussion with the principal with a knowledge base, with some preparation. Then, maybe he will give a little bit too.

Sally: Isn't there a happy medium here where you can do something of yours and also what the curriculum might dictate? Just so that it's not completely one way or the other. You get to do some of what you want, what you know is right, what will work with kids, and you do some of what they want too.

Ronald: So, it's ok to do the harmful stuff, as long as you do the good stuff too?

Sally: Yeah, well, I mean . . . to some extent, maybe. No, I guess I wouldn't do the bad stuff. That doesn't make sense. I'm thinking there is stuff that needs to be taught that addresses the standards, but I guess actually, no, I won't do it if it's wrong.

We liken this evolving conversation to "spinning plates." As students formulate their positions and develop their own insights they are forced to consider the ideas of others through this dialectical exchange, thereby positioning another "plate" to be spun, another thought that must be considered. It is this emerging complexity that allows insights to move towards solutions. Notice how the following excerpt concerning teaching-to-the-test evolves with increasing clarity.

Jane: As a student teacher, I'm going to be in a predicament next semester. I'm going into a fourth grade class and I've already been told that we will be making a final push to prepare students for statewide assessments in the spring. Here, in our program, we're all told that we're not supposed to teach to the test, but I mean, my cooperating teacher couldn't have made it any clearer to me.

Canestrari: Testing has become a yearly event. The results are published in the paper and the schools are ranked from low to high performing. Do you have to pay attention to these results, or should you simply teach the way you know is best for your students?

Ryan: Well, again, as a beginning teacher, if I'm told that it's imperative that we do better on the tests, I would highly recommend that you teach more to the test. But, obviously, I mean you could maintain your teaching and still address the test issue.

Jane: Do I drop social studies? Science? My cooperating teacher didn't say specifically, "We're going to drop science," but there's no doubt in my mind that's what she meant when she said, "We need to prepare the students for the test."

Ronald: If we teach the right way won't students be prepared for the test anyway?

Kate: No. If there's a state-wide assessment in 5th grade in mathematics, and your job is to prepare students to do well on this test, what do you have to give up to do that? I agree that you can do lots of things the right way that will help them in math, but even if you do everything well to teach them math, but drop the rest of the curriculum to prepare for the math test, are you serving your students well?

Although not always sure of why these conversations are important, all of the students, as you will see in the exchange below, are certain that such conversations are a critical part of teacher education, and perhaps more importantly, should be part and parcel of the on-going professional development of in-service teachers as well. In fact, students are so certain of the importance of these conversations that once given the opportunity it is like the opening of the flood gates.

Megan: Isn't this what it's really about, carefully listening to and analyzing each other's views? I mean do real teachers do this? Do they ever really get to reflect on their practice, or do they just go through the motions?

Ted: I know I'm only beginning my student teaching, but I don't see this happening in my school. Is this what faculty meetings are like?

Ryan: I've been a long-term substitute for a whole semester and I've never been in a faculty meeting where there was a conversation like this. And I don't get it. Shouldn't teachers be engaged in this kind of discussion? Isn't this what should happen in a faculty meeting?

This exchange, and many more like it, underscores the perceived importance—even urgency—of addressing the "Yes, but ..." question. The taped transcripts reveal not only deep student reflection about weighty educational issues, but also important insights. Further, there is clearly an evolution in thinking unfolding here that underscores the value of engaging teachers in the kind of dialectical process advocated in the past by notable educators like Dewey (1938) and today by a whole host of critical theorists (e.g., Giroux, 1985; Zeichner, 1983).

Our students also came to some important conclusions about how deliberate attempts at creating a chorus of teachers' voices may be the profession's greatest hope for continuous renewal—a discussion that echoes an interview we conducted with Deborah Meier earlier last year. When asked, "Can teachers be effective in changing their conditions?" Meier responded:

Of course, once they learn to survive. The second strategy is to organize—join with others. It starts with being a good colleague in one's own schools. Not easy work. Another way is through teacher and staff organizations. The power of solidarity among working people is still, or once again, obviously vital ... Teacher unions also provide us with links to other organized working people. But, it's important to remember that it's not just joining with the teachers. For example, you may also be a parent. Don't hesitate to speak out in that role also . . . Then, there's using your professional voice. I don't just mean your teacherly voice, but your broader professional voice. (Canestrari & Marlowe, 2004, 214–215)

And, here is what our students had to say after a similar question.

Canestrari: How do good teachers get heard when they have a different vision than the administration about what a classroom should look like?

Mike: You are teaching a science kit lesson and you decide that it is going really well and so you ask the principal to sit in. Everybody is interactive, it's going great, learning is taking place or maybe someone else in the school is interested in a demonstration, and so you invite them into the room.

Ronald: Or you teach together. Let's try something here and approach this unit all from the same standpoint, teaching across content areas.

Ryan: Teaming through integration is powerful . . . building consensus, doing things even across grade levels by showing what really works.

Carissa: I think change requires one person first, and then you talk with someone else, and you have a partner and then it grows. Soon, collectively, you can make a push. At some point when districts will realize that it's come to the point where you have pockets of teachers yelling so loudly that you can't cover your ears up any more and even legislators, people dictating policy, administrators . . . they're going to have to start listening to what we know about good teaching.

As we probed further about how the "Yes, but . . ." conversation should be initiated, students expanded the focus of the discussion to larger questions about who should participate in such discussions and where they should occur. It was during this part of the conversation that many students realized for the first time that those above them face pressures too. We probed further, "Don't educational leaders have the most and best opportunities to engage in critical discourse?" Together, we came to some important conclusions. Like teachers, educational leaders can also cave in to internal and external pressures. These collapses are often exacerbated by hierarchical school cultures that have evolved into sorts of feudalistic protectorates where each layer of authority protects the layer below it; superintendents protect principals, principals protect teachers, in return for loyalty, compliance, and silence.

It also didn't take long for our students to see the very real ways in which the mandates they will soon face as teachers mirror those that we face as professors. This became abundantly clear as we pushed our students to reflect more deeply about exactly why they thought the discussion was so fruitful. Students were quick to point out that even at the post-secondary level mandatory assessment and grading policies often interfere with learning. As Schap has argued (in Kohn, 1994) grading policies interfere with learning when teachers use them as a way to assess the extent to which students have complied with their demands as opposed to using grades as supportive feedback to help guide student learning, to inform instruction, and to help teachers understand whether or not their pedagogy is effective. Discussing this demand versus support model of grading was eye-opening for many students; while they expressed discomfort with many of their grading experiences, they had never before really reflected on how, and for what purposes, grades might be employed. Some expressed surprise, and relief, that our discussion was ungraded. Because after reflection, the number of instructional activities students identified in their program that were explicitly evaluated struck many as inconsistent with what professors were telling them about good teaching and learning for its own sake. The fact that this activity was not graded was unique, even liberating. But, like our students who will soon be teachers, we too often have little say about whether to give grades. Similarly, as university professors in a teacher education program, we must worry about how our students will fare on standardized tests, as the state will make judgments about our program based on our students' performance. But assessment information based on standardized tests is often misleading and can be used to make dubious claims about how much students are actually learning or about the success of academic programs. It is for these reasons that we too perpetually face the "Yes, but . . ." question, a revelation for many students.

Canestrari: What's different about the conversation we're having now compared to discussions in other classes? What accounts for this very high level of engagement?

Steve: Look at the situation. Is this high risk or low risk? Are we getting graded? *No*, we're just having a conversation with no stakes attached and we're really learning the most in this kind of setting. Everyone wants to get involved. Remember what we read about the affective filter? [Laughter in class] To get back to the original question, yeah there is a place for this. We need this at both the undergraduate and graduate level. Look how everyone gets involved.

Ronald: In this university setting where everything is graded, everything is assessed, how can you maintain this level of engagement given a threatening environment? I mean we're still in a classroom where every experience, every paper, every assignment is graded and analyzed and evaluated and then we have pre-evals, in-process evals, post-evals . . . I just realized something!!! This is why kids hate school. Because the energy, the enthusiasm for learning gets sucked right out of them with all the obsessive focus on assessment.

Carissa: So you're really in the same position as we will soon be in as teachers. You have people above you telling you that you must give grades, as just one example. You don't really have a choice either.

The students that we engaged in conversation were junior and senior undergraduates and graduate masters degree students that were very close to their final field placements. Ironically, it is at the end of the program when they are closest to classrooms of their own, that our students become less secure as they reflect on the incongruity between what they are learning at the university and what they are seeing in public school classrooms. At a time when our students should be feeling more confident, more certain about the skills they have acquired, the dispositions they have adopted, they are instead feeling increasingly adrift; dissonance abounds. The "Yes, but . . ." question dominates their thinking and causes them to second guess their education and their good instincts.

Have we prepared our future teachers for the challenges that await them? Do our teacher education programs have enough emphasis on scholarship and tolerance for differing viewpoints? Have we engaged students in a way that allows them to think critically? Have we given them substantial preparation in articulating what's right in a way that either facilitates or causes others to rethink their classrooms? Have we prepared them in the art of resistance and dissent? Our suspicion is that we have not and our conviction is that these questions must frame teacher education.

But, perhaps, there is hope for those teachers who are prepared differently. Hope for those who have internalized Freire's (1970) desire for liberation in the form of "problem-posing education" or Giroux's (1985) insistence that teachers think of themselves as "transformative intellectuals" or even Postman and Weingartner's (1969) urging that teachers be vigilant "crap" detectors. Ohanian (2004) warns us that teachers must be educated rather than trained, that offering recipes leads only to the deskilling of teachers, that teaching practice be informed by philosophy and art and music rather than simply by experts "who promise the keys to classroom control and creative bulletin boards, along with 100 steps to reading success."

It was through the back and forth of our conversation, the student-to-student exchange, the horizontal communication between faculty and students where all participants were peers, that reminded us all of the importance and power of these kinds of discussions to inform teaching and learning.

REFERENCES

Canestrari, A., & Marlowe, B. A. (2004). *Educational foundations: An anthology of critical readings*. Thousand Oaks, CA: Sage.

Dewey, J. (1938). *Experience and education*. New York: Touchstone.

Freire, P. (1970). *Pedagogy of the oppressed*. New York: Continuum International Publishing Group.

Giroux, H. (1985). Teachers as transformative intellectuals. *Social Education, 49*(5), 376–379.

Kohn, A. (1994). Grading: The issue is not how, but why. *Educational Leadership 52*(2), 38–41.

Marlowe, B. A., & Page, M. L. (1998). *Creating and sustaining the constructivist classroom*. Thousand Oaks, CA: Corwin.

Ohanian, S. (2004). On stir and serve recipes for teaching. In *Educational foundations: An anthology of critical readings*, Canestrari, A., & Marlowe, B. A. (Eds.). Thousand Oaks, CA: Sage.

Postman, N., & Weingartner, C. (1969). *Teaching as a subversive activity*. New York: Delacort.

Spinner, H., & Fraser, B. J. (2002). *Evaluation of an innovative mathematics program in terms of classroom environment, student attitudes, and conceptual development*. (ERIC Document Reproduction Service Number ED464829)

Tyack, D., & Cuban, L. (1995). *Tinkering toward Utopia: A century of public school reform*. Cambridge: Harvard University Press.

Zeichner, K. M. (1983, May-June). Alternative paradigms of teacher education. *Journal of Teacher Education 34*(3), 4.

FOR FURTHER EXPLORATION

Canestrari, A. S. (2005). Social studies and geography: Beyond rote memorization. In *Integrating Inquiry Across the Curriculum* (R. H. Audet & L. K. Jordan (Eds.), Thousand Oaks, CA: Corwin.

Donnell, K., Yang, L., Winfield, A., Canestrari, A. S., Marlowe, B. A. & Kamii, M. (2008). Conversations about social justice. *Encounter: Education for Meaning and Social Justice, 21*(4).

Marlowe, B. A., & Canestrari, A. S. (2006). *Educational psychology in context: Readings for future teachers*. Thousand Oaks, CA: SAGE.

Thombs, M. M., Gillis, M. M., & Canestrari, A. S. (2008). *Using WebQuests in the social studies classroom: A culturally responsive approach*. Thousand Oaks, CA: SAGE.

PART VII

How Do We
Move Forward?

James is a single parent. He now lives in Providence, Rhode Island, with his daughter, Naomi. He is a devoted father who dreams of a bright future for her and does all he can to help Naomi take advantage of every opportunity that life has to offer, especially when it comes to schooling. He makes it a priority to know her teachers. He keeps abreast of what is going on at the school and in her classroom. And, when he can, he finds ways to extend and enhance her learning with as many resources that he can get his hands on. After a long day of work for James and school for Naomi, the two relax a bit before Dad starts the home version of the extended school day helping Naomi with homework and projects. Naomi does well in school.

Prior to living in Providence, James, so concerned with Naomi's learning and unimpressed with her teachers, actually withdrew his daughter from an elementary school in another city in Rhode Island and moved in order to enroll her in what he determined to be a better school. Naomi is happy. But for James . . . not so much.

He has discovered, over time, that the kind of attention and opportunities that he remembers being provided have become like folklore, barely existing in many teachers' memories. The pressures to do well on tests like the New England Common Assessment Program (NECAP) have crowded out from the curriculum a range of subjects that he remembers from his own school experience. He has noticed, for example, that science and music have disappeared. Good teachers, he says, "are between a rock and hard place." So James is spending more and more time not simply helping Naomi with homework but making up for what he thinks the school has come to ignore by buying science kits and enriching her opportunities for learning to make up for gaps in her schooling. Since attending a university forum, titled *Putting Equity into Action*, he has even more questions about his daughter's education and her future. Unsure about what to do, he wonders if he should enroll Naomi in the local charter school lottery?

21

Poor Teaching for Poor Children . . . in the Name of Reform

Alfie Kohn

L ove them or hate them, the proposals collectively known as "school reform" are mostly top-down policies: divert public money to quasi-private charter schools, pit states against one another in a race for federal education dollars, offer rewards when test scores go up, fire the teachers or close the schools when they don't.

Policy makers and the general public have paid much less attention to what happens inside classrooms—the particulars of teaching and learning—especially in low-income neighborhoods. The news here has been discouraging for quite some time, but, in a painfully ironic twist, things seem to be getting worse as a direct result of the "reform" strategies pursued by the Bush administration, then intensified under President Obama, and cheered by corporate executives and journalists.

In an article published in *Phi Delta Kappan* back in 1991, Martin Haberman, a professor at the University of Wisconsin, coined the phrase "pedagogy of poverty." Based on his observations in thousands of urban classrooms, Haberman described a tightly controlled routine in which teachers dispense, and then test students on, factual information; assign seatwork; and punish noncompliance. It is a regimen, he said, "in which learners can 'succeed' without becoming either involved or thought-ful"—and it is noticeably different from the questioning, discovering, arguing, and collaborating that is more common (though by no means universal) among students in suburban and private schools.

Now, two decades later, Haberman reports that "the overly directive, mind-numbing . . . anti-intellectual acts" that pass for teaching in most urban schools "not only remain the coin of the realm but have become the gold standard." It's how you're *supposed* to teach kids of color.

Earlier this year, Natalie Hopkinson, an African American writer, put it this way in an article called "The McEducation of the Negro": "In the name of reform . . . education—for those 'failing' urban kids, anyway—is about learning the rules and following directions. Not critical thinking. Not creativity. It's about how to correctly eliminate three out of four bubbles."

Those who demand that we "close the achievement gap" generally focus only on results, which in practice refers only to test scores. High-quality instruction is defined as whatever raises those scores. But when teaching strategies *are* considered, there is wide agreement (again, among noneducators) about what constitutes appropriate instruction in the inner city.

The curriculum consists of a series of separate skills, with more worksheets than real books, more rote practice than exploration of ideas, more memorization (sometimes assisted with chanting and clapping) than thinking. In books like *The Shame of the Nation*, Jonathan Kozol, another frequent visitor to urban schools, describes a mechanical, precisely paced process for drilling black and Latino children in "obsessively enumerated particles of amputated skill associated with upcoming state exams."

Not only is the teaching scripted, with students required to answer fact-based questions on command, but a system of almost militaristic behavior control is common, with public humiliation for noncompliance and an array of rewards for obedience that calls to mind the token economy programs developed in prisons and psychiatric hospitals.

Deborah Meier, the educator and author who has founded extraordinary schools in New York and Boston, points out that the very idea of "school" has radically different meanings for middle-class kids, who are "expected to have opinions," and poor kids, who are expected to do what they're told. Schools for the well-off are about inquiry and choices; schools for the poor are about drills and compliance. The two types of institutions "barely have any connection to each other," she says.

Adds Kozol: "The children of the suburbs learn to think and to interrogate reality," while inner-city kids "are trained for nonreflective acquiescence." (Work hard, be nice.) At one of the urban schools he visited, a teacher told him, "If there were middle-class white children here, the parents would rebel at this curriculum and stop it cold."

Among the research that has confirmed the disparity are two studies based on data from the periodic National Assessment of Educational Progress. One found that black children are much more likely than white children to be taught with workbooks or worksheets on a daily basis. The other revealed a racial disparity in how computers are used for instruction, with African Americans mostly getting drill and practice exercises (which, the study also found, are associated with poorer results).

Yet another study, by a researcher at Michigan State University, discovered that students in more affluent neighborhoods were given more choice in their reading, more opportunities to talk with one another about books, the chance to analyze and write poetry and to learn skills in the context of real literature.

Well before his brief tenure last year as New Jersey's Commissioner of Education, Bret Schundler expressed considerable enthusiasm about the sort of teaching that involves constant drill and repetition and "doesn't allow children not to answer." This approach is "bringing a lot of value-added for our children," he enthused. *Our* children? Does that mean he would send his own kids to that kind of school? Of course not. "Those schools are best for certain children," he explained.

The result is that "certain children" are left farther and farther behind. The rich get richer, while the poor get worksheets.

To be sure, the gap is not entirely due to how kids are taught. As economist Richard Rothstein reminds us, all school-related variables combined can explain only about one-third of the variation in student achievement. Similarly, if you look closely at those international test comparisons that supposedly find the U.S. trailing, it turns out that socioeconomic factors are largely responsible. Our wealthier students do very well compared to other countries; our poorer students do not. And we have more poor children than do other industrialized nations.

To whatever extent education does matter, though, the pedagogy of poverty traps those who are subject to it. The problem isn't that their education lacks "rigor"—in fact, a single-minded focus on *"raising the bar"* has served mostly to push more low-income youths out of school— but that it lacks depth and relevance and the capacity to engage students. As Deborah Stipek, dean of Stanford's School of Education, once commented, drill-and-skill instruction isn't how middle-class children got their edge, so "why use a strategy to help poor kids catch up that didn't help middle class kids in the first place?"

Essentially the same point has been made by one educational expert after another, including two prominent African Americans in the field: Linda Darling-Hammond (who observed that the "most counterproductive [teaching] approaches" are "enforced most rigidly in the schools serving the most disadvantaged students") and Claude Steele ("a skills-focused, remedial education . . . virtually guarantee[s] the persistence of the race gap").

Rather than viewing the pedagogy of poverty as a disgrace, however, many of the charter schools championed by the new reformers have concentrated on perfecting and intensifying techniques to keep children "on task" and compel them to follow directions. (Interestingly, their carrot-and-stick methods mirror those used by policy makers to control educators.) Bunches of eager, mostly white, college students are invited to drop by for a couple of years to lend their energy to this dubious enterprise.

Is racism to blame here—or perhaps behaviorism? Or could it be that, at its core, the corporate version of "school reform" was never intended to promote thinking—let alone interest in learning—but merely to improve test results? That pressure is highest in the inner cities, where the scores are lowest. And the pedagogy of poverty can sometimes "work" to raise those scores, which makes everyone happy and inclined to reward those teachers.

Unfortunately, that result is often at the expense of real learning, the sort that more privileged students enjoy, because the tests measure what matters least. Thus, it's possible for the accountability movement to *simultaneously narrow the test-score gap and widen the learning gap.*

What's to be done? In the short run, Deborah Meier is probably right when she remarks, "Only secretly rebellious teachers have ever done right by our least advantaged kids." To do right by them in the open, we would need structural changes that make the best kind of teaching available to the kids who need it most.

And we know it *can* work, which is to say, the pedagogy of poverty is not what's best for the poor. There's plenty of precedent. A three-year study (published by the U.S. Department of Education) of 140 elementary classrooms with high concentrations of poor children found that students whose teachers emphasized "meaning and understanding" were far more successful than those who received basic-skills instruction. The researchers concluded by decisively rejecting "schooling for the children of poverty . . . [that] emphasizes basic skills, sequential curricula, and tight control of instruction by the teacher."

Remarkable results with low-income students of all ages have also been found with the Reggio Emilia model of early-childhood education, the "performance assessment" high schools in New York, and "Big Picture" schools around the country. All of these start with students' interests and questions; learning is organized around real-life problems and projects. Exploration is both active and interactive, reflecting the simple truth that kids learn how to make good decisions by making decisions, not by following directions. Finally, success is judged by authentic indicators of thinking and motivation, not by multiple-choice tests.

That last point is critical. Standardized exams serve mostly to make dreadful forms of teaching appear successful. As long as they remain our primary way of evaluating, we may never see *real* school reform—only an intensification of traditional practices, with the very worst reserved for the disadvantaged.

A British educator named David Gribble was once speaking in favor of the kind of education that honors children's interests and helps them to think deeply about questions that matter. Of course, he added, that sort of education is appropriate for affluent children. For disadvantaged children, on the other hand, it is . . . *essential.*

FOR FURTHER EXPLORATION

Comer, J. P. (2009). *What I learned in school: Reflections on race, child development, and school reform.* New York, NY: Jossey-Bass.

Noguera, P. (2003). *City schools and the American dream: Reclaiming the promise of public education.* New York, NY: Teacher's College Press.

Oakes, J. (2005). *Keeping track: How schools structure inequality.* New Haven, CT: Yale University Press.

Payne, C. M. (2008). *So much reform, so little change: The persistence of failure in urban schools.* Cambridge, MA: Harvard Education Press.

Alfie Kohn is an author, speaker, and social critic.

22

Necessary Muddles

Children's Language Learning in the Classroom

Darlene Witte-Townsend

A decade ago, as the result of an act of Congress, the kinds of language emphasized in classroom curricula began to narrow and take on a more technological, less natural character. Under the stricture of this act of Congress—the No Child Left Behind Act of 2001 (NCLB)—there is less room than previously for interactive, relational, and meaningful language learning to take place. In many classrooms, there is plenty of form but little that is significant. Teachers are now required to use what is called *research-based*, pre-scripted, formulaic methods for teaching language in order to ensure increased test scores. (Unfortunately, the term *research*, as it is presently used in the new technology of Congress-driven education, seems to refer to masses of recently produced, "approved" curriculum materials for which actual research data appear to be very thin and largely unavailable for scrutiny: a brave new world, indeed.)

In this world, driven by powerful others, children may be asked to learn the rules for language without personal meaning, without knowing them as connected to the moving of their own bodies and their own emerging awareness and experience. Regulation and structure are heavily imposed, the intent being to teach language directly and efficiently. However, when we spend even a few minutes with children, listening to their language as they play, we can see that in the delicious muddle they create, a special kind of structure emerges in a very natural way. Play is not mindless, rather, it "is use of mind" (Bruner, 1983).

There is evidence of thought, of work, of play, of problem solving, of engagement with ideas, of doing, of cognitive growth on the go and in the flow, and from this natural process, something more springs. Children seem to bring forth their own development when provided with a rich learning environment that includes caring adults who provide only as much external structure as needed and have an appreciation for the genius of play (Brown, 2010).

Think of the last time you observed a child playing with words. Perhaps he or she was generating a list of rhymes while jumping up and down or rolling across the floor. A rhyme for "gum" was necessary. "Some" and "mom" were tried, and then "bum" popped out, and a giggle or a grin followed as the raw power of language took over. This is the way children are. This is the way human beings are. We are subsumed, melted, turned into slush by our own nonsense and linguistic cleverness. This is important.

While it is typical for healthy young children to embody an innate drive to learn, for most, schooling eventually results in reduced interest (Smilovitz, 1996). The quality of engagement shifts, in many cases, to the pursuit of instrumental rewards, including gold stars and grades. This is problematic because the motivation to learn also shifts from being intrinsic to extrinsic (Kohn, 1999). Does this shift in engagement happen, in part, because we distrust and discourage language playfulness in classrooms? We need to realize that when we fail to encourage this kind of play, we discourage engagement and cognitive growth. Play with language brings forth meaning and moves us forward socially, emotionally, and cognitively. To lose this quality, this significance, is to lose too much. We risk removing children's greatest resource for the integration of new information, for making sense of experience, for self-healing, and for managing the difficulties of life in general (Elkind, 1987).

Children need legitimate struggle, ambiguity, playful interaction to learn language, and they need *muddle*. All of these are part of our linguistic and social heritage and erupt in the lives of ordinary, everyday children. Play with language facilitates and extends cognitive capabilities. Yet over the past decade and looking far into the future, American educational practice has set on a course in direct opposition to the need for freedom in thinking. Is education practice at a critical juncture at the far side of a swinging arc? Do we not now face a pedagogical fracturing of major proportions? Let us ask how to revive a safe, playful, meaningful, thinking space in classrooms, where teacher and child may risk learning something new within the ambiguous muddle of real language play-with-structure. Let us try to understand the negative effect of an overly restrictive language environment driven by education policies that seem to have ignored consideration of the sociolinguistic development of children. Let us move forward.

When making decisions about what to teach in classrooms, we need to respond in the moment to the language of the children in the class because they will give us clues as to where their interests lie. Are they wondering about valentines, or letters, or invitations? Are they writing lists? Are they printing the letter *E* over and over in every orientation possible and in every color in their crayon box? Do they arrive one morning, bursting with interest in pig latin and by this interest now showing that they are ready to tackle code breaking at a new, higher level (Witte-Townsend & Whiting, 2005)?

Children's interests show us what they are ready to practice. They will practice on their own, and more often than many realize, teachers' instruction and guided practice can follow: Teachers do not need to always lead the children. In some of today's schools, in some classrooms, there is precious little of the spontaneous. Instead of supporting children in the zone of making, an overly zealous culture of testing has taken precedence. Testing and assessments have expanded until they now overwhelm the routine of the classroom for days at a time and go further than needed for giving teachers useful information needed for supporting children's learning. Let us aim to find a "just right" balance of information gathering that is appropriate but not overwhelming.

Let us understand that pre-scripted, mechanistic programs with empty, nonlanguage experiences cannot replace natural language. We must also use play, the arts, and rich language to balance the whole. Many schools have replaced the arts with a very heavy emphasis on structured literacy practice. Let us move toward structured literacy practice that arises from rich experiences in the arts. Too many playgrounds have been replaced with crushed gravel and asphalt. Let us recognize that children need access to natural, physical environments for healthy overall development and move toward providing healthier learning environments (Louv, 2011). For too many children, recess has been eliminated or reduced, and all the need a child has for the choreography of the whole has been left behind.

NCLB-induced culture in schools has provided a world of nonmeaning in which children predominantly experience language as stable and ordered. A real language is one where meaning is a fleeting thing: Lawmakers, parents, and educators who neglect the significance of this are likely to throw up unintended roadblocks that tamp down learning.

While structure in learning is necessary, it has inherent limits. Who of us cannot remember the agony of being held back by structures that just didn't fit our minds and our bodies? Do teens sometimes need to be invited to write in the style of a stream of consciousness novel, to develop a dictionary of slang, or to imitate a J. D. Salinger approach to language? If they are so invited, will their thoughts flow effortlessly out of their emotional core? Sometimes the unconventional is more productive, with the permission to speak freely making it all the more appealing *because* it is dangerous, socially unacceptable, and somewhat muddled.

When linguistic and cultural research has long shown that children create their own reality from the milieu in which they are immersed (Chukovsky, 1963), why do we insist on *teaching* conventional language forms in the absence of play and exploration? Why do we approach *literacy* as if it were a system of objects? What if language cannot be taught directly, moving from page to brain, but can only be created from within a living, moving, human being? Interaction and experience are important in language learning, especially in the early stages (Wolf, 2008), despite the pronouncements of the National Reading Panel (National Institute of Child Health and Human Development, 2000). Literacy, or use of language in conventional ways, is not a matter of reason and structure only. It is also a matter of the art of being and is of the heart as much as it is of mind and experience.

In play, children learn how language works. They learn to manage themselves as much as they learn to manage language. Through use, they practice and come to understand rules of language such as correct verb and noun placement and how to make question-and-answer formats work. At the same time, they achieve a social back-and-forth, a reading of social meaning that quickens the memory and stimulates the mind, even as they try to outdo each other. Why can't we encourage this sort of activity more often and recognize it for the evidence of language development that it reveals?

Most adults are comfortable when children sit quietly in desks in orderly rows, filling in tidy blanks on worksheets. The difficulty with this is that when we look closely, we realize that out of a class of children so occupied, some will not be paying attention and getting it right. If you observe carefully, perhaps you will see those who are patiently resisting this excessive structure by doodling, chatting, dropping pencils and finding them, stuffing papers into the backs of their desks, sitting with their eyes half shut, their pencils not moving at all. Pretending. Playing. Ironically, the children who know the answers and don't *need* to practice writing them down are the ones most willing to slot them into the blanks on workbook pages. They do it partly because it is easy for them but mostly because they love their teachers and will do anything to please them. The students who refuse to complete the assigned work may actually have the most integrity, because they refuse to be compromised. But these students, in today's schools, are, "failing." What truth could be brought to bear if we were to describe them differently? We must provide classrooms where the fluid moments when a child's eyes are alight with sensed meaning as inner movement is valued.

Unfortunately, in today's schools, most of the language children experience is in one mode, the regulatory mode—for example, "Put the candy down. Don't touch it." Halliday (1977) described this mode as one of seven that make up natural uses of language, and all need to be part of a child's daily learning. Smith (1977) described an additional three modes of language that children also use naturally. What happened to the integrity of classroom language and literacy teaching practice when the foundational work of researchers such as Halliday and Smith was ignored by the National Reading Panel (National Institute of Child Health and Human Development, 2000) and subsequently deemphasized to the point where their insights disappeared? If you were to spend a day following children in school, you might see cause for concern—as I have. Some classrooms cause me no concern: In those classrooms where educators employ language arts/literacy approaches such as those developed by Lucy Calkins (1994), Debbie Miller (2002), and Irene Fountas and Gay Su Pinnell (2006), I see empowered, personal thinking; I see doing and meaning-making that is of and for the child. I see the children learning using a full range of language modes and more tolerance for muddle.

But in classrooms where some of the approved, overly structured programs are used, there is little room for thinking, and the regulatory mode predominates. I propose that curriculum should flow naturally and effectively from the child's language acquisition and experience; it should be complemented by their teachers' professional knowledge of language development and a child-friendly structure. Beyond this, classrooms need a supply of high quality and varied fiction and nonfiction books; reference materials; the ability to nurture classroom conversation; technological portals to the wide, wide world; and an excellent system for adapting to and keeping track of individual student progress.

The previously given curriculum would not impose unnatural ambiguity and could be alive with the understanding that study of language forms must occur in use. Children would be empowered to develop a sufficient understanding of how language works without being forced to continually and predominantly study and be tested primarily on only the forms, most notably the regulatory forms.

Of course, children *do* need to learn conventional forms, but we must be wary of our egocentric, cultural biases that predispose us, as adults, to confuse the underlying issues involved, whether we are teachers, parents, or members of Congress. When we want children to learn correct language use, they must have interactive experiences that allow natural use and expression. The study of form will not lead them to an understanding of form unless they already have an embodied sense of the language through their experience. While useful in its place, the regulatory mode is technological, and it is always and only about structure. Too heavily imposed, it weighs down the natural energy of learning. Emerging research in the field of psychology tells us that learning is optimal when it occurs within a synchronistic, sensual flow, not when it is linear and stripped down (Csikszentmihalyi, 2008).

The need for us to respond to children's learning needs in complex ways is exemplified by the nature of American culture. Individual differences in background can be extreme, which results in difficulty in matching the mechanized curricula favored by proponents of NCLB and like measures, to children's learning needs: Some have 500 books in their bedrooms and daily conversations with their parents; others have few, if any, books in their homes and rarely, if ever, engage in conversation. In the community where I live and work, kindergarten teachers observe that fewer than 50% of children have ever been cuddled and read to, even once, when they arrive at school on their first day of kindergarten. Think of all of these children thrown together in classrooms where the most common form of language used is regulatory—is it adequate for any of them?

What does this mean in the context of the everyday classroom? Effective instruction in the literacy classroom should involve all the natural uses of language, on a regular basis, in interactive situations. Language learning requires real, interactive situations—not only formal grammar lessons. We must not assume that reducing language by removing ambiguity, fun, and liveliness from the learning experience will be of help. Traditional grammar lessons are about language, but they are not real language in use and contribute little to the moments of shared satisfaction that should spontaneously arise when new levels of language mastery are achieved.

It is the child who must find his/her way through the ambiguous while working with real language if meaning is to emerge. However, such concepts are not easily communicated. Parents and the U.S. secretary of education alike may demand that young children receive lessons in formal grammar, taught in a formal way, not realizing the inefficiency of this method if it is overused or used at the wrong time. It can be difficult to explain why another method that might seem open and muddled could actually be more efficient. We must remember that every language interaction that has meaning does so because of, not in spite of, the social context within which it emerged. Conversation, emotion, and shared understanding are essential to active minds, healthy lives, and vibrant classrooms.

If children are allowed to retain an instinctive, natural, spontaneous, playful approach to language learning, will they trust their instinct for making appropriate choices in other life situations? If they have the freedom to sense and move freely in cognitive space, are they more likely to continue to trust their own perceptions? When children play with language, they are not losing control or acting without control, sense, or meaning. Rather, like poets, they are using their language to achieve new, higher levels of form, of control, and of meaning. Confidence emerges. Awareness of and respect for this process will help educators to ensure an appropriate choreography of structured/ nonstructured learning events for the children in our classrooms.

Educators cannot pretend that a heavily structured learning environment provides for anything more than a heavily structured—and heavily restricted—thinking environment. There is a way to undo the decade-long assault on thinking that has overtaken public schools. While we are determined to teach children to use the conventions of written and spoken language, let us remember this: In any given moment, children naturally move toward and make necessary structure, but their moves are more like those of artists and poets than like machines. While we teach them necessary structure, let us remember the nature of the process of thinking. Let us turn toward an educational vision that will nourish the full range of capabilities of the children of Homo sapiens: we who know that we know.

REFERENCES

Brown, S. (2010). *Play: How it shapes the brain, opens the imagination and invigorates the soul.* New York: Avery Trade Books.

Bruner, J. (1983, Spring). Play, thought, and language. *Peabody Journal of Education, 60*(3), 60–69.

Calkins, L. (1994). *The art of teaching writing.* Portsmouth, NH: Heinemann.

Chukovsky, K. (1963). *From two to five* (Rev. ed.). Berkeley: University of California Press.

Csikszentmihalyi, M. (2008). *The psychology of optimal experience.* New York: Harper Perennial.

Elkind, D. (1987). *Miseducation: Preschoolers at risk.* New York: Knopf.

Fountas, I., & Pinnell, G. (2006) *Teaching for comprehending and fluency: Thinking, talking and writing about reading.* Portsmouth, NH: Heinemann.

Halliday, M. A. K. (1977). *Learning how to mean.* New York: Elsevier.

Kohn, A. (1999). *Punished by rewards: The trouble with gold stars, incentive plans, A's, praise, and other bribes* (2nd ed.). New York: Mariner Books.

Louv, R. (2011). *The nature principle: Human restoration and the end of nature deficit disorder.* Chapel Hill, NC: Algonquin Books.

Miller, D. (2002). Reading for meaning. Portland, ME: Stenhouse Publishers.

National Institute of Child Health and Human Development. (2000, April). *Report of the National Reading Panel: Teaching children to read* (NIH Pub. No. 00–4769). Bethesda, MD: Author.

No Child Left Behind Act of 2001. Pub. L. No. 107–110, § 103–104, 115 Stat. 1425 (2002).

Smilovitz, B. (1996). *If not now, when? Education, not schooling.* New York: Routledge & Kegan Paul.

Smith, F. (1977). The uses of language. *Language Arts, 54*(6), 638–644.

Witte-Townsend, D. L., & Whiting, A. G. (2005). Seeking best practice in reading fluency development: Children, parents and teachers tell stories of complex relations. *New England Reading Association Journal, 41*(1), 51–63.

Wolf, M. (2008). *Proust and the squid: The story and science of the reading brain.* New York: Harper.

FOR FURTHER EXPLORATION

Witte-Townsend, D. L., & DiGiulio, E. (2004). Something from nothing: Exploring dimensions of knowing through the repeated reading of favourite books. *International Journal of Children's Spirituality, 9*(2), 127–142.

Witte-Townsend, D. L., & Hill, A. E. (2006). Light-ness of being in the primary classroom: Inviting conversations of depth across educational communities. *Educational Philosophy and Theory, 38*(3), 373–389.

Witte-Townsend, D. L., & Hill, A. E. (2006). Toward a pedagogy of depth in everyday classrooms: Exploring relational consciousness among teachers and young children. In B. A. Marlowe & A. S. Canestrari (Eds.), *Educational psychology: Readings for future teachers* (pp. 79–90). Thousand Oaks, CA: Sage.

Witte-Townsend, D. L., & Whiting, A. G. (2005). Seeking best practice in reading fluency development: Children, parents and teachers tell stories of complex relations. *New England Reading Association Journal, 41*(1), 51–63.

23

Teacher Unionism Reborn

Lois Weiner

I n the past five years, we have witnessed a demonization of teachers
unions that is close to achieving its goal: destruction of the most
stable and potentially powerful defender of mass public education.
Teacher unionism's continued existence is imperiled—if what we
define as "existence" is organizations having the legal capacity to bargain over any meaningful economic benefits and defend teachers'
rights to exercise professional judgment about what to teach and how
to do it.

As I explain elsewhere, financial and political elites began this project forty years ago when they imposed school reform on Latin America,
Africa, and Asia as a quid pro quo for economic aid. Though specifics
of this global social engineering differ from one country to another,
reforms have the same footprint: School funding is cut and school systems are broken up to promote privatization under the banner of
"choice"; teachers and curriculum are controlled by tying pay to standardized test scores and eliminating tenure; standardized testing measures what is taught to most students, reducing content to basic math,
reading, and writing. Teachers' unions have been singled out for attack
because throughout the world they are the most significant barriers to
this project's implementation.

Rhetoric about equalizing school outcomes for groups long denied
access to adequate, let alone quality education, masks the real aim of
the last twenty years of reform, creating a docile workforce that
receives no more than the 8th grade education needed to compete with

NOTE: Weiner, Lois. "Teacher Unionism Reborn" in *New Politics Journal*.
Winter 2012, Vol: XIII-4, # 52. Reprinted with permission by *New Politics
Journal*. http://newpol.org/node/579

workers elsewhere for jobs that can be moved easily from one city, state, or country. World Bank materials lay out the assumptions seldom articulated in this country: Money educating workers beyond the level most will need wastes scarce public funding; and minimally educated workers require minimally educated teachers, whose performance can be monitored through use of standardized testing. The newest World Bank report, "Making Schools Work" takes the reasoning (and policy) even further, insisting that "contract teachers" who work for one-quarter of what civil service employees receive, have no benefits, no job protection, and no rights produce good enough outcomes.

The attack has been fueled by right-wing foundations and advanced by Democrats and Republicans alike. The corporate media, including traditionally liberal elements, like Hollywood, *The New Yorker* and The *New York Times,* have blanketed TV, radio, and the press with bogus premises about education's relationship to the economy and the role of teachers unions in blocking much-needed change. The Obama Administration substitutes educational reforms straight out of the playbook of right-wing foundations as the panacea to unemployment and poverty. When Secretary of Education Arne Duncan avers that education is the "one true path out of poverty" he displays the administration's intention to divert attention away from unemployment, health care, child hunger, and homelessness. School improvement supplants all the economic and social reforms that have, historically, been used to ameliorate poverty. Defenders of public education frequently answer these inflated claims for education with protestations that schools can do nothing to alter the fate of poor children. Unfortunately, their response serves to heighten public perceptions that school people—teachers—refuse to take responsibility for what occurs under their watch. The more accurate and politically effective response is that schools can do more and better if we have well-prepared and well-supported teachers at work in well-resourced schools, and yet, even with these conditions, schools are hostage to powerful forces that depress achievement—factors that are beyond their control. This more nuanced defense of public education and teachers undercuts one of the most difficult problems we face in defending public education, neoliberalism's exploitation of historic inequalities in education. This is especially true in the United States, where the rhetoric of the civil rights movement has been totally hijacked in defense of charter schools and improving "teacher quality" by eliminating seniority and tenure. Even *The Nation* has bought the reification of individual teacher performance as the sine qua non of school improvement.

Teachers' unions globally have experienced an astoundingly well-orchestrated, well-financed attack, and resistance elsewhere in the world has been forceful and persistent. In contrast, U.S. teacher unions have been easy targets. Most teachers belong to a local affiliate of the NEA or the AFT. Both the NEA and AFT are national unions with state-level organizations. In general, teachers in the largest cities are in the AFT, which is a member of the AFL-CIO. The NEA functions as a union and collaborates with labor on legislation and in politics but is not in the AFL-CIO. In the NEA, state organizations are the most powerful component. In the AFT, the local affiliate is key. Staff generally control the NEA, officers the AFT. In most school systems, the union apparatus is intact, but the organizations are shells, weakened by their embrace of the "business union" or "service model" that characterizes most U.S. unions. The synergy of business unionism's hierarchical ethos and the legal framework giving unions the right to bargain on behalf of teachers, namely exclusive representation as bargaining agent, the right to collect "agency fee" (payment to the union of what is generally the equivalent of dues, to cover expenses the union expends in negotiating and enforcing the contract), and dues check-off (automatic deduction of dues from the member's paycheck) has encouraged a totally bureaucratic approach to contract enforcement, member passivity, and erosion of the union's school-site presence. Local union officers and activists have often been clueless about how to respond to the blitzkrieg of vitriol, and the national unions have been little help. They have been unwilling to "rock the boat," desiring above all to stay politically moored to Obama, a president who has pressed for a thoroughly anti-teacher, anti-union, anti-public education agenda. Another factor is, of course, the personal power and privilege national officers and staff enjoy as a result of their cozy relationship with powerful elites.

From the start of mass public education, teachers unions, like most of organized labor, turned a blind eye to racism and anti-immigrant sentiment. Teachers' unions' failure to acknowledge this history has facilitated their being cast—incredibly, by billionaires who have plundered the nation's resources—as a special interest group, more interested in protecting teachers' jobs than in helping poor children succeed in school. Many parents and citizens, even some teachers, have been persuaded that tenure and seniority protect "dead wood," not realizing that when tenure and seniority are lost, so is democratic space in classrooms. The unions' unwillingness to acknowledge schooling's past and current role in reproducing social inequality, their reluctance to work as partners with activists to take on racism, sexism, militarization, and anti-immigrant prejudice, have weakened their credibility with groups who should be teacher unionists' strongest allies.

This problem is exemplified by Diane Ravitch's defense of teacher unions. Unlike Chester Finn, a former ally who brags about his desire to destroy public education, Ravitch understands that once public education is destroyed, like Humpty Dumpty, it won't be put back together again—and when public education goes, so will a powerful force for democracy. Another explanation for Ravitch's about-face on the neoliberal reforms she advocated as part of the Bush Administration is that she is an intellectual and unlike her former neo-conservative allies is genuinely interested in education. She is, rightly, horrified by the anti-intellectualism that is writ large in neoliberalism's successful efforts to vocationalize education. Most of what she writes is eloquent, passionate, and accurate. Unlike the disoriented bureaucrats who run the unions, Ravitch understands that a fight needs to be made and she is willing to wage it. Ravitch criticized mayoral control of the New York City schools as undemocratic when the president of the union representing New York City teachers supported the measure. Ravitch has come out against linking teacher pay to test scores while the national unions have caved. Ravitch has shown the union bureaucrats how they could, if they wished, defend the union and public education more effectively. She is Albert Shanker's doppelganger, that is, while he still acted like a union president rather than a labor statesman.

However, as was the case with Shanker and is true of NEA and AFT officials today, Ravitch's defense of teacher unionism and public education is constrained by an ideological commitment to defending U.S. capitalism at any cost. Because she can't or won't acknowledge what has been wrong with U.S. society and public education, she can't devise a compelling alternative to the neoliberal reforms. She embeds, subtly, in her current defense of public education the claim that there was no crisis in U.S. public education before the neoliberal reforms were imposed. But there was. The Left historians she blasted in the 1960s and 70s in her defense of the status quo had it right. The schools did—and do—reproduce social inequality. In her recent essay in the *New York Review of Books* (September 29, 2011) she reduces current educational inequality between Whites and minorities to yet another in a series of over-blown crises U.S. schools have endured since their creation. She argues that "poverty matters," which it does, of course. So does racism, which she does not mention. So do other forms of discrimination which she ignores. Elsewhere, Ravitch states her desire for public education to be what she experienced in high school, in Houston, Texas. (In the PBS history of U.S. public education, Ravitch fondly recalls her days as a high school cheerleader.) But how many Black and Hispanic parents will fight for a return to the status quo that barred their children from schools that served Whites?

AN EMERGING RESISTANCE

The nation's largest cities were home to teacher unionism's original birth and its rebirth in the 1960s. Today opposition caucuses have emerged once again in cities, where conditions have deteriorated to an extent unimaginable even a decade ago. Charter schools, as their proponents freely admit, are one of the main weapons to make school systems free of union influence. A charter school is essentially its own school district, free of district regulations—and union involvement. In most large cities, teachers' unions gave up seniority in transfer when the first wave of school closings began. Now, when schools are closed because of poor test scores and replaced by charter schools, experienced teachers are often thrown into pools of "displaced teachers." They must compete for jobs with new hires who earn one-half the salary. Teacher pay now comes out of a school's budget, so many principals, especially those with little or no teaching experience themselves, prefer hiring two new teachers for the price of one more-experienced teacher. A fact little publicized by the unions is that older minority teachers face intense racism when they interview for jobs, especially with young, white principals. Readers familiar with labor history will see the dismaying parallels to "shape up" on the docks and fields, before unionization brought hiring halls and protections for older workers.

Although tenure has been dismissed as irrelevant in K–12 teaching, its importance is greater today than ever before. As principals' pay is increasingly tied to improving test scores, and the noose between teacher pay and student test scores is tightened, teachers who want to give their students a richer diet than test prep are facing the prospect of losing their jobs if they follow their moral and professional principles. Even more chilling is schools' use of corporate propaganda, obtained through seemingly trustworthy vendors, as occurred with *Scholastic Books* promoting a fourth-grade curriculum written by the coal industry with its perspective. Even where it still exists in state law, tenure has been greatly weakened because administrators can easily give teachers spurious unsatisfactory ratings due to weakened enforcement of evaluation procedures. In many city schools, principals can and do function without any check on their power, other than what is exercised by distant officials whose only concern is test scores. Over and over one hears of teachers who have bought the anti-union propaganda that is so prevalent in the media, or are too overworked and demoralized to do anything other than what they are told, or are too afraid of retribution to voice a contrary opinion. The union's presence has been so eroded and its credibility so damaged that "transforming the union" in many districts probably means building it from scratch.

At the same time, some teachers have become politicized by the vicious, unfair political attacks on their ability, character, professional authority, and economic well-being. Still, they often cling to the "service model" of unionism and expect "the union" to somehow, magically, intervene. The idea that they ARE the union is slowly percolating through the ranks, and increasingly, a new generation of teacher union activists is emerging. Union renewal is taking many forms, but the most important developments from a strategic perspective are occurring in the nation's cities. Not all major cities are experiencing the kind of change that's needed. For example, in Washington, D.C., a protracted, ultimately successful court challenge by a former union official who vied for the presidency did little to mobilize teachers and community. On the other hand, in the Chicago Teachers Union (CTU), a vibrant leadership, mostly new to union office, has brought their commitment to mobilize the membership, explicitly rejecting business unionism. In Milwaukee, long-time education activist Bob Peterson, a founder of the magazine *Rethinking Schools,* now heads Milwaukee's teachers union. Radical teachers who previously shunned the union now understand that they need it to protect teachers' economic rights, and like Peterson, see the union capable of fighting on a "tripod" of concerns: "bread and butter unionism . . . professional unionism . . . and social justice unionism." Peterson points to the need for truly mutual alliances, building strong relations with parents and community groups "not just to ensure adequate support for public education, but so that we as a union are also involved in improving the community."

Though *Rethinking Schools* and others use the term "social justice" union, I think the idea of a "social movement" union is more useful because it addresses the need for transformation of the unions internally, especially the need for union democracy. Union democracy is a thorny issue for radicals, especially those who assume leadership of moribund organizations. "Social justice" unionism addresses the positions the union takes on various political, social, and economic issues. One temptation for radicals who take office without a mobilized base to support them is that union democracy becomes a hindrance to the union acting on a "social justice" program. On the other hand, "social movement" unionism gets at the need for empowering members, building the union from the bottom-up, making the union itself a social movement. A social movement union not only endorses social justice demands in education and the society, working with social movements to further these aims, it also exists as a social movement itself, pressing as much as it can against the constraints of its being a membership organization—with the responsibility to protect its members.

The CTU is probably the most important testing ground for social movement unionism. The union is now led by activists from CORE (Caucus of Rank-and-File Educators). Using newfangled social media and old-fashioned face-to-face meetings and organizing, CORE defeated the older guard leadership loyal to the national AFT office. With scarcely a second to catch their breath, CTU's new leaders were confronted with ferocious attacks by the state and city on the contract and teachers' pensions. In gaining their political footing, the inexperienced leadership made mistakes that were both natural and damaging, for instance, trusting that state union officials would be more expert about policy decisions and allowing the local president to participate in meetings with high-ranking state officials by herself. The CTU leadership faces a stunning phalanx of opponents, ranging from Mayor Rahm Emmanuel, who flaunts the prestige and support he has in the White House and from powerful "friends of labor" in the Democratic Party, to Republican and Democratic state politicians, eager to destroy all public employees unions, mostly especially those representing city teachers. CTU leaders must simultaneously take from the state and national union resources that are needed while simultaneously doing all that is necessary to oust these officials who impede the movement's objectives. In my opinion, CORE activists are an inspiration, heroic and wise.

Like teachers in other cities, Los Angeles teachers face a viciously anti-teachers union mayor. But what differentiates LA's Mayor Antonio Villaraigosa is that he parlayed his position as a staffer for the teachers' union, United Teachers of Los Angeles (UTLA), and his close relationship with two of UTLA's highest ranking officers—well-known leftists—to become a labor bigwig and then mayor. UTLA was the first teachers' union in a major U.S. city in which a reform caucus succeeded in sweeping the old guard out of office. However, only a small fraction of the membership voted in the election (and in the most recent election as well). The reformers have been in the unenviable position of responding to horrific attacks while also managing the union's bureaucratic operations, without being able to count on much support from the membership. Unfortunately, the reformers, who took office in a coalition that did not permit accountability among the factions, maintained many of the bureaucratic practices of the previous administration. The leadership's disastrous decision to support mayoral control—because their buddy was the Mayor—was a function of an emphasis on playing power politics rather than addressing the union's bureaucratic functioning. In the most recent elections, a long-time activist running as an independent but aligning himself with a more conservative caucus won the presidency. At the same time, a progressive caucus, PEAC, took a majority of seats on the union's board of directors. What needs to be done now—and quickly—is for leaders and activists to focus financial and human resources on reviving the union at the school site. Probably one-third of the schools, campuses as they're called, lack functioning chapters. This admittedly painstaking work of educating members that they "own" the union, to help them in organizing themselves, is inescapable. One bright spot from the reformers' victory is that UTLA's Human Rights Committee has embraced international work with Canadian and Mexican teachers unions, under the umbrella of the Trinational Coalition to Defend Public Education.

Of all the teachers unions in major cities, it appears at first glance that New York's union, the United Federation of Teachers (UFT), has done the best job in protecting teachers and public schools. Many of the worst abuses teachers have suffered elsewhere have been forestalled by the union's political clout in Albany. Charter schools have not mushroomed as fast as they have elsewhere, for instance California. Schools being closed due to low test scores are not being auctioned off to the highest bidder, as is occurring in Los Angeles. But appearances are deceiving because while the UFT has indeed been able to protect many of the vestiges of the old system by calling in its political chips, it has done so at the expense of alienating its natural allies, insulating the bureaucracy and allowing the union to all but disappear at the school, and seriously erode at the district level, where union staff may decline to provide chapter chairs with the most minimal forms of support, like meeting with principals about grievances. One estimate I've heard from a loyalist to the current leadership puts the number of schools with no functioning union chapters at far more than one-third, probably closer to three-fifths. Many teachers are too frightened to attend union meetings or even meet privately with union staff at the school site. What they may consent to do, when pressed, is to put union materials in teachers' mailboxes, but they will do so only in secret. One fine young teacher in a selective Manhattan high school touted to be "progressive" and favored by leftish parents was given "unsatisfactory" ratings by the principal for "harassing" colleagues. He put a notice in their mailboxes informing them of a get-together to discuss the school's admission policies. The chapter chair refused to help because she wanted to stay in the principal's good graces, and union staff were unwilling to be involved. Their job as they see it is to file grievances that they are sure will succeed. The UF clearly lacks the capacity—and will—to defend its members and the schools. Some activists theorize that the union is morphing, perhaps through conscious intent, from a "service model" of unionism into a membership organization that wears the mantle of union but in fact is a provider of consumer services, like low cost auto insurance.

Still, the UFT bosses have not yet seen a serious challenge. In the last change of rule, the crown was passed to Michael Mulgrew, who actually taught in the city schools, unlike Randi Weingarten, a lawyer who served as UFT President and is currently AFT national President. Mulgrew's face is new, but the apparatus remains impenetrably bureaucratic and the union's politics are essentially as they were under Shanker. There is little sense from the way the union leadership presents itself or acts that teacher unionism has experienced an assault that challenges its existence. The union newspaper's coverage of school struggles—or rather lack of it—shows how little engaged the UFT is in protecting the contract, schools or teachers, as well as how remote it is from community-based groups fighting on social justice. In the October 27, 2001, issue of the union newspaper, Michael Mulgrew's picture appeared 9 times in the first 11 pages. An article applauded the success of Junior ROTC at one of the city's many racially segregated city high schools. No mention was made of the anti- militarization campaigns that are occurring elsewhere in the nation, for instance in Los Angeles, with UTLA's support. Another story informed teachers about their rights—in handling disruptive students. No mention was made of advocacy groups' work about racial discrimination in school disciplinary policies, of activists working to alter school organization and culture so that "disruptive" students are less so. Stories on charter school organizing painted a glowing picture—another victory! There was one nod to the fact that Occupy Wall Street was a few blocks away from union headquarters, a story (with a picture of Michael Mulgrew) described the union's participation in a coalition demanding no tax breaks for millionaires. But mostly the newspaper contained sentimental snapshots of teachers doing charity work. In light of the real conditions in the school system, including thousands of teachers who are paid (for now) but jobless, draconian cuts in funding felt in loss of money for supplies and class sizes that often exceed the contractual norms (not enforced), and the absence of union chapters in at least one-third of the schools, the paper's contents are almost surreal. Clearly, this is a union leadership that doesn't understand that publicity about teachers walking in support of breast cancer awareness will not suffice to defend their schools, their jobs, or their right to have a real union represent them.

The UFT's one victory in recent memory was organizing family daycare workers, that is, making them union members. The UFT, in alliance with ACORN, used its political muscle to win the right to have family daycare workers have union representation and have their dues deducted from their wages, which are paid by the state. An election for the bargaining agent occurred, a small fraction of the workers in the unit voted, and the UFT won the vote. While this seems to be a win-win, strengthening the union and giving exploited workers union representation, in fact the "top-down" process fails to build the resiliency union members will need to win or defend gains. Often what occurs in this kind of organizing is that shortly after the election for representation, the new members are forgotten. In this familiar scenario not limited to the UFT, union officials use the new members to strengthen their bureaucratic hold on the union apparatus. Union membership gives workers access to some protections, much needed and deserved to be sure; but especially when members are not in the majority constituency (teachers in the case of the UFT), they are trapped in a union that does little to represent them. The case of the family daycare workers is especially poignant because the UFT/ACORN alliance muscled out what had been the authentic community-based organizing of family daycare workers, by a Brooklyn group, Families United for Racial and Economic Equality.

One bright spot in the New York City teachers union's political horizon is Teachers Unite, which is trying to bring activists on social justice in schooling together with teachers who want to see the UFT transformed. Teachers Unite is small but growing. One of its most successful activities has been providing workshops on building the union at the school site, taught by teachers who are themselves chapter leaders.

Teachers Unite's activity demonstrates what could be done to build the union if the UFT bureaucracy really wanted to do so. Teachers from other activist groups, including Grassroots Education Movement (GEM), which produced a splendid video countering the misinformation in *Waiting for Superman*, are collaborating with Teachers Unite on social justice campaigns in the city schools, including helping to organize against school closings. Another hopeful development is that Teachers Unite is part of a still-emerging national network of reform groups.

OCCUPY THE UNIONS!

If teachers' unions are to continue to exist as a meaningful form of workers' representation, members need to transform them—and fast. The future of the movement depends on activists realizing that they, not staff or officers on the state and national levels, have to be the catalysts for change. Just as there is no escape from building the union at the base, there is no getting around the hard work of developing authentic alliances with parents and community activists, coalitions that acknowledge historic inequalities and support communities in their needs, rather than being paper organizations that are dusted off when the union wants to display community support. Elected officials, from school boards to governors, are violating union contracts with impunity. Lawsuits, by themselves, the favored method of dealing with law-breaking officials, can't stop this. What can is direct action undertaken with parents and community, as the CTU has done in combating school closings in Chicago.

In contrast, the AFT and NEA national leadership pursue a strategy of cozying up to their "friends" in the Democratic Party, including President Obama. This undercuts the brave activity of many teachers battling in their schools against the policies Obama and Duncan are pushing. For instance, both national unions have accepted use of standardized tests to judge student performance and teachers' pay, in order, they say, to stay "credible." But "credible" to whom? Certainly not teachers who risk their livelihoods by speaking out against the harm done by education having been reduced to teaching to/for the test. The president of the AFT chapter in his charter school shared with me his outrage and dismay at what occurred when he called the state union for help in dealing with the principal's demand for pay increases linked to student test scores. He was told the changes the principal demanded were official AFT policy.

In July 2011, the NEA officially endorsed Obama for President. The AFT will undoubtedly follow suit, once organized labor decides the time is right to make this commitment. Although the AFT and NEA nationally are in the Democrats' hip pocket, a different scenario might occur in local school board elections. Teachers unions are beginning to run candidates for school boards. Often local unions support candidates with the same "lesser evil" rationale the national and state unions use in endorsing Democrats. But in some places, this strategy is being challenged. Instead of electing someone, anyone, who is marginally better, teachers unions are thinking of how they might use the races as an opportunity to build support from the ground up. Campaigns for school board elections can be testing grounds for building new electoral alliances, alliances that are wholly independent of both parties, speak truth to corporate power, and advance a vision of public education that supports collaboration among schooling's constituencies. As Occupy Wall Street has demonstrated, the country is hungry for leaders who will speak out against capitalism's excesses. Neither the NEA nor AFT can provide that leadership, nor be partners in a movement that challenges Wall Street, as long as its top officials want the unions to be included as collaborators in maintaining U.S. capitalism's domination of U.S. society and the globe.

As labor researchers Mayssoun Sukarieh and Stuart Tannock explain, though the AFT supports its far-flung global operations with "high-minded rhetoric of global labor solidarity, philanthropic good-will, and democracy promotion," the union wants most of all to further U.S. hegemony. The AFT's international operations are vast, ranging from "Bolivia to Burma and Kenya to Kazakhstan." Ironically, the AFT aims to educate teacher unionists elsewhere in the world to desert the traditions of social movement unionism that we in the United States should be learning—and imitating—here at home. Given claims by some progressives that the AFT changed with the end of the Cold War and Shanker's death, it's important to note Sukarieh and Tannock contend that the AFT "continues with its cold war legacy largely uninterrupted. Its current director of international affairs, David Dorn, was also director during the Shanker era. Rather than question, apologize for, or distance itself from any of its past international work, the AFT celebrates and explicitly claims to be continuing with this exact same line of activity . . . The AFT continues to expand its international programs . . . from its 1990s base in Eastern Europe to the current focus on the Middle East" (p. 186).

AFT and NEA rely on their size, wealth, and connections with the U.S. government to dominate politics of the Education International (EI), the global federation of teachers unions. There used to be significant foreign policy differences between the NEA and AFT, with the NEA being more liberal. However, those distinctions, even ephemeral, seem to have been lost. Both joined in squashing democracy at the EI conference in Capetown this past summer, where they used their control of the EI's administrative apparatus to push through a palatable (to them) resolution on Palestine and Israel. According to a conference participant with whom I spoke, AFT and NEA shocked Western European delegates with their brazen (and successful) effort to control debate and force an outcome that was more in line with U.S. foreign policy.

Three different resolutions on Palestine and Israel were presented to the conference. One came from the EI board, another from the UK higher education union, Universities and Colleges Union, and the third from the National Union of Teachers (NUT). Operating much as the AFT leadership does at its own conventions, the AFT and NEA maneuvered to suppress the NUT resolution, which was a forthright condemnation of Israel's actions towards Palestine. They first tried to persuade the presiding NUT officer to withdraw the resolution. This effort at intimidation failed, so they warned NUT delegates that should they persist in presenting their resolution, the AFT delegation would bolt from the conference. An NEA staffer being groomed for leadership in the EI's administrative office handled negotiations on behalf of the AFT and NEA, and ultimately, a "compromise" resolution was approved, one that dropped sharp criticism of Israeli policy. Delegates from the Middle East were enraged at the resolution and by their having been silenced in the debate.

With all of the political struggles going on in the world, with the concerted attacks against teachers unions, why did the AFT and NEA make the NUT's resolution on Palestine the main focus of their political intervention at the EI? Why would the leadership of NEA and AFT' jeopardize their political legitimacy by flaunting their control over the EI's administrative apparatus? The answer is in the lopsided nature of the AFT and NEA's political compass, permanently stuck in the direction of the U.S. government's desires. Nothing counts as much for the NEA and AFT leadership as the prerogatives of U.S. capitalism and the government that protects it. Their political loyalties to U.S. imperialism are seen in almost every political decision. For example, the NEA and AFT ban membership by the Chinese and Cuban unions in the EI because they are not free of government control. Fair enough, but why then permit participation of the Egyptian union—entirely controlled by the Mubarak dictatorship—until the union fell in arrears on its dues, shortly before Mubarak was overthrown? Teacher union leaders from the global south object to the contradiction between EI's professed support for free trade unions throughout the world and its, that is, the NEA and AFT's, one-sided application of criteria that coincide with the desires of the U.S. government. Under life-and-death pressure from their own governments and fearful of further attacks by international agencies that answer to Washington, teacher unionists in Asia and Africa are understandably reluctant to challenge the AFT and NEA. Given this imbalance of power between unions in the global south and the AFT and NEA, the Western European unions have a special responsibility to fight for democracy in the EI and for consistent application of the ruler measuring whether unions are indeed "free" of government control.

When Naomi Klein spoke at Occupy Wall Street she noted that the rest of the world had been waiting for this challenge at capitalism's heart. The same is true of U.S. teacher unionism's renaissance. Teachers and students around the globe need teachers in this country to occupy their unions. At this writing, the eyes of the world are on the courageous activists who are facing down the world's most powerful elite in downtown Manhattan. Our eyes should also be on the heroic activity of teachers moving to occupy their unions. The future of public education globally depends in great measure on them.

FOR FURTHER EXPLORATION

Weiner, L. (1993). *Preparing teachers for urban schools: Lessons from thirty years of school reform.* New York, NY: Teachers College Press.

Weiner, L. (1999). *Urban teaching: The essentials* (2nd ed.). New York, NY: Teachers College Press.

Weiner, L. (2001). *Urban education in the U.S., A Reader.* Xanedu.com.

Weiner, L. (2008). *The global assault on teaching, teachers, and their unions: Stories for resistance.* New York, NY: Palgrave Macmillan.

Epilogue

The Quest

Achieving Ideological Escape Velocity—Becoming an Activist Teacher

Ann Gibson Winfield

WHERE WE ARE

In the fourth century B.C., Chinese philosopher Motse wrote:

> When nobody in the world loves any other, naturally the strong will overpower the weak, the many will oppress the few, the wealthy will mock the poor . . . (quoted in Heubner, 1999, p. 78)

Clearly, we are still struggling with what Motse observed in the fourth century B.C.! How can teachers contribute to changing this state of affairs? Teachers must advocate for their students' right to empowered lives, and must envision a society that values, supports, encourages, and revels in every student's talent, curiosity, and creativity. There is a heavy pressure to conform, to stay quiet, to obey and even to promote policies and practices that are damaging but are so deeply engrained in the system that they have become the "hidden curriculum" (Giroux, 2004). A transformative, activist teacher does not submit to this pressure because they know that to do so is "not

---

NOTE: Reprinted with kind permission from the author.

only unprincipled, deeply cynical and cowardly, it's suicidal, a slippery slope with lots of miserable historical precedent" (Ayers, 2006).

WHERE WE MIGHT GO

So, you ask, what do activist teachers do? Activist teachers understand that much of what is commonly assumed about education is a relic of the past, that these assumptions are socially constructed and are therefore open to be reconstructed. Activist teachers understand that schools are contexts where meaning is actively made by students, teachers, and administrators on a daily basis and that therefore those meanings can change and be a source of transformation. Activist teachers analyze school policies and practices in relation to the economic, political, social, and cultural forces that shape, and are in turn shaped by them. They consider race, class, gender, ethnicity, sexual orientation, language, religion, and physical and mental abilities and disabilities as social relations of power that often differentially determine school experiences and individual and collective identities.

Activist teachers also ask big questions and reflect on how and why U.S. schools continue to contribute to the reproduction of unequal educational opportunities and outcomes for our children. Activist teachers are, first and foremost, self-reflective. They do not blame students, their families, or their environments for any perceived lack. Instead, they continually strive to identify, evaluate, and critique their own assumptions, teaching practices, and willingness to conform by putting the interests of their students and a vision of a socially just society as the goal that supersedes all other goals.

You might be wondering at this point how one goes about achieving all this, and such a question is an example of the residue we all carry from our own experience in the educational system. We must resist the desire for a quick fix, a synopsis, or a recipe that will allow us to suddenly understand what it takes to become a transformative teacher. Rest assured that this is a lifelong process, an orientation toward the future if you will, that develops and grows over time. There is no doubt that every individual will have their own version of how to proceed, and it is in that spirit that I suggest the cultivation of the following habits:

• Read often, and deeply. As Appelbaum (2008) says, we read "because reading helps us to experience what is necessary to reconsider what we think to be true about our personal worlds of experience, for imagination, interpretation, and insight" (p. 12). From quick scans of thi newspaper coverage to the kinds of books you have to keep re-reading sentences in order to understand, read as much as possible. There is no substitute for exposure. Read book reviews and books, historical fiction and things written by and about people and places that are unfamiliar. When you aren't sure about something, look it up. Talk to people about what you read. Think about what you read. Write about what you read.

• Expose yourselves to as much art, theatre, music, and literature as possible, as often as possible. We are most free to recognize and support creativity, imagination, and multiple forms of expression in our students when we have an appreciation of the possibilities. Find and cultivate your own artistic talents.

• Seek out a variety of sources for the news, and change back and forth frequently. As you do this, you will begin to recognize the assumptions, biases, and ideological residue that pervade the media. Become a media critic, unearth hidden (intended or otherwise) messages, and teach your students to do the same.

• When you are unsure about what to do, always put your students' well being at the forefront of anything you are considering—when you do that, the answer usually becomes much clearer. Also, become comfortable with ambiguity—it is an authentic, thoughtful place to be that provides room for growth and change.

• Interact, examine, explore, compare, and critique with your colleagues as much as possible, but be a savvy judge of character and avoid toxicity, negativity, or anything that disrespects, denigrates, or puts limitations on students and their families.

• Never lose sight of the big picture; context is essential. It is never frivolous to ask difficult or seemingly unanswerable questions. What do schools teach? What should schools teach? Who should decide what schools teach? Is the primary aim of education to instill basic skills or to foster critical thinking? Should education aim to mold future citizens, create an efficient workforce, engender personal development, or inspire academic achievement? Must education have an aim? What beliefs, values, or attitudes are learned from classroom practice? What lessons are acquired but taken for granted, taught but not planned?

Good teachers are, to use Giroux's term, "transformative intellectuals," practicing theoreticians, willing and able to reflect the fluid nature of the world around them. Resist any implication that teaching

n, that teaching doesn't require a special form of
ning is a skill that can be easily measured and moni-
ᴧ, or the commitment to progressive education and a
ociety that recognizes and values all people, occurs in the
,s—activism is embedded in the questions you ask, in the
ore you respond, in the strategic building of knowledge,
ᴄe and insight, in the patience, in the security that your path
ᴛ and that the right answers are available, in the resistance to
ᴐn one's laurels, to self-congratulate, to cling to old fears. Activism
ᴛhe recognition that we are all connected. It means demanding of
ᴜr democracy the representation, the ideals, and the vision contained
in our founding documents.

WHAT WE MIGHT SEE

We are all understandably reticent to ask questions and pursue goals that
undermine the bedrock of our society—the status quo. We do not want
to believe that societal institutions may not reflect our deepest beliefs
about a just society. We want to get along, we are afraid of conflict, of
being "wrong," of not knowing what to do. This, though, is an evasion
of the fundamental responsibility for the lives of students that teachers
take on. As Ayers (2006) has suggested, good teachers "must embody a
profound threat to the status quo" by challenging "the imposition of
labels and all the simple-minded metrics employed to describe student
learning and rank youngsters in a hierarchy of winners and losers."

Teachers, good teachers, teachers who recognize, appreciate,
respect, and embolden their students; those teachers do not have the
luxury of failing to interrogate their own assumptions, nor the assumptions embedded in the institutional policies and practices that surround them at every turn. Teachers are morally obligated to do no
harm (someone should write a Hippocratic Oath for teachers), and in
order to achieve that they embark upon a quest to understand that is
unflinching, lifelong, and metabolic.

This is no easy task. It requires that you create within *yourself* the
kind of learner that reflects your aspirations for your students. Human
beings are born with an insatiable curiosity and any experience for a
child, educational or otherwise, that damages, hinders, or deflects the
passion for more and more knowledge is unacceptable. It is just here
that the motivation to engage in the constant disassembly of assumptions and a relentless pursuit of knowledge comes.

As teachers we must adhere ourselves to something more, something deeper, something that withstands political, economic, and ideological winds.

REFERENCES

Appelbaum, P. (2008). *Children's books for grown-up teachers: Reading and writing curriculum theory.* New York, NY: Routledge.

Ayers, W. (2006). Love me, I'm a Liberal. *Monthly Review.*

Dewey, J. (1933). *The quest for certainty.* Oakville, Ontario: Capricorn Books.

Giroux, H. A. (2004). Teachers as transformative intellectuals. In A. S. Canestrari B. A. Marlowe (Eds.), *Educational foundations: An anthology of critical readings.* Thousand Oaks, CA: Sage.

Heschel, A. J. (1966/1959). *The insecurity of freedom: Essays on human existence.* Philadelphia, PA: Jewish Publication Society.

Heubner, D. (1999). *The lure of the transcendent: Collected essays by Dwayne E. Heubner. Mahwah, NJ: Lawrence Erlbaum.*

FOR FURTHER EXPLORATION

Burke, J. M., Eaton, L., Wilson, A. V., Atkins, K & Winfield, A. G. (2005). Epiphimania: A study of boundaries in curriculum pedagogy. *International Journal of Education and the Arts.*

Winfield, A. G. (2007). *Eugenics and education in America: Institutionalized racism and the implications of history, ideology, and memory.* New York: Peter Lang.

Winfield, A. G. (2010). Eugenic ideology and historical osmosis. *Curriculum Studies - The Next Moments: Exploring Post-Reconceptualization.* E. Malewski (editor). New York: Routledge.

Winfield, A. G. (2012). Resuscitating bad science: Eugenics past and present. In *The Assault on Public Education,* Watkins, W. H., editor, New York: Teachers College Press.

Ann Gibson Winfield is a professor of education at Roger Williams University in Bristol, Rhode Island, and the author of *Eugenics and Education in America: Institutionalized Racism and the Implications of History, Ideology and Memory* (Peter Lang, 2007).

Index

⦿SAGE research**methods**

The essential online tool for researchers from the world's leading methods publisher

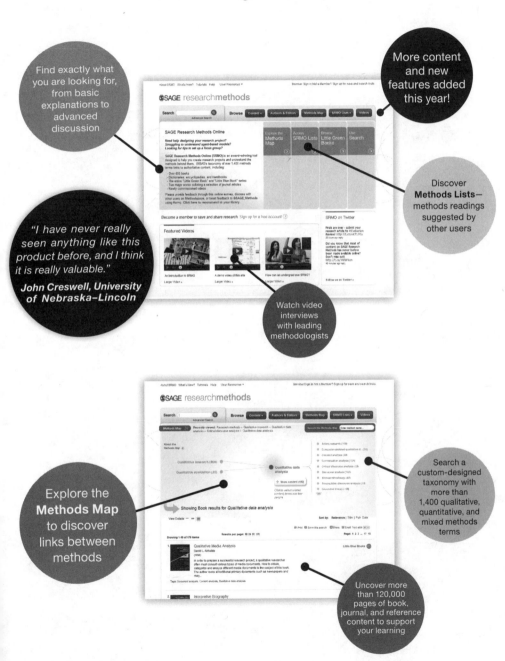

More content and new features added this year!

Find exactly what you are looking for, from basic explanations to advanced discussion

Discover Methods Lists— methods readings suggested by other users

"I have never really seen anything like this product before, and I think it is really valuable."

John Creswell, University of Nebraska–Lincoln

Watch video interviews with leading methodologists

Explore the Methods Map to discover links between methods

Search a custom-designed taxonomy with more than 1,400 qualitative, quantitative, and mixed methods terms

Uncover more than 120,000 pages of book, journal, and reference content to support your learning

Find out more at
www.sageresearchmethods.com